THE FIRST LADIES

The First Ladies

THIRD EDITION

BETTY BOYD CAROLI

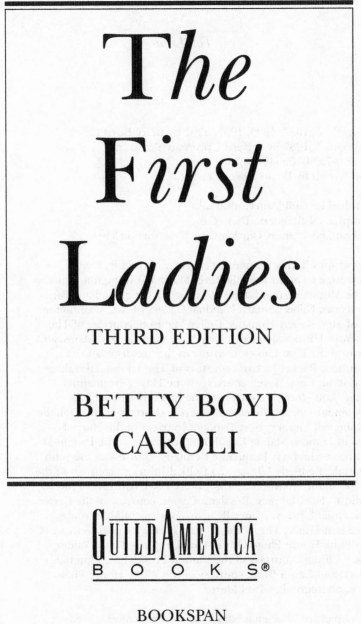

GUILDAMERICA
B O O K S®

BOOKSPAN
GARDEN CITY, NEW YORK

For Livio

Published by GuildAmerica® Books,
an imprint of BOOKSPAN, Dept. GB,
401 Franklin Avenue, Garden City, New York 11530

Photographs in this volume are courtesy of the Library of
Congress, except for the following: Martha Washington, courtesy
of The Mount Vernon Ladies' Association; Abigail Adams, *Mrs.
John Adams,* Gilbert Stuart, National Gallery of Art, Washington,
Gift of Mrs. Robert Homans; Dolley Madison, courtesy of The
New-York Historical Society, New York City; Louisa Adams, and
Gowns of the First Ladies, courtesy of the Smithsonian
Institution; Rachel Jackson, courtesy of The Ladies' Hermitage
Association; Lucy Hayes, courtesy of the Hayes Presidential
Center; Lou Hoover, courtesy of the Herbert Hoover
Presidential Library; Eleanor Roosevelt, courtesy of the Franklin
D. Roosevelt Library; Bess Truman, courtesy of the Harry S.
Truman Library; Mamie Eisenhower, courtesy of the Dwight D.
Eisenhower Library; Jacqueline Kennedy, courtesy of the John
Fitzgerald Kennedy Library; Lady Bird Johnson, courtesy of the
Lyndon Baines Johnson Library; Betty Ford, courtesy of the
Gerald R. Ford Library; Rosalynn Carter, courtesy of the Carter
Presidential Library; Nancy Reagan, courtesy of Mary Anne
Fackelman-Miner, The White House; Barbara Bush, courtesy of
The White House Photo Office. Photographer: David Valdez;
Hillary Clinton, courtesy of the Clinton Presidential Materials
Project; and Laura Bush, courtesy of the White House Photo
Office, photographer Paul Marce.

This expanded book club edition of *The First Ladies*
is published by arrangement with Oxford University Press, Inc.

ACKNOWLEDGMENTS

F OR PERMISSION to quote from the following manuscript collections, I wish to thank: Cornell University Library, the Moore Family Papers; New Britain Public Library, Elihu Burritt's Journal; the University of Tennessee Library, the Papers of Margaret and Smiley Blanton; Penfield Library of State University at Oswego, the Papers of Millard Fillmore; Massachusetts Historical Society, the Adams Family Papers; the Virginia Historical Society, the letters of Martha Washington; the Library of Congress, the Papers of Woodrow Wilson; and the Ohio Historical Society, the Papers of Warren G. Harding.

New York City is rich in libraries and I have used many of them during the course of researching this book. I am particularly grateful to the staffs of the libraries of New York University, Columbia University, the Graduate Center and Kingsborough Community College of the City University of New York, and the Forty-second Street Public Library, where I worked in the Wertheim Room. The National Endowment for the Humanities granted me a Fellowship that freed me from teaching during the 1985–86 academic year when I finished the project. I also wish to thank Susan Rabiner, of Oxford University Press, and Mary Jatlow, of Nelson Doubleday Books, who edited this book through several different versions.

Livio Caroli arrived in New York in 1965 with very little interest in American history (which he found lacking in political intrigue when compared with that of his native Venice) but he has gradually revised his opinion. His "outsider's view" that the institution of First Lady was an interesting American invention helped convince

me that the subject required a book, and he has enthusiastically
supported the project to its completion.

B.B.C.

New York City

Contents

INTRODUCTION

A T FIRST, the prospect of writing a book on presidents' wives did not interest me. What value could there be in studying a group of women united only by the fact that their husbands had held the same job? My curiosity was piqued, however, when I looked at what had been published on the subject. Even a cursory reading of the standard works revealed striking patterns among presidents' wives. Most of them came from social and economic backgrounds significantly superior to those of the men they married. Many of the women wed in spite of strenuous parental objection to their choices, and some of the men were younger than their brides. Recurring phrases hinted that the women assumed more control over their lives than I had imagined. Several of the wives had eased the financial burdens of their households by managing family farms, teaching school, and working as secretaries after their marriages. Other information pointed to a pattern of early exposure to politics, and I was struck by the number of uncles, fathers, and grandfathers who had at one time held political office. Perhaps the women deserved a closer look.

As soon as I examined the women's unpublished letters, I was intrigued. Who could read Lucretia Garfield's poignant puzzlings in the 1850s about what being a wife meant and not then go on to learn how her marriage turned out? What about the indomitable Sarah Polk, whose blunt letters showed her to be particularly opinionated and astute? Was the handwritten memorandum on the subject of Mary Lincoln's insanity trial to be believed? What about the mysterious Eliza Johnson, who was much maligned as a hill woman of little education? Why did her son, then enrolled at Georgetown, write her a beautifully penned, grammatically perfect letter and ask her to "excuse the mistakes"? These and dozens of other questions arose.

A handful of presidents' wives achieved great fame, of course, but others of equal or greater interest and significance have been allowed to drop into obscurity. Nearly 170 years before Jackie Kennedy charmed Paris, James Monroe's wife, Elizabeth, was dubbed "la belle Américaine" in the French capital. Abigail Adams is remembered for her spirited vitality while her daughter-in-law Louisa, wife of John Quincy Adams, who showed considerable courage by traveling from St. Petersburg to Paris during the Napoleonic Wars, is almost forgotten. Eleanor Roosevelt's break with precedents is well documented, especially her agreement to meet regularly with women reporters, but her predecessor, Lou Hoover, gained little credit for the feminist speeches she delivered on national radio or for the fortitude she showed in her personal life. Living in China during the Boxer Rebellion, she witnessed gun battles in front of her house but refused to show fright or to flee. Such courageous women surely deserved more attention than they had received.

Although the Constitution mentions no assignments for the chief executive's spouse, she has become a prominent part of the presidency. Both outspoken Eleanor Roosevelt and reticent Bess Truman were named during their husbands' administrations as among the "most powerful people in Washington," while the vice-presidents were conspicuously absent from such lists. President Ford, whose wife Betty explained that she resorted to "pillow talk" to convince her husband of her point of view, admitted that she was frequently successful. Her opinion had carried weight, he said, on some very controversial issues, including the pardon of Richard Nixon. Rosalynn Carter admitted that the enlistment of a president's wife in almost any project is of inestimable value. At the conclusion of the 1985 Geneva Summit Conference, President Reagan appeared in front of the United States Congress and thanked his wife Nancy for being "an outstanding ambassador of goodwill for us all."

Tracing the evolution of the title "First Lady" is particularly fascinating. Back in 1789, crowds accustomed to the pomp of royal persons heralded the wife of their new president as "Lady Washington." Usage soon changed, however. When the United States reaffirmed its democratic vows and "plain folks" politics, a "First Lady" made no sense at all. Presidential campaigns that boasted of candidates' humble origins, including log cabin births and little formal schooling, could hardly fasten noble-sounding titles on the wives of the winners. The women were addressed as "Presidentress" or "Mrs. President" or, as was frequently the case, not mentioned at all outside Washington.

Eventually the country's familiarity with its chief executive grew and expectations for the president's wife also heightened. In the 1850s, James Buchanan's young niece, who served as his official hostess, was praised as "our Democratic queen," and in the Republican administration that followed, Mary Lincoln became the "Republican queen." Even a century later some people likened Jackie Kennedy's position to that of Princess Grace of Monaco.

During the last quarter of the nineteenth century, as mass circulation magazines made presidents and their families more familiar figures across the continent, the presidents' wives began to assume a popularity of their own. Lucy Hayes, who accompanied her husband on the first trip a president ever took from the Atlantic coast to the Pacific, heard herself heralded as the "first lady of the land."

As the New Deal drew power and attention to Washington in the 1930s, and World War II added a large dose of unifying patriotism, the use of "First Lady" seemed to flourish, and even began to appear in dictionaries. However, many women who held the title detested it—the question arose about what to call their husbands and jests were made about "First Mate," "First Gentleman," or "First Spouse." None of these objections had any effect, though, and popular magazines continued to publish prominent articles about the current "First Lady," while television correspondents superimposed their own stamp of approval on the phrase.

Since the institution of "First Lady" is an American one, it seems reasonable to ask what in the United States provided for such growth. Did a quirk in the presidential system nurture it? Or did it develop out of peculiarly American attitudes about leaders?

The United States' presidency, as established by the Constitutional Convention in 1787, includes two jobs that are performed by separate individuals in other types of representative governments: a head of state who presides over ceremonial functions and a head of government who makes major appointments and takes a decisive role in legislation. The American president, charged with both tasks, frequently resorted to sending substitutes on ceremonial and other occasions when a mere physical presence was required. Members of the president's household made excellent surrogates—they signaled the president's approval and also his continued control of government. Martha Washington began what became a tradition when she attended a New York church service while George was ill, and her example inspired her successors. Nearly two hundred years later, Nancy Reagan left her husband's hospital room to return to the White House and announce to guests assembled for a large reception that she was "the president's stand-in." Political wives substituted in other ways for their spouses, sometimes maintaining a facade of civility while their husbands feuded. John Quincy Adams observed in 1824 that Andrew Jackson and William Crawford, contenders for the presidency, were avoiding each other socially but "the ladies have exchanged visits."

The president's living arrangements also increased his wife's role. Once the decision had been made to combine the president's official residence with his private quarters, his spouse dealt with more than just guest lists at official dinners. With a husband who "worked at home," John Quincy Adams's wife Louisa liked to point out, she could not escape knowing something about his job—who supported him and who opposed him.

The election process provided another push into prominence for candidates' wives. Although it was considered inappropriate for women to campaign openly until well into the twentieth century, the groundwork was laid a century earlier. Since presidents must seek a popular mandate rather than the approval of their party caucus as a prime minister does, they cannot rely on the contacts and trust accrued from years of working with colleagues but must go to the population at large. A stand-in campaigner is always useful and enjoys some advantages over the candidate. Rosalynn Carter went off on her own in quest of votes for Jimmy fourteen months in advance of the 1976 nomination because she recognized the need to reach many voters. Lady Bird Johnson, confident that Southern chivalry would accord her courtesies not granted her husband, campaigned on her own through several states in 1964. She called campaigning "one of the bills you have to pay for the job your husband has."

The enlistment of presidents' spouses in prominent roles required the concurrence of the women, several of whom compiled remarkable records. Eleanor Roosevelt's unprecedented energy over twelve years raised the possibility of just what a president's wife could accomplish; Lady Bird Johnson moved the distaff side of the White House off the family pages of the country's newspapers and into the mainstream of her husband's "Great Society"; Betty Ford took public stands at odds with those of her husband; Rosalynn Carter attended cabinet meetings, defended her approach to mental health care in front of a Senate committee, and conducted talks of a "substantive" nature on a Latin American trip. During Ronald Reagan's convalescence in the summer of 1985, Washington watchers pointed to three people in control at the White House: the president, his chief of staff, and the First Lady.

A few First Ladies marked watersheds in the history of the job. Dolley Madison's popularity does not stem solely, as many believe, from her having introduced ice cream to Americans. (That distinction belongs more likely to Thomas Jefferson, who recorded in his own hand the preferred recipe for the cold dessert that he had liked so much in France.) For almost half a century, Dolley Madison remained a central figure in the capital, showing an uncanny ability to use social occasions to her husband's political advantage. She had laid the foundation for her prominence in the Jefferson administration (1801–1809) when the widowed president turned to her to help him entertain. Later, when James Madison succeeded Thomas Jefferson, Dolley had two terms of her own (1809–1817) to solidify an important role for the president's consort. After her husband retired from office, she continued to act as unofficial tutor to young White House hostesses, making her last, very celebrated appearance at President Polk's party in 1849.

The two decades embracing the Lincoln (1861–1865) and Grant (1869–1877) administrations offered a similar turning point. For two generations preceding them, presidents' wives had made themselves nearly invisible in Washington. Some pled poor health or grief over family tragedies, but most felt justified in sending in substitutes to preside over social gatherings. Neither Mary Lincoln nor Julia Grant showed a similar reticence when confronted with the spotlight; both obliged photographers and reporters who requested pictures and information. The public appetite was whetted for trivia about important persons, and Jenkinsism (the nineteenth century equivalent of what later came to be called paparazzi) had its day.

Some presidents' wives paralleled their husbands' interpretations of the job of chief executive. While Theodore Roosevelt (1901–1909) took advantage of what he termed the "bully pulpit," his wife Edith streamlined the executive mansion and hired a staff for herself. Theodore officially renamed the mansion the "White House" and Edith helped transform it into an important national monument. Together they drew the nation's attention to the energetic young family residing at 1600 Pennsylvania Avenue and set the stage for the increased attention in the following decades.

The thirty-odd women who shaped First Ladyship (counting is complicated by the fact that daughters, daughters-in-law, and sisters of presidents used the title) ranged in age from early twenties to late sixties, from superbly educated for their time to poorly schooled. Some showed themselves immensely courageous and adventuresome; others were emotionally unstable, withdrawn, and beset by enough personal tragedies to defeat even gargantuan wills. Each woman worked within a set of expectations for her time and place, often within the confines imposed by the special needs of marriage to a politician. Each was given "a magic wand" of sorts, with no instructions on its use—each woman had to figure that out for herself.

Note to the reader: The question of what name to use for women who are married to famous men remains a difficult one. Writers commonly refer to men by their last name alone (as in "Washington's Farewell") so that wives, when they are mentioned at all, are left with the cumbersome combination of first and last names (Mary Lincoln) or first name alone (Jackie, Nancy). Since famous couples are my subject here, I decided to treat both partners equally and use given names or full names as appropriate.

THE FIRST LADIES

Setting Precedents:
The First Presidents'
Wives
1789–1829

MARTHA DANDRIDGE CUSTIS WASHINGTON

O<small>N A MAY MORNING IN</small> 1789, President Washington's barge docked at the southern tip of Manhattan and a short, matronly woman stepped ashore. After thirty years of marriage to the tall general beside her, Martha Washington was accustomed to fitting her life to his, but the direction of that accommodation was no longer clear. His role in this new government remained undefined, falling somewhere between monarch and commoner; her part was even less clear. If George would not be king, then she could not be queen; yet the thirteen-gun salute and shouts of "Long Live Lady Washington" suggested some kind of special prominence.

To deal with many problems, including some of the questions about her role, George Washington had preceded Martha to the new nation's temporary capital in New York, and when he went over to New Jersey that morning to escort his wife into the city, he supplied the answer to at least one of those questions. Rather than let Martha Washington travel in a private conveyance, he brought her over in the presidential barge. Thus, the president and Martha arrived to fanfare, signaling the beginning of what would become an American tradition—the presidential spouse had a public role in the ritual and ceremonial aspects of the presidency.

The crowds that lined the streets as the Washingtons made their way from the Battery to their rented house on Cherry Street were not the first that Martha had faced. On her trips to join George each winter during the Revolution, she had already responded to cheers for "Lady Washington." Those earlier outbursts had seemed almost part of the war mood and may have been directed as much to raising the morale of the spectators as to expressing tribute to the general's wife. When the shouts continued after the war ended, their meaning was less clear.

Other kinds of uncertainty surrounded much of the new government's activity in 1789. The Constitution writers, in their attempts to assign neither too much power to the chief executive nor too little, had debated for weeks without resolving all matters involving the president. They had not even specified how he should be addressed. The Senate suggested "His Highness, the President of the United States and Protector of Liberties," but the more democratic House of Representatives would hear of nothing other than "Mr. President." One newspaper editor argued vehemently for "His Excellency," and John Adams pointed out that a simple "Mr. President" showed too little deference and sounded like the officer of some local, insignificant association. Suggestions of titles for the president's wife ranged all the way from "Marquise" and "Lady" down to a simple "Mrs."

George Washington canvassed widely for advice, going to personal friends, a Supreme Court justice, congressmen, and his own vice-president for counsel on how to balance the need for accessibility with the other demands of his job. Alexander Hamilton, an outspoken advocate of a powerful executive, advised his mentor to keep social contacts to a minimum, in order to preserve the dignity of the office. A president might issue invitations, Hamilton suggested, but not more often than once a week, and when he met his guests, he should spend very little time with them. As for visits to other people's homes, Hamilton thought these entirely inappropriate and he warned against them. John Adams, who had never gained a reputation for catering to the masses, came out on the more liberal side in this discussion when he ventured that the president might call on close personal friends and hold as many as two parties a week.

Finally George Washington took space in the local newspaper to announce his general calling hours: persons simply paying their respects should limit themselves to Tuesday and Friday afternoons between two and three o'clock, while those on business could come any time except Sunday, when the president wanted to see no one at all.

George also resolved that he would host a reception for men only, called a "levée," each Tuesday afternoon and that Martha would preside on Friday evenings at another party, called a "drawing room," which both men and women could attend. To mark this latter occasion as official but slightly less formal than the first, the president would attend but he would carry neither sword nor hat.

Martha Washington had not even arrived in the capital for these discussions, so she could hardly have been consulted as to her views, but George's wide canvass for advice set the stage for his successors to admit that they included their wives in important presidential matters. Martha's acquiescence in her role is confirmed by the fact that immediately upon her arrival in New York she began performing tasks that resulted from her husband's office. The first morning she awakened to face dozens of curious women who had directed their carriages to her Cherry Street house, and that afternoon she sat down to dinner with guests whom George had previously invited. This was no mere social event but one of the president's first attempts at political brokerage. Although political

parties had not yet developed, George had reasoned that congressmen from different parts of the country needed an opportunity to
meet socially and work out possible differences.

The next day, a Friday, Martha held her first "drawing room," a
party that brought out New York's curious to evaluate the hostess's
efforts to entertain graciously without seeming to carve a superior
niche for herself. Whether or not Martha satisfied these competing
claims to everyone's satisfaction remains unclear. But she certainly
tried. While stewards brought in guests, she remained seated in
queenly fashion and the president moved among those present,
escorting them to the refreshment table and supplying introduc-
tions. When guests stood around uncertainly, not knowing how to
end the party, Martha took control. Those present had wondered
whether they should wait respectfully for the hostess to exit, as they
would have done for royalty, or, in good democratic style, leave at
whim. Martha's solution could hardly have offended or been interpreted as taking on airs. "The General always retires at nine," she
stood and announced, "and I generally precede him." Then she
walked out.

Before her marriage to George, Martha had acquired a reputation
for having a mind of her own, although the stories about her may be
as apocryphal as those of George and the cherry tree. She slapped
the face of an offensive suitor at a fashionable ball and rode her
horse up the stairs of her uncle's house. Later, after her first husband died, she found herself at twenty-six with two young children
and one of the largest estates in Virginia. Writing to an English
merchant, she outlined the conditions under which she would sell to
him and her hopes that he would be fair. The many corrections in
the manuscript draft indicate that she could not have found the task
easy but the wording shows she could be firm: "It will be proper to
continue this Account in the same manner as if my husband was
living, as most of the goods I shall send for will be for the good of
the family." She signed herself simply, "Martha Custis." Later, after
she had married George Washington, she advised her young niece

to be "as independent as your circumstances will admit because dependence is, I think, a wretched state."

Her marriage to George Washington was only the first in a long list of upwardly mobile unions for presidents. The two met in 1758, shortly after her first husband had died, leaving her in possession of thousands of acres of land and nearly 30,000 pounds in colonial Virginia currency—the equivalent of several million twentieth-century dollars. A few months later, after having seen her only a few times, George married Martha. Almost a year younger than his bride—and a foot taller—he cut a dashing figure. The young widow evidently perceived in him some potential that other women missed since she married him after they had turned him down.

His own money could hardly have figured in George's attractiveness because his holdings amounted to far less than Martha's. The Mount Vernon estate had already gone to George's half brother. Not until about the time George married did he inherit the bulk of his father's estate, and even then, it took his bride's holdings to make him a really rich man.

Mention of financial gain from his union with Martha always rankled George. Many years later, after he had become president and was negotiating to purchase land for the new capital, the matter came up again. David Burns, a blunt old Scotsman, happened to own some property that George wanted for the new Federal City, but Burns rejected all arguments that his patriotic duty extended to selling the land. When the president pressured him, Burns blurted out, "I suppose, Mr. Washington, you think people are going to take every grist from you as pure grain; but what would you have been if you hadn't married the rich widow Custis!" According to the often-repeated story, the president stalked out and refused to communicate further with Burns.

In the first weeks of the Washington presidency (1789–1797), it was curiosity more than criticism that drew New Yorkers to the chief executive's house. Despite the firm limits George set for himself, Martha reasoned that she should do otherwise. Custom dictated that a gracious lady, no matter what her husband's title, returned the calls of all women who had come to her door and left their calling cards, so Martha resolved to return each visit, and to accomplish this within three days of the original call.

Even the vice-president's wife, Abigail Adams, soon got caught up in this activity, noting in a letter that she had "returned 60 visits in 3 or 4 afternoons." Following the Washingtons' lead, the Adamses invited all the congressmen and their wives to dine with them: "Indeed I have been fully employed," Abigail Adams wrote, "in entertaining company, and tho we have a room in which we dine 24 persons at a Time, I shall not get through them all for a month."

When the Washingtons' house on Cherry Street failed to accommodate their invited guests, George and Martha moved to larger quarters on Broadway. But before settling completely into their new house, they had to prepare to move again—this time to Philadelphia, where the nation's capital was transferred in the fall of 1790.

The move to Philadelphia pleased Martha in some ways—she thought her new Market Street address afforded more privacy than she had found in New York—and by Christmas day, she was ready to open her house to local residents. A week later, many of them returned for her New Year's reception, a repeat performance of the party she had given the year before in New York. Her regular Friday drawing room occurred on January 1 in 1790, and George had postponed his Tuesday levée to coincide, thus beginning a tradition that the president and his wife would open their house on New Year's to all who wanted to come. Except in wartime or periods of mourning, the event was a regular feature of the president's schedule and eventually drew thousands, until it so taxed the energies of the hosts that the Hoovers stopped it in 1933.

By the time George Washington's two terms had been completed, some aspects of the president's role had been settled (although by no means all) and some of his wife's responsibilities had taken shape (although they would change). In meeting the obligations of the two roles he had assumed—as head of state and head of government—

the president would enlist his spouse's help openly in the first job but only covertly, if at all, in the second. Since the ceremonial side of the job required presenting a democratic image but also including enough formality to retain respect, a wife who was willing to do so could help maintain a balance. When her husband appeared pompous, she might stress humility; if he chose to move casually among guests, she could hold court in queenly fashion. Her calls at people's homes substituted for contacts that her husband's schedule did not permit.

George and Martha Washington thus set some precedents that would continue relatively undisturbed for more than a century, until gradually the job of president's wife changed to involve her more openly in the substantive part of the office. Martha gave no evidence of playing anything other than the hostess role—and George gave no evidence of ever requesting that she do more—but the role she filled should not be dismissed lightly. When he was too ill to attend church services, her presence was duly recorded, as though people in a pretelevision age needed a glimpse of their leader for reassurance. She even helped her husband circumvent the prohibition against a president's accepting gifts. When Pennsylvania offered her a costly carriage, George decided she could keep it since it had not actually been bestowed on him.

Newspapers that survive from the eighteenth century show that considerable attention was paid to Martha Washington. On her first journey alone after George's inauguration, the *Pennsylvania Packet* reported on each segment, including how troops had marched outside Philadelphia to meet her and escort her entourage to the party that had been prepared for them at Gray's Ferry on the Schuylkill River. By the time Martha arrived at Robert Morris's Market Street house, where she was to spend the night, she felt obliged to acknowledge the crowds, and in her one speech on record, she stood in her carriage and thanked Philadelphians for their hospitality. When she continued her journey the next morning, troops accompanied her out of the city until rain threatened and she insisted they turn back. The *Pennsylvania Packet* concluded its lengthy description of that visit with its own judgment that the president's wife was a "most amiable woman."

Interest in Martha Washington's activities continued during her eight years as First Lady and even afterward. When George died in 1799, Congress officially recognized Martha Washington by granting her the franking privilege, which she used until her death in 1802 at her Mount Vernon home.

ABIGAIL SMITH ADAMS

THE NEXT FIRST LADY, Abigail Smith Adams (1797–1801), brought very different ideas to marriage and women's role in it— opinions that could not help but make themselves felt in how she handled the role of president's wife. Speaking out had always come naturally to her, and John's first mention of her in his diary, when she was only fourteen, was as "a wit." By the time she reached maturity, her sharp tongue and strong views had become more obviously part of her personality. When her husband ascended to the country's highest office in 1797, rumors multiplied concerning her influence. Rather than Lady Adams, she was dubbed "Mrs. President."

From very early in her husband's administration, Abigail Adams was accused of playing politics. When she spoke out on the split developing between Jeffersonian Republicans and Federalists, she had, in the opinion of many political figures, stepped beyond the proper bounds for her sex. Albert Gallatin, an Adams opponent, in

a letter to his wife, described how Abigail had been observed singling out some members of Congress and labeling them "our people." Such partisanship in a woman offended Gallatin and he ridiculed Abigail as "Mrs. President not of the United States but of a
faction." He much preferred his own apolitical spouse, whom he
called "infinitely more lovely than politics."

Such criticism failed to silence Abigail Adams. A woman might
"not hold the reins of government," Abigail once wrote, but that
should not stop her from judging how government was "conducted." Hundreds of letters she wrote to family and friends reveal
her opinions on many matters and several leading political figures.
In Alexander Hamilton's eyes she saw "the very devil itself." She
judged a Massachusetts congressman uninformed; Albert Gallatin
was a dangerous, "sly, artfull, insidious" man who, by openly favoring France, had misled people about how much influence the French
had on the United States government.

In seeking the reasons for Abigail's strong voice, the record of her
marriage is not inconsequential. She had wed John Adams in spite
of family objection. His Harvard education might have seemed rec-
ommendation enough for his seeking the hand of Abigail Smith, but
her parents refused to think so. John's legal profession made him
suspect, and even if his earnings increased, he could not offer the
economic security and social prestige that the Reverend Smith
thought his daughter deserved.

Abigail's mother openly disapproved of John Adams; her father
did little better at concealing his dislike. When the young couple
decided to marry anyway and asked her father to perform the ceremony, he puzzled the congregation by taking as his biblical text a
verse from the Book of Luke that reads, "John came neither eating
bread nor drinking wine and some say he has a devil in him." The
bridegroom remained unruffled by his cool welcome and boasted to
a friend that he had married into the family of the "richest clergy-
man in the province."

During the early years of their marriage, when her husband absented himself for long periods, Abigail eased his rise in politics by her willingness and ability to raise their five children (their eldest son, John Quincy Adams, later became President), run the family farm in Quincy, Massachusetts, and keep the household solvent.

Abigail occasionally complained of the weight of her responsibilities, but her family appreciated her contribution to the men's careers. In 1776, nearly a century and a half before the publication of Virginia Woolf's *A Room of One's Own,* Abigail lamented the lack of time and space for herself: "I always had a fancy for a closet with a window which I could more peculiarly call my own." Abigail's grandson may well have had her complaint in mind when he noted how her careful management had helped the Adamses escape the financial worries that plagued both Thomas Jefferson and James Monroe. In the introduction to his grandmother's letters, Charles Francis Adams wrote that she was "a farmer cultivating the land and discussing the weather and the crops; a merchant reporting prices current and the rates of exchange and directing the making up of invoices, a politician speculating upon the probabilities of war, and a mother—and in all she appears equally well."

Finally, in 1784, she was able to join her husband in France when the family rented a house in Auteuil. Because she could not speak French, although she read it, Abigail found dealing with servants difficult; dinner parties with non-English speakers made her uncomfortable. She worried about her clothes in a country where style obviously mattered. "To be out of fashion is more criminal than to be seen in a state of nature," she observed, "to which," she added primly, "Parisians are not averse." But her curiosity and genuine interest in French ways proved more powerful than her complaints; and her own letters, as well as those of her daughter and husband, indicate these were some of the family's happiest times.

The French stay was cut short when John Adams was appointed Ambassador to the Court of St. James in 1785. It was an extremely awkward post since his presence served as a reminder to Britons that they had recently lost thirteen of their American colonies. Abigail found her reception icy, and she informed her sister that she had never been treated so badly as when forced to stand in line for four hours waiting "for a gracious smile from majesty." She could not wait to leave England. When the English Queen Charlotte was later reported to have her own worries, Abigail showed little sympathy, and she wrote her daughter that the woman deserved whatever humiliation she received.

After five years in Europe, Abigail could not hide her nostalgia for home. She had seen enough of the world, she wrote her friend Thomas Jefferson, and she was ready to retire to her little farm that had "more charms for my fancy than residing at the Court of St. James where I seldom meet characters so inoffensive as my hens and chicks or minds so well improved as my garden. Heaven forgive me," she added primly, "I wish they deserved better at my hands."

After John achieved high office, Abigail continued to devote her managerial abilities to promoting his success, relieving him of family responsibilities and training a careful eye on expenses. She had missed his inauguration in 1797 because she was nursing his sick mother in Massachusetts, and when he complained that he needed her with him, she replied she would come as soon as she could—she would not wait for "courting."

By the time Abigail arrived in Philadelphia in May 1797, inflation had so diminished the value of the chief executive's salary that entertaining became a financial, as well as an emotional, burden. In her diary she noted that for the Fourth of July reception that the president traditionally gave for representatives and senators, she would have to supply 200 pounds of cake and two 1/4 casks of wine and rum. True to form, she managed to save part of the president's salary while still fulfilling what she perceived as social obligations. Few of her successors would be able to do so; her loud complaints indicate, however, that she had intended to save even more.

Demands her husband's job imposed on her time became nearly as objectionable as those on her purse, and she complained of having to rise at five in order to have some time to herself. Her mornings were devoted to "family arrangements," but the after-noons were filled with First Lady work—receiving guests and making calls.

John's biographers found clear evidence that he discussed many important problems with her, engaged her help in drafting semi-official letters, and in the words of historian Page Smith, treated her as "minister without portfolio." It comes as no surprise that people who sought the president's approval sometimes went to his wife first. Nor did they hesitate to blame her when things went awry. After John Adams had made an unpopular appointment while his wife was ill in Massachusetts, he wrote to inform her how much she was missed. His friends judged her "a good counsellor," he wrote, and if she had been with him, he might have avoided his mistake. "This ought to gratify your vanity enough to cure you," he concluded.

To the minority who approved of opinionated women, Abigail Adams became something of a heroine. Henrietta Liston, wife of the British minister, wrote her uncle in 1797 that she was "much pleased with Mrs. Adams, and hoped to acquire her sort of spirit in time "but the thing is new to me yet." Albert Gallatin's kind of disapproval was the more common response, and Abigail found herself caricatured in both song and drawing. An English ballad of the time had popularized the story of an elderly married couple, "Darby and Joan," who were devoted to each other but woefully out of touch with their times, and Abigail was distressed to see herself and her husband referred to in print as America's "Darby and Joan." However strong the criticism, Abigail persisted in her efforts to help John in whatever way she could.

Near the end of John Adams's single term, Abigail had to oversee the transfer of the President's Palace, as it was still called by some people, to the new capital on the banks of the Potomac. In letters to her family she made little attempt to conceal her displeasure with the unformed city that she found in December 1800. Streets remained unfinished in Washington, Abigail wrote to her daughter, and Georgetown "is the very dirtyest Hole I ever saw for a place of any trade, or respectability of inhabitants—a quagmire after every rain." Vacillating as usual between wanting the president to live in comfort and frowning on too much splendor, Congress had been stingy with appropriations for his new permanent residence, and the Adamses arrived to find the house unfinished. Not all the rooms had been plastered, "bells are wholly wanting," Abigail complained, "and promises are all you can obtain." When the time came for the requisite entertaining, Abigail herded her guests into the one fully furnished hall, but understanding the political cost of appearing too critical of what had been provided, she alerted her daughter, "When asked how I like it, say that I wrote you the situation is beautiful."

Abigail hardly had time to settle into the Washington house before the results of the 1800 election signaled that she would have to move out. The election had gone on for weeks because a tie in the electoral college between Jefferson and Burr threw the decision into the House of Representatives. Abigail Adams understood that her husband was out of the running but she could not bring herself to leave Washington until the final balloting on February 11, 1801, less than a month before the inauguration. Deeply disappointed but philosophical about Jefferson's victory, which ended the administration she had frequently described as "ours," she wrote to her son, "The consequences to us personally is that we retire from public life. If I did not rise with dignity, I can at least fall with ease, which is the more difficult task." Although Abigail and John Adams retired to their home in Quincy, Abigail kept up her interest in politics until her death in 1818.

Nearly half a century would pass before Americans again voted into the presidency a man (James Polk) who appeared to hold such high regard for the counsel of his spouse as did John Adams. This was respect, it should be noted, which resulted from experience. During their long marriage, Abigail showed both wisdom and strength, never permitting concern with domestic details to shut her off from important issues facing the country. When John was absent from Massachusetts, she kept him informed of political sentiment there, and she exchanged letters with many astute women, including Mercy Warren, the historian of the Revolution. Abigail's voicing of strong opinions after her husband became president represented no change in her behavior—she had always spoken her mind—and she demonstrated that a president's wife could, with her husband's support, move beyond a merely ceremonial role to involve herself in substantive issues.

The Adams administration also demonstrated, however, that a president would be criticized by the Gallatins of the time, who preferred the model left by Martha Washington. She had always stayed well within the confines of domesticity, and as the president's wife, she continued in a docile, supportive role. Which of the two examples became the pattern would be determined by those who followed.

DOLLEY PAYNE TODD MADISON

T HOMAS JEFFERSON'S TWO TERMS (1801–1809) offered an excellent opportunity to introduce different expectations for hostesses at the White House because he was a widower. His wife, Martha Wayles Skelton Jefferson, had died in 1782, and his oldest daughter, Martha Jefferson Randolph, was busy with her own large family. But etiquette dictated the presence of a hostess if women guests were to attend a dinner party, and so President Jefferson asked his good friend, Dolley Madison, to "take care of the female guests expected." His choice of Dolley came naturally. Jefferson's home,

Monticello, was within a few miles of the Madisons' Virginia estate and in the first years of her marriage, when her husband's fame had drawn crowds of admirers, Dolley had frequently fled to the quiet of Jefferson's house to avoid the confusion at her own. James Madison's appointment as secretary of state in 1801 legitimatized her new prominence in Washington society, and she thoroughly enjoyed the elevation. Martha Washington and Abigail Adams accepted a portion of the president's ceremonial tasks for themselves, and Dolley Madison used Jefferson's two terms to assure a central role for whoever served as the president's hostess and to develop her own formidable reputation for adroitly mixing politics and parties. An older, less energetic, or more insecure woman in her place might have hesitated to assert herself, but Dolley Madison, at thirty-two, showed no reluctance.

Dolley Madison's emergence as a superior hostess is somewhat ironic since she was raised in the Society of Friends, where frivolity and extravagance had little place. From a childhood among the "plain people," she grew to put great importance on what she wore and on having a good time, ordering her shawls and turbans from Paris and losing money at cards with considerable aplomb. Much of the change in her life can be attributed to her marriage, surely one of the most unusual unions in presidential history.

Dolley Payne Todd's marriage to James Madison had not been her first. Like Martha Washington and Martha Jefferson, she had been a widow when she wed a future president. The third-born child of failed shopkeepers in Philadelphia, Dolley had first married a young lawyer from her family's Quaker congregation. Within three years, both he and one of their young sons had died, leaving Dolley at age twenty-five to fend for herself and her remaining son, She moved back to her mother's to help run a boardinghouse. Within months, Aaron Burr introduced her to one of the most famous men in America—James Madison—who had passed age forty without taking a wife. Because he was several inches shorter than she but of obvious intellect and even then of enormous reputation, she immediately dubbed him the "great little Madison."

Shy, even dour in public, he could be a wit in private and evidently admired a woman who could take her gaiety everywhere. Within months of their meeting and less than a year after her first husband's death, Dolley Payne Todd and James Madison were married in 1794. For the forty-odd years they lived together, he complained if he had to be separated from his "Dolley" and she ran here and there in the service of the man she always called "Madison."

The first woman to witness her husband's swearing in as President, Dolley immediately indicated her intention to play a visible role by opening her Georgetown house for a reception following the inauguration ceremony. Perhaps because the event fell on a Saturday, larger than usual crowds had come to Washington and hundreds of people lined up to sample the Madisons' punch and cake. The President's House would have accommodated a larger crowd, but ex-presidents did not vacate speedily in those days and Jefferson took a week to get his things together for the trip back to Monticello.

At the first inaugural ball, planned by Washington's Dancing Assembly for Long's Hotel that evening, Dolley continued to hold center stage. Heavy demand for tickets (only four hundred were issued) led to great confusion, and the room became so congested that someone had to break a window to provide ventilation. People stood on benches to catch a glimpse of the new president's wife, who behaved, one woman wrote glowingly, "with perfect propriety, dignity, sweetness and grace." John Quincy Adams, who rarely enjoyed social gatherings and never shone at them, stood in the minority when he pronounced this party "excessive . . . oppressive and bad."

The president's official residence remained unfinished at the beginning of the Madison administration (1809–17), and one young visitor from New York described its exterior as appallingly grim, more suitable for a "State Prison" than anything else. Dolley insisted that improvements begin at once. When Congress appropriated $11,000, she spent almost one-quarter of the total on just the East Room (which Jefferson had neglected to furnish). For help in her selections, she turned to Benjamin Latrobe, the English-born architect who had become President Jefferson's surveyor of public buildings. Fewer than eight weeks after the inauguration she was ready to show off the results at her first drawing room.

At these parties the public's curiosity was divided between the president and his wife, so the weaknesses of one partner were offset by the strengths of the other. James Madison, who could be appealing in private but appear disinterested around people he did not know, gained from Dolley's ability to charm almost everyone. Washington Irving, who attended a Madison reception soon after he arrived in the capital in 1811, captured the difference when he described Dolley as "a fine, portly buxom dame who has a smile and pleasant word for everybody, but as to Jemmy Madison, ah poor Jemmy—he is but a withered little applejohn." The president preferred an inconspicuous seat at the dinner table so he could avoid having to play the host, and his guests frequently went away thinking he had not even noticed them.

Dolley's entertaining had its political side and she often showed the skills of a candidate running for office, rarely forgetting a name or making an inappropriate comment. Aware of the criticism that had surrounded Abigail Adams, Dolley showered her husband's enemies with the same attention that she gave his friends. Frances Few, who visited the capital during Dolley's first season, pointed to her inscrutability when she wrote, "It is impossible to know what Mrs. Madison is thinking because she tried to be all things to all men." Some critics claimed that Dolley paid too much attention to other men; one White House visitor reported that the president's wife had told an old bachelor that she was "no prude, and then held up her mouth for him to kiss." A political opponent had hinted broadly during a campaign that James "had impaired" himself "by an unfortunate matrimonial connection," but such attacks were rare. Dolley Madison achieved a popularity that her successors would envy for decades to come.

The reputation resulted from more than the style of her parties. In delicate political maneuvering, she could soften a cruel dismissal. After her husband eased Robert Smith, secretary of state, out of his cabinet in 1811, she gave a dinner in Smith's honor. When Smith failed to appear, Dolley took her sister and "called twice," Smith wrote, "with professions of great affection."

The desire to cultivate political support for her husband sent Dolley out visiting all the congressmen's families who moved to Washington. The fact that she called first was important—it signaled humility in the president's attitude toward legislators. But the number of congressmen and their aides had grown since the days of Martha Washington and Abigail Adams, so the number of calls multiplied. Although often perfunctory (with Dolley leaving her carriage only long enough to drop her card on the silver tray in the front hall), the calls took her from one end of Washington's unpaved streets to the other, consuming entire days so that she had only Sundays for herself. Yet tampering with tradition carried political risks that she understood all too well, since any family slighted might take revenge on her husband.

The expectation that Dolley would not only call on each family but also invite them to the President's House imposed a large burden even on someone who thrived on playing the hostess. "We have members in abundance with their wives and daughters," Dolley wrote to friends in Paris, "and I have never felt the entertainment of company oppressive until now."

Dolley Madison's task became more difficult as the presidential election of 1812 approached. James Madison's first term had not been easy. Both the British and French had continued to interfere with American shipping on the Atlantic, and boundary disputes with Indians erupted frequently in the Great Lakes region. Yet James very much wanted another term and Dolley remained optimistic about his chances. As early as December 1811, she had observed that "the intrigues for President and Vice President go on," but she correctly predicted that the next election would terminate in victory "as the last did."

Dolley well understood the importance of keeping discontented congressmen in line so that they would not be tempted to vote for DeWitt Clinton, the opponent. Six months before the election, she wrote her sister that a large number of legislators were annoyed with the President "and refused to dine with him," but a week later she had them there "in a large body." James Blaine, who later tried for the presidency himself, credited Dolley with a large share in her husband's second presidential victory. Her cheerful impartiality brought the disenchanted around, Blaine wrote, and she convinced them to stick with the incumbent.

Historians who have carefully studied the Madison administration tend to agree that Dolley proved a valuable asset to her husband. In the continuing debate between a democratic chief executive and a regal one, she played both sides; and for every critic who thought she went too far on one side, she acquired an admirer on the other. One woman described approvingly how the Madisons maintained a royal setting at their parties where custom dictated that each female guest curtsey to the President and then find a seat, but a senator from Massachusetts stressed the egalitarianism at the Madisons' parties. For his tastes, Dolley went a bit too far in implementing democracy, mixing "all classes of people from the Minister from Russia to under clerks of the post office and the printer of a paper— greasy boots and silk stockings." Such contrasting evaluations of Dolley Madison led one historian to conclude that she was "brilliant in the things she did not say or do."

Even actions deemed inappropriate for her peers earned accolades for Dolley. Stained fingers left little doubt that she used snuff, not an acceptable habit for nineteenth-century ladies but one that was excused in her. "In her hands the snuffbox seems only a gracious implement with which to charm," one woman offered in Dolley's defense, and another admirer described the snuffbox as a "perfect security from hostility as bread and salt are among many savage tribes." Some of Dolley's observers considered the possibility that she used cosmetics, with some deciding that she surely "painted," while others offered evidence that her heightened color resulted from natural enthusiasm. "I do not think it true that she uses cosmetics," one contemporary wrote, "I saw her color come and go at the naval ball."

Dolley Madison's vivacious personality guaranteed her fame, but in her most celebrated act, she performed as a wife engineering the transfer of her house's furnishings. That the item she arranged to save happened to be a portrait of George Washington rendered this a patriotic act. According to Dolley, British troops were approaching the capital in August 1814, and the president was out of town consulting with his military advisers. She had been warned that she should "be ready at a moment's warning to enter my carriage and leave the city; that the enemy seemed stronger than had at first been reported, and it might happen that they would reach the city with the intention of destroying it." But Dolley insisted to her sister that she would not budge "until I see Mr. Madison safe so that he can accompany me." When a friend came to "hasten" her departure, she consented to go "as soon as the large picture of General Washington is secured. I have ordered the frame to be broken and the canvas taken out."

After leaving that day, Dolley never again lived at the White House. When the Madisons returned to Washington, the President's residence had been burned by the British, and Dolley had to move her entertaining elsewhere. But neither this obstacle—nor others that dogged her path—deterred the indomitable Dolley. After James's presidency ended in 1817, the Madisons returned to live at their Montpelier estate in Virginia but she kept an eye on the social life of the capital. When he died in 1836, she moved back to Washington, where her final years were marked by financial worries. Her son by her first marriage had never learned to manage money and he drove her nearly to ruin. Only by selling her husband's papers to Congress was she able to remain solvent. Washington hostesses sought her counsel and politicians continued to make courtesy calls at her house until her death in 1849 at age eighty-one. Just months earlier, she had attended her last White House party, this one given by President Polk nearly half a century after she had first made history there by hostessing for President Jefferson.

ELIZABETH KORTWRIGHT MONROE

U NLIKE HER PREDECESSOR, Elizabeth Kortwright Monroe acted to reduce dramatically the social obligations of all future First Ladies. The results of the 1816 presidential election had hardly come in when it became clear that Elizabeth Monroe had no intention of allowing her daily schedule to be dictated by others, certainly not by provincial wives of Midwestern congressmen. Born to wealthy New Yorkers, she was acquainted with the courts of Europe, having accompanied her husband James Monroe when he held diplomatic posts in both London and Paris.

Her single act of public courage occurred well before she became First Lady—when her husband was minister to France, in 1794. James and Elizabeth Monroe had arrived in Paris resolved to assist Marie-Adrienne Lafayette, wife of America's Revolutionary War friend Marquis de Lafayette, who was being held in a Paris prison during the French Revolution. To stir up sympathy for her plight, the Monroes bought a private carriage and painted it so it would draw the curious. Then Elizabeth Monroe rode alone, through the crowds that pressed in around her, to the prison gates, where a frightened and surprised Marie-Adrienne Lafayette came out to meet the American. The two women chatted and embraced in full view of the crowds. Mme. Lafayette, who had feared she was heading for the guillotine when she was summoned that morning, could hardly conceal her delight at seeing Elizabeth Monroe instead. The crowds appeared every bit as moved as she, and their cheers had the intended result—as James Monroe rather dryly summed up in his diary his wife's successful mission, "The sensibility of all the beholders was deeply excited" so that the Committee on Safety consented to Mme. Lafayette's release.

Back in America while her husband served as secretary of state (1809–1817), Elizabeth Monroe showed much more reticence and made clear that she expected to have little to do with the wives of other department heads. After seven years in the capital, she and her husband remained "perfect strangers," one social leader wrote, "not only to me but all citizens." James's elevation to the presidency (1817–1825) caused no deviation in the Monroes' custom. Some hope prevailed that invitations to the President's House would flow more freely after the mansion, destroyed in the 1814 burning of Washington by the British, had been rebuilt. However, Elizabeth's handling of her daughter's wedding ended that speculation.

In a "first" for a president's family, Maria, the younger of the two Monroe daughters, was married in 1820, and many Washingtonians expected to find their names on the wedding guest list. This was the chance, reasoned congressmen and diplomats, for the president to make them all one family, sharing the festivities associated with the nuptials. However, Elizabeth Monroe had other ideas. She insisted that the wedding remain strictly private, and she invited only the family's closest friends. Later presidents' sons and especially their daughters who chose to be married in small ceremonies might well thank Elizabeth Monroe's stubbornness. She resisted all requests that she increase the number of guests invited, and when the diplomatic corps persisted, she dispatched the secretary of state to set them straight.

Dubbed "la belle Americaine" when she lived in Paris, Elizabeth Monroe retained her spectacular beauty at age fifty-four when her husband became president. Portraits made of her at that time show a regal woman, dark and poised, flattered by the new fashions that exposed more arm and breast than had previously been considered proper. She preferred to order her dresses from France and reportedly paid $1,500 per dress for the privilege. Her exquisite clothing, remarkable both for its design and workmanship, later added interest to the popular Smithsonian exhibition on First Ladies, but it produced a great deal of envy among her contemporaries.

Elizabeth Monroe's open refusal to court public favor puzzled observers during the first Monroe administration; during her husband's second term, when Elizabeth put even more distance between herself and everyone else, the public reaction became severe. She stayed away from Washington for months at a time visiting her two married daughters.

When Elizabeth Monroe refused to go around Washington to court the favor of congressmen's wives, they retaliated by boycotting the few parties she did give. "The drawing room of the President was opened last night," one woman wrote in December 1819, "to a beggarly row of empty chairs. Only five females attended, three of whom were foreigners." Louisa Adams, wife of Secretary of State John Quincy Adams, received an equally severe reprimand. On one occasion, after inviting "a large party, only three came." Louisa was caught up in the dispute over how accessible the wives of government leaders should be to other citizens. Elizabeth Monroe offered poor health as the reason for not calling on the families of all new congressmen in the capital; and although Louisa Adams returned all visits, the fact that she did not *initiate* the visits was what some newcomers to the capital objected to.

This was no insignificant matter to John Quincy Adams, particularly when it spilled over into criticism of his own behavior. President Monroe called John Quincy in to discuss the "etiquette of the visits" and to relay the displeasure of senators who had complained "that the Secretary of State refuses to pay them the first visit." A cabinet meeting on the subject followed a few days later, and when no agreement could be reached, John Quincy Adams wrote letters to both the president and vice-president to outline his own position.

The letters served their purpose and settled the matter. Wives of cabinet members would not be expected to act as the Welcome Wagon to every legislator's family who moved to Washington, and the president's wife would similarly be relieved of the responsibility to call. Elizabeth Monroe had thus won her point about the need for presidents' wives to have some privacy and not be required to devote full time to the hostessing that would promote their husbands' careers. She left Washington at the end of James's presidency and retired with him to their Virginia home, where she died in 1830.

LOUISA JOHNSON ADAMS

As the wife of John Quincy Adams, a candidate for the presidency in 1824, Louisa Johnson Adams could ill afford to assert her independence in the matter of visits to the families of new legislators in Washington. "It is understood," she wrote in her diary, "that a man who is ambitious to become President of the United States must make his wife visit the Ladies of the members of Congress first. Otherwise he is totally inefficient to fill so high an office." Each morning her husband prepared a set of cards for her "as carefully as a commercial treaty," and she started on her hated rounds, going sometimes to as many as twenty-five different houses in one day even though it meant traveling from one end of the city to the other.

Nor did the visits end her responsibilities because each time Congress convened, a new round of callers came to her door—representatives, their wives, relatives, and aides—to pay their respects to her husband. John Quincy made a meticulous accounting of the time thus consumed: "I have received in the course of this month two hundred and thirty-five visitors, which is an average of about eight a day. A half hour to each visitor occupies four hours a day; but that is short of the average. The interruption to business thus incessantly repeated is distressing, but unavoidable," he wrote in March 1824, as the date of the next presidential election approached.

However, as hard as she worked to keep social commitments, Louisa Adams did not win unanimous approval. She had been born in England and, although her father came from Baltimore, seemed a bit too foreign to suit some Americans, including her mother-in-law, Abigail Adams. Louisa had met her husband in London and did not set eyes on his country until age twenty-six, when she arrived with him and their three-month-old son. The encounter was a disaster. "Had I stepped into Noah's Ark, I do not think I could have been more utterly astonished," she wrote, recognizing at once how unacceptable her husband's family found her.

Part of Louisa's discomfort resulted from embarrassment. Her father's London-based empire had provided a luxurious life for his eight children (all but one of them daughters) before his business collapsed in the summer of 1797, just at the time of Louisa's nuptials. She could not forget the shame of it, and more than a quarter century later, in a memoir written for her children, she repeated the details once more. Her father's substantial wedding gift had never materialized and "the injury Mr. Adams received by his marriage with me was the loss of the 5,000 pounds and the having connected himself with a ruined house."

John Quincy offered little support to bolster his wife's confidence, and although she followed him back and forth on his diplomatic duties, from Berlin to Massachusetts, then from Washington to St. Petersburg and Paris, she never ceased to complain about his insensitivity. In Russia, she became depressed because she regretted having left her two young sons back in Massachusetts with their grandparents. Her condition worsened in 1813 when her infant daughter died. She blamed herself for the baby's death, explaining in her diary, "Necessity alone induced me to wean her and in doing so I lost her." Tutoring the one son who had come with her gave her some pleasure but she understood that her husband disdained her efforts. When the time came to select a gift for her, he chose a book on "the diseases of the mind." He refused to discuss anything relevant to his diplomatic work, although Louisa shrewdly pointed out that she could hardly remain ignorant of what went on around her. In commenting to her son many years later that the Adams men made poor husbands, she may well have had the St. Petersburg years in mind.

Louisa Adams's diary and unpublished autobiography, which she titled "Adventures of a Nobody," show evidence of a trained, inquisitive mind but one easily pushed into acquiescence. During the winter of 1812–1813 she noted that she had read more than twenty books, including many biographies and memoirs. The records of women, especially those attached to famous or powerful men, particularly interested her. After reading a biography of Diane de Poitiers, mistress of France's King Henry II, Louisa pondered how Diane's life had been shaped by others. The book convinced her, Louisa wrote, "how little we can do of ourselves." She had hoped to study astronomy but bowed to advice that it was too difficult for her, and when warned away or kept ignorant of political intrigues, she showed a similar obeisance. "I am continuously told that I cannot by the Constitution have any share in the public honours of my husband," she wrote after returning to the United States, and when a congressman broached a political subject, "I was again forced to repeat that I had nothing to do with affairs of State."

Louisa Adams revealed considerable courage when given the chance. While her husband was stationed in St. Petersburg in 1814, he was called to Ghent to work out the details of the peace treaty that ended the War of 1812. With that assignment finished, he wrote to Louisa, instructing her to sell everything and join him in Paris. Although it was the middle of winter and she would have to go through war-damaged areas, if not through actual fighting, she disposed of their belongings and prepared in a matter of weeks to begin the journey. For company she had only her eight-year-old son and three servants whom she hired the day she set out.

The account of Louisa's trip from St. Petersburg to Paris reads like a concocted adventure, filled with danger, intrigue, and murder. When her carriage sank into the snow, she called "out the inhabitants with pick axe and shovel to dig us out," she later wrote. Warned that there had been a "dreadful murder" the night before on the "very road over which I was to pass," she refused to stop. Told that one of her servants had the reputation of a "desperate villain of the worst character" she had little alternative but to continue with him. Her informant begged her not to fire the man on the spot for fear he might uncover the source of her information and retaliate. Because she feared her servants might try to rob her, she carefully hid the gold she carried and then waved letters of credit in front of them so they would be misled into thinking that she picked up small amounts in cities along the way. When her servants deserted her, she hired others, and when impertinent border officials treated her rudely, she threatened to report them to their superiors. Her health was "dreadful," she later wrote, but she persevered, stopping to rest at houses where she knew no one. Sometimes she sat up all night because she feared for her life if she slept.

When Louisa arrived in Paris, after weeks of difficult and dangerous travel, her husband was waiting at the Hotel du Nord "perfectly astonished" at her adventures. His diary makes light of the whole trip, and he wrote matter-of-factly to his mother, "Mrs. A performed the journey from St. Petersburg in 40 days and it has been of essential service to her and Charles' health. She entered France precisely at the time when the revolution was taking place." Although her maid needed two months of bed rest to recover, Louisa

Adams, whom her family and historians portrayed as frail and sickly all her life, immediately resumed her regular schedule.

But Louisa rarely got the chance to earn her husband's favorable notice. Politics formed the center of his life, and she understood that he relegated her to the domestic sphere. "Politics is absolutely essential to my husband's existence," she wrote, but not for her. Since the beginning of her marriage, she had hated participating in the ceremonial parts of her husband's job, especially since her opinions on important matters did not count for much. She once complained, "I have nothing to do with the disposal of affairs and have never but once been consulted."

At any public appearance, Louisa knew that she was carefully observed for some indication of her husband's position. "Trifling occurrences are turned into political machinery—even my countenance was watched at the Senate during Mr. Pinckney's speech as I was afterward informed by some of the gentlemen." She had been among the first women to attend congressional debates during the Madison administration, but what had started out as a way to keep herself informed had turned into another opportunity to be scrutinized and evaluated.

Louisa Adams had frequently remarked that "friends grow warmer as Mr. Adams rises in popularity," and she saw the new attention focused on her as just one more example of the fickleness of politics.

The fact that John Quincy Adams performed so poorly on social occasions increased his dependence on his wife, who had a reputation for charming everyone. As part of the 1824 campaign, he decided that they should give a large party marking the anniversary of Andrew Jackson's great victory in 1815 at New Orleans. Though Louisa lacked enthusiasm for the idea, she bowed to her husband's conclusion that such a party could help win votes. "It was agreed this day," she wrote in December 1823, "that we should give a Ball to General Jackson on the 8th of January. I objected much to the plan but was overpowered by John's argument and the thing was settled." She had less than three weeks to prepare. In addition to sending invitations, which went out by the hundreds up until the day before the event, she had to arrange that beds be folded up and furniture moved so that their house could accommodate the crowd. While preparations continued, she maintained a full social schedule, even giving a small party on January sixth.

The ball became the season's most spectacular social affair, singled out for years to come as the model of everything a party should be. Dolley Madison, then living in Montpelier, Virginia, could not attend but she received a glowing report from a good friend, who wrote, "Mrs. Adams' reception on the 8th was really a very brilliant party and admirably arranged. The ladies climbed on chairs and benches to see General Jackson and Mrs. Adams very gracefully took his arm and walked through the apartments with him, which gratified the general curiosity. It is said 1,400 invitations were issued and about 800 guests present."

John Quincy Adams captured the presidency in 1825 (but only after a bitter contest was finally decided in the House of Representatives) and served as president for one term. Louisa might well have hoped that four years as First Lady would end her reluctant tenure as political wife but it was not to be. In an unusual move for an ex-president, John Quincy returned to Congress, where he served until his death in 1848. Thus, the Adams marriage, made more tense by the demands of a public career, lasted more than half a century. Although the gesture hardly compensated for her sacrifice, Congress adjourned for her funeral when Louisa died in 1853.

In many ways, the early presidents' wives, along with their husbands, form a distinct group. In attempting to define just what demands their husbands' jobs imposed on them, they collectively built the foundation for those who followed, and they anticipated most of the problems. With one eye on the rules of protocol and another on their husbands' popularity, they sought (some more diligently than others) to find the middle ground. They worked to

improve the President's House, which served as their home as well
as a national monument, and they struggled with the publicity that
focused on them as a result of their husbands' jobs. In the evident
and continuing debate over just how much distance a president
should keep between himself and the people, the presidents' wives
took an important part, striking a balance between commoner and
queen.

Young Substitutes for First Ladies
1829–1869

ANDREW JACKSON'S inauguration in 1829 signaled a new mood in the country—one that would affect presidents' wives for decades to come. Crowds converged on the capital from all over the eastern seaboard, arriving in carriages and carts, wearing silk and homespun. Never one to disappoint crowds, the tall, white-haired war hero gave his speech, took the prescribed oath, kissed the Bible, and then in an immensely popular gesture bent in a low bow to the people. Word immediately went out that the President's House was now the People's House and open to all without distinction. Thousands headed toward it.

No precautions had been taken to protect the mansion's furnishings, but the unexpectedly large crowd would have rendered such measures ineffective anyway. Glasses shattered and furniture broke as the hungry and curious surged toward tables where food, prepared for hundreds, proved insufficient. People filled their pockets as well as their stomachs. When the president was nearly crushed, one Jackson admirer and staunch defender of "people's rule" decided this was going too far: "Ladies and gentlemen only had been expected at this Levée," Margaret Bayard Smith, a newspaper editor's wife wrote, "not the people en masse. Of all tyrants, they are the most ferocious, cruel and despotic."

Political Changes and Social Pressures

The 1820s and 1830s eventually altered the entire political process for presidential aspirants. Instead of looking to a small party caucus for nomination, anyone hoping to be president had to appeal to a convention of delegates, many of whom were strangers. Most states gradually changed the qualifications for voting so that all adult white males—rather than just property owners—had the suffrage. Old traditions of deference to the rich and the well educated weakened, paving the way for new ideas about who was qualified for high office.

Presidential style changed after 1829 so that new importance was put on appearing "natural" rather than "cultured," and "good" rather than "learned." Heroes seemed to come from the ranks of the common folk rather than the obvious elite.

The presidents' wives would come to "the head of female society" with entirely different experiences from their predecessors. These later women had not had the opportunity to develop Elizabeth Monroe's familiarity with French philosophers or Louisa Adams's habit of sprinkling letters with Latin phrases. Nor had they had the pleasure, or pain, of having been presented at the Court of St. James as had Abigail Adams. Many had not ventured far from the town where they were born until they journeyed to Washington.

Thus, presidents' wives after 1829 lacked some of their predecessors' training in etiquette, a lack deemed important by a segment of the Washington population that had taken upon itself the responsibility of formulating and enforcing rigid rules of protocol and style. Called the "cave dwellers," because of their long and continued residence in Washington while elected officials and their families came and went like "a kaleidoscope that changed every four years," the locals scrutinized each newcomer, including each president's family.

For several decades in the nineteenth century, presidents' wives chose to abdicate their public roles rather than risk the censure of the "cave dwellers." Most First Ladies moved to Washington when their husbands were inaugurated, but they delegated responsibility for official entertaining to someone else. From 1829 to 1869, it is the exceptional First Lady who carves out for herself a public role—most administrations had stand-in chatelaines in charge at the President's House.

Three presidents in the forty-year span had no choice but to rely on substitute hostesses in the White House. Andrew Jackson and Martin Van Buren were both widowers and James Buchanan never married. While they could have followed Thomas Jefferson's example and relied on the wife of a cabinet member or on some other mature woman for official hostessing, each chose, instead, a niece or daughter-in-law, all less than thirty years of age. The other nine presidents in this period did have wives but six of these women (Anna Harrison, Letitia Tyler, Margaret Taylor, Abigail Fillmore, Jane Pierce, and Eliza Johnson) pled poor health or grief and escaped performing the tasks that had come to be seen as traditional for a president's wife. Each maintained very low visibility throughout her husband's administration and turned to a daughter or daughter-in-law to serve in her stead. Elizabeth Monroe (1817–1825) had taken a similar course, but what had been an exception during the first few administrations became a pattern now. The long reign of substitute hostesses and the repeated claims of illness by the presidents' wives during this period can hardly be explained away as mere coincidence. What remains undisputed—particularly in the case of Margaret Taylor, Abigail Fillmore, Jane Pierce, and Eliza Johnson—is that each of these women had a thorough dislike of the prospect of heading up Washington social life.

That presidents' wives in the middle of the nineteenth century were wary of a public role is not remarkable. It was a time of significant change in women's lives. Industrialization took much of the work out of the home and put it in the factory, leaving wives who had supervised domestic production with less to do. The kind of household that Martha Washington had managed at Mt. Vernon, or Abigail Adams at Quincy, was now altered or had vanished. The division between women's work and that of men became clearer, and even the women who went out each day to work the machines aspired to the leisurely life and lack of responsibility that seemed to go with being a "lady."

The nation was undergoing enormous geographic expansion at the same time. With just a few large acquisitions, the western boundary jumped to the Pacific Ocean by 1850. Behind the boasts about "manifest destiny" lay many problems, including how to distribute and govern the new land, how to service the people who settled there, and most troubling of all, what role, if any, slave labor should play. The "stretch marks" of the rapid growth would prove disfiguring for decades to come, and it is not surprising that presidents' wives kept aloof from the major debates of their time.

RACHEL DONELSON ROBARDS
JACKSON;
EMILY DONELSON

WHEN WORD REACHED Rachel Jackson of Andrew's victory in the 1828 election, she commented, "I had rather be a doorkeeper in the house of my Lord than live in that palace in Washington. For Mr.

Jackson's sake, I am glad, for my own part, I never wished it." Earlier brushes with the "cave dwellers" had soured Rachel on the capital, and she made no secret of her distaste for returning to live in that city.

Staying in Tennessee and not going near Washington would have been Rachel's preference, but she changed her mind after one of her husband's supporters informed her that everyone was watching to see what she did. John Eaton, who later became Andrew Jackson's secretary of war, wrote that if she failed to arrive she would not only disappoint her friends but also allow her "persecutors" to "chuckle" that they had scared her into staying away. Whether unwilling to disappoint her fans or stubborn about facing down her critics, Rachel started packing and called in friends to help update her wardrobe. She understood she would have to face the same old charges once again.

Rachel's difficulties had begun many years before when she was just a teenager with more than her share of admirers around Harrodsburg, Kentucky. Described by a contemporary as of "medium height, with a beautifully moulded form, full red lips rippling with smiles and dimples," she could ride a horse as well as anyone her age, tell the best stories, and dance the fastest. Among those who noticed her was Lewis Robards, and when she was eighteen, he married her. The couple went to live with his mother, who reigned as a kind of frontier aristocrat in that part of Kentucky. The elder Mrs. Robards got along well enough with Rachel but Lewis found fault with her every move. Abusive and jealous of even the slightest attention given her by other men, he soon sent her back to her mother. Attempts to patch up the marriage failed, and Rachel resolved to put as much distance as possible between herself and her husband. Neighbors said she feared bodily harm.

On her trip down the Mississippi to stay with relatives, Rachel had the company of two men—an elderly family friend and young Andrew Jackson, a boarder at her mother's and an open admirer of the daughter. After settling her in Natchez, Andrew returned to Nashville but before long was back at her side. Believing that Lewis Robards had secured a divorce, as he had announced he would do, Rachel and Andrew were married in August 1791.

The young couple misjudged Robards's actions; after obtaining permission from the Virginia legislature to end his marriage, he had failed to follow through. Whether from simple negligence or from other, more sinister motives, Robards waited three years and then asked for a divorce on the grounds that his wife was then living with another man. As soon as they heard what had happened, the Jacksons promptly remarried, but their mistake furnished their enemies with ammunition for years.

Such legal snags occurred frequently on the frontier and Rachel seems to have troubled herself very little about this one, but Andrew kept his dueling pistols oiled for thirty-seven years. His widowed mother had advised him as a youth not to expect law courts to protect him when words were at issue but to "settle them cases yourself." He may well have smarted from the charge that a gentleman would have verified his bride's divorce before marrying her; but whatever his reasons, his readiness to fight kept the subject alive long after gossip about it might have died out. In the process of defending his wife's reputation, he invited many quarrels and received a bullet which he carried in his shoulder for twenty years.

Rachel's divorce was more than two decades old when she first accompanied Andrew to Washington in 1815 to celebrate his military victory at New Orleans. The Jackson marriage, although childless, appeared to be a happy one. The fact that the capital gave Rachel such a cool welcome suggests that more than propriety was at issue. Her far bigger sin was her lack of both sophistication and education. As one social arbiter put it, "Mrs. Jackson is totally uninformed in mind and manners," adding gratuitously, "although extremely civil in her way."

Money was not the issue. Rachel's parents were of some means, and her father, John Donelson, had served several terms in the Virginia House of Burgesses. But Rachel was a child of the frontier.

One of eleven children, she had moved with her family from western Virginia to Tennessee and then to Kentucky, where schools were scarce. Nobody claimed her husband had benefited from much education but he had acquitted himself on the battlefield, an opportunity his wife never had. The same qualities of naturalness and strength that had contributed to his immense popularity and had provided his nickname, "Old Hickory," became in his wife grounds for ridicule and exclusion. Women, especially the mature ones, were expected to represent culture, etiquette, and sophistication—not unstudied naturalness.

In no way did Rachel Jackson approach the accepted model of femininity. Nearing fifty by the time she made her first trip out of the Kentucky-Tennessee area, she had become set in her country ways. Tanned, leathery skin had replaced the creamy complexion of her youth. She preferred to ride a horse rather than sit in a carriage, and she cared little for fashions and cosmetics. Outside her family and friends, the Presbyterian church constituted her one interest, and a quiet evening at home smoking a pipe with Andrew remained her idea of a good time.

Rachel Jackson's additional transgression against prevailing standards of femininity was her stoutness. A miniature painted of her about 1815 shows a plump woman with dark curls under a lacy cap. Her eyes are placid and resigned rather than sharp or alert. She was, one observer noted, "fat, forty, but not fair." Her girth had already provided a source of amusement in New Orleans, where Rachel had gone to help her husband celebrate his military victory. She had been dazzled by the sights of the city, but the local women had exhibited less enthusiasm for her and they had revived an old French saying to describe her: "She shows how far the skin can be stretched." A cartoon made the round of New Orleans: it depicted Rachel being laced, without complete success, into a fashionably small-waisted dress. When she danced with Andrew, someone present described her as "a short, fat dumpling bobbing" opposite him.

Hardly oblivious to the insults, Rachel preferred staying home.

She reluctantly accompanied Andrew to Florida, where he served as governor, but she caused him to turn down a subsequent appointment as ambassador to Mexico when she refused to go. Although she would have gladly confined herself to their Hermitage plantation near Nashville the rest of her life, she braced herself for Washington and made her way there again in 1824 when Andrew took his Senate seat amid speculation that he stood next in line for the presidency.

At first, Rachel Jackson tried to keep to herself in the capital and, except for church twice a week, rarely left her rooms at Gadsby's Hotel. But on January 8, 1825, a party honoring her husband required her attendance. The hostess did little to make Rachel feel comfortable and the party became an ordeal for her. The other guests singled her out as "stout, vulgar, illiterate" and they made fun of her bad grammar.

By the time of the 1828 presidential campaign, Rachel's fitness to occupy a conspicuous place had become a political issue. A North Carolina paper, admittedly hostile to Andrew Jackson, advised voters to consider carefully the wisdom of putting Rachel "at the head of the female society of the United States." When rumors about her character multiplied, the Jackson camp sent out investigators to line up supporting evidence for its version of the divorce. Rachel understood that the attacks on her were politically motivated, but that hardly eased her discomfort. "The enemies of the Genls have dipt their arrows in wormwood and gall and sped them at me," she wrote, adding in her curious spelling, "thay had no rite to do it."

While preparing to move to Washington in December 1828, prior to her husband's inauguration, Rachel Jackson suffered a heart attack. At sixty-one, she was older than any previous president's wife. Rachel Jackson's decision just before her death to ask her niece, Emily Donelson, to substitute for her might have been based on her own failing health. But that explanation fails to suffice when it becomes clear that Emily Donelson is only the beginning of a long list of youthful chatelaines. After Emily's untimely death at twenty-eight in 1836, another Jackson niece came from Tennessee to take her place until the end of Jackson's term in 1837. In the subsequent administration, Angelica Van Buren, wife of Martin's son, played a similar role. She was followed in subsequent administrations by several other substitutes for First Lady. All were sweet, young models of girlish innocence, and they fit well the mood of a nation that expected little more of prominent women than cheerful acquiescence.

Actually Andrew Jackson's niece, Emily Donelson, was, in many ways, just a younger version of her Aunt Rachel. When she married Major Andrew J. Donelson, Rachel Jackson's nephew, at seventeen, Emily had traveled little and boasted no superior education. But when she arrived in Washington three years later, her age evidently excused her limitations. Fanny Kemble, the British actress, described Emily approvingly as "a very pretty person with simple and pleasant manners," and John R. Montgomery, a lawyer from Pennsylvania, wrote his daughter that he had found the young Emily Donelson "a very agreeable woman." It is difficult to account for Emily's popularity in the same city that had so castigated her aunt, except by pointing to her youth. The very same adjectives ("sweet," "simple," "pleasant") that had been directed at Rachel in sarcasm became compliments for her young niece.

Youth had a privileged place in American culture by the 1830s. Respect for age and experience had begun to fall away in America by the early 1800s, and old people less often were given special seating in churches or were able to hang on to political appointments in their last years. The new respect for youth enticed people to shave a few years off their real ages, so that they "rounded off" forty-five to "early forties," and moved from one decade to the next with great reluctance.

Concurrent developments in fashion reinforced the advantages of youth. The white wigs and powdered hair, favored by George Washington and Thomas Jefferson, disappeared. Knee breeches, which had flattered the older man by exposing his legs, often the last part of the anatomy to go, gave way to leg-concealing trousers.

Women's fashion also changed to flatter youth. The large posterior and sagging bodice, styles of the late eighteenth century, accommodated more comfortably a matronly figure than did the high-waisted, slim-hipped styles of the early 1800s. Women's clothes in the early nineteenth century resembled children's frocks: thin muslin that clung to the body and shorter skirts that revealed the white stockings and flat slippers so often associated with little children.

Many foreigners commented on the new admiration for youth in America; some connected the change to democracy. Eventually the United States earned an international reputation for being "youth conscious," but the phenomenon began inconspicuously. The president's residence, with its long string of youthful mistresses between 1829 and 1869, offers just one more example of the result.

ANGELICA SINGLETON VAN BUREN

ANDREW JACKSON relinquished the White House in March 1837 to Martin Van Buren, the New York Democrat whose nomination for vice-president Andrew had carefully engineered in 1832. In one term in Jackson's administration (1833–1837), Van Buren carefully groomed himself for the top office. A widower for many years, he maintained a mostly male preserve until his son's marriage in 1838. Then he quickly acted to install his son's bride, Angelica Singleton Van Buren, as his hostess in the White House.

His own wife, Hannah Hoes Van Buren, had died almost two

decades earlier and she remains one of history's shortest footnotes. The small record she left points, however, to the rigors of childbearing in early nineteenth century America. Hannah had married at twenty-four and given birth to four children in five years. Then, after becoming ill (probably with tuberculosis), she gave birth to another son and died in 1819 when she was only thirty-five.

Angelica Singleton, who married the oldest Van Buren son, might have expected an easier life than the elder Mrs. Van Buren. Born in 1816 to a wealthy South Carolina family, Angelica did live to age 61. But her White House years were hardly free from tragedy. She gave birth to a daughter in March 1840, and then saw the baby die a few months later just as Martin Van Buren's single term as president was ending.

In spite of her own personal difficulties, Angelica earned high marks as White House hostess. She claimed Dolley Madison as a distant relative and frequently called on the older woman for tutoring and advice. Soon the president's parties became livelier. After an 1839 New Year's reception, the *Boston Post* raved, "Angelica Van Buren is a lady of rare accomplishments, very modest yet perfectly easy and graceful in her manners and free and vivacious in her conversation. She is universally admired."

Angelica's portrait, painted by Henry Inman, would eventually become one of the most famous in the White House. It shows a smiling woman with plumes in her hair—her head is tilted to one side as though she meant to be a model of the youth and submissiveness that was in style for women of her time.

ANNA SYMMES HARRISON;
JANE HARRISON

B EGINNING WITH Anna Harrison in 1841 and ending with Eliza Johnson in 1869, there is a curious pattern of invalidism in which many of the presidents' wives cited illness and avoided the responsibilities of First Lady. Anna Harrison's case is remarkable because the onset of her sickness coincided with the elevation of her husband to the presidency.

Anna's early years had prepared her well enough for Washington social life. Born in 1775 to a New Jersey family that traced its American roots back to New England in the 1630s, she had been raised by her grandparents who sent her to two of the best schools on the East Coast—Clinton Academy on Long Island and Isabella Graham's school in New York City. Her father had remarried after Anna's mother died, and he held a succession of prestigious posts including associate justice of the state's supreme court.

On a trip west with her father, Anna met young army officer William Henry Harrison and, even though her father protested, she married William in 1795 when she was twenty. Throughout their long marriage (until his death in 1841) Anna followed him loyally from one job to another—governor of Indiana Territory, military commander, and a series of elected offices including congressman and senator. Nothing about her health suggested illness —in fact, she gave birth to ten children and outlived nine of them.

But Anna Harrison did not follow her husband to the White

House. One son had died in 1840 during the election campaign, and Anna became despondent and refused to appear in public. Cincinnati newspapers began to describe her as an "invalid." Rather than travel to Washington for the inauguration, she sent her daughter-in-law, Jane Harrison. The younger woman had little opportunity to establish a reputation because the president died within one month of taking office. Contemporaries spoke approvingly, however, of the "attractive, young" White House hostess.

LETITIA CHRISTIAN TYLER; PRISCILLA COOPER TYLER

FOLLOWING William Henry Harrison's death, his vice-president, John Tyler, brought a large, supportive family with him to Washington. His wife Letitia was only 51 but she had suffered a stroke two years earlier, and her health failed just when her husband reached the pinnacle of American politics. Daughter of a wealthy Virginia planter, Letitia had married John Tyler when she was twenty-two. While he pursued a political career, she gave birth to nine children of whom seven survived infancy. By 1841 she could do little more than supervise White House management from behind the scenes and let her daughters and daughter-in-law preside at social functions. Within a year she was dead—the first presidential wife to die in the White House.

Her daughter-in-law, Priscilla Cooper Tyler, gladly filled in. Then in her mid-twenties, Priscilla appealed to a country infatuated with youth. For her part, she loved the attention, having become accustomed to it while touring the country as an actress in plays featuring her father, Thomas Cooper. She could not believe she was actually hostess at the country's most famous home, and she wrote her sister in 1841: "Here I am actually living in and what is more, presiding at the White House, and I look at myself like the little old woman and exclaim 'can this be I?' "

Priscilla Cooper Tyler took great pleasure entertaining at other people's expense and adding to her already large circle of admirers. "I am considered *'charmante'* by the Frenchmen, 'lovely' by the Americans and 'really quite nice, you know' by the English," she wrote with more than a little accuracy. One French minister ridiculed a country where a woman could pass from being an actress to "what serves as a Republican throne." But most of her guests thought she did her job well. John Quincy Adams, not an easy man to please, found that Priscilla entertained with as much style as the most accomplished European court. The *New York True Sun* reported approvingly that Priscilla made "no enemies."

JULIA GARDINER TYLER

P RISCILLA COOPER TYLER gave up her White House role in the spring of 1844 so that an even younger woman could take her place. In the fall of 1842, her mother-in-law, Letitia Tyler, became the first woman to die during her husband's presidency, and eighteen months later John Tyler remarried. At fifty-five, he selected a wealthy twenty-four-year-old New Yorker, Julia Gardiner, who had taken Washington by storm when she visited there with her family.

Among the many marriage proposals offered the "Rose of Long Island," the president's evidently took precedence and in a very small ceremony at an Episcopal church in New York City, she became his bride on June 26, 1844.

A model of youthful exuberance and energy, Julia Gardiner Tyler served less than a year as First Lady but she worked hard to leave her mark. She initiated the custom of musicians greeting the president with "Hail to the Chief," and she hired a press agent to sound her "praises far and near." This latter was an unnecessary gesture since she had always shown a knack for attracting attention. Before her marriage she had shocked her parents' socially conscious friends by posing for a department store advertisement at a time when ladies did not lend their likenesses to any commercial announcement. The Gardiners had whisked Julia off to Europe to save them all from further embarrassment.

Julia's impish, impetuous nature continued to gain her attention in the White House. Some people thought her extravagant to drive four horses, "finer horses than those of the Russian minister," and a bit self-centered when she "received guests seated, her large armchair on a slightly raised platform, three feathers in her hair and a long trained purple dress." One woman compared Julia unfavorably to her predecessors and concluded, "Other Presidents' wives have taken their state more easily," but for the most part, people indulged Julia. Her husband doted on her and the public watched approvingly one more young woman preside over the President's House.

The Tylers vacated the White House in March 1845, so that the hardworking Polks could move in for four years, a time in which Sarah Polk showed herself every bit as diligent in her role as her husband did in his. No substitutes would take her place, either in the limelight of executive mansion entertaining or in the close working relationship she had with her husband. Sarah Polk represents an exception, however, to be considered in the next chapter.

MARGARET SMITH TAYLOR;
BETTIE TAYLOR BLISS

MARGARET MACKALL SMITH TAYLOR appeared to reject fashionable city life to marry Zachary Taylor. Educated in a New York City finishing school, she had to learn frontier ways as she followed her husband from one military post to another. While he built a military reputation (including acquiring the nickname "Old Rough and Ready," which extended beyond army life), she gave birth to five daughters and then finally to a son, when she was thirty-eight. By the time the Mexican-American War ended in 1848, she was looking forward to quiet retirement on their Southern plantation, but a surge of popular sentiment pushed Zachary into political office. His admission that he had never cast a ballot in his life failed to quell enthusiasm for his candidacy. After he won the presidency in 1848, Margaret resigned herself to one more assignment with him—this time to the White House.

From the beginning, Margaret Taylor refused to have any part of the capital's social life and designated her daughter, Bettie Taylor Bliss, as her substitute at official functions. Only twenty-two years old and a recent bride, Bettie Bliss appealed to youth-conscious Washington while Margaret Taylor's vague explanations of having "delicate health" and being an "invalid" sufficed as reason for her to stay upstairs at the White House and entertain her family and close friends there.

Margaret Taylor's low visibility prompted many rumors about

her, including the charge that she lacked sophistication. One contemporary explained that Margaret did little more than knit in her room and smoke her pipe—a description that persisted well beyond her death in 1852. Forty years later, a writer for a popular magazine reported that Margaret had "moaned to the accompaniment of her pipe," and other authors continued to refer to the pipe long after it became clear that she never touched one.

Family and close friends of Margaret Taylor pointed out that she had such a strong aversion to tobacco that no one who knew her smoked in her presence. As for resorting to moaning rather than talking intelligibly, she "ably bore her share in the conversation," according to guests who were present. Margaret's grandson, whom she raised, described her as a "strict disciplinarian, intolerant of the slightest breach of good manners."

The Taylor administration ended abruptly in July 1850, when the president suddenly took sick and died. Margaret did not attend her husband's state funeral, such ordeals then considered beyond the capacity of widows. Two years later she died, so obscure that no authentic likeness of her, either in painting or photograph, survives. Her obituary in the *New York Times* did not even give her full name— referring to her only as "Mrs. General Taylor."

ABIGAIL POWERS FILLMORE;
MARY ABIGAIL FILLMORE

ABIGAIL FILLMORE, whose husband Millard Fillmore assumed the presidency at Zachary Taylor's death in 1850, followed her predecessor's example and turned to her daughter to substitute for her on official occasions, even though eighteen-year-old Mary Abigail had not yet had the chance to develop very clear ideas of her own.

Abigail Powers was a schoolteacher when she met nineteen-year-old Millard Fillmore, two years her junior. During the early years of their marriage, her large library and good conversation had made her home a gathering place for Buffalo's literati, and an insatiable curiosity and desire to learn continued to motivate her all through her life. As an adult she taught herself French and began studying piano. Thurlow Weed, Millard's political associate, reported that Millard always returned from business trips with books for Abigail because she was a "notable reader." A Washington newspaperman described her as "remarkably well informed."

Throughout her marriage, Abigail followed the issues related to her husband's career and acted as a sounding board for him. She had a thorough understanding of pending legislation and could discuss knowledgeably current affairs. Millard's respect for her opinions is well documented, including his admission that he never could destroy "even the little business notes she had sent him." One of their friends described the great courtesy Millard always showed Abigail, "like that which a man usually bestows upon a guest," and went on to note that he often said that he "never took any important step without her counsel and advice." In the spring of 1850 when he was vice-president, Millard wrote to her after she had returned to Buffalo, "How lonesome this hotel room is in your absence. I can hardly bear to sit down. But you have scarcely been out of my mind since you left. How I wish I could be with you!" After filling her in on the details of a Senate debate, over which he had presided, he ended the letter by outlining a political problem and then disclosing how he planned to resolve it.

But Abigail Fillmore apparently had no interest at all in the social leadership role that went along with being the president's wife. She preferred an evening with a book rather than meeting strangers at a party. Although she attended weekly receptions and evening levées "health permitting," she followed the lead of her contemporaries, who tired of the formal entertaining in the capital, and took every chance they could to withdraw and leave the parties to the young women.

In her early fifties during her husband's term, Abigail Fillmore was by no means an invalid (although she complained of a weak ankle that sometimes required her staying a day in bed if she had to stand for hours in a receiving line). A lively conversationalist at small dinners for family and close friends on Saturday evenings, she rarely accepted invitations. Preferring a "cheerful room" on the second story of the White House, where her daughter could play her piano and harp, Abigail surrounded herself with books and spent her happiest hours there. Her one significant contribution as First Lady was the establishment of a White House library because she was disappointed to find that none existed. Her life ended with her husband's presidency. At the inauguration of his successor in 1853, she caught cold and within a month she died.

JANE APPLETON PIERCE

WHEN JANE APPLETON married the Democratic Congressman Franklin Pierce in 1834, her prominent New England family had objected that he came from a different political party and that his family stood well below theirs in wealth and prestige. Jane's wedding had none of the festive quality that marked the ceremonies of her sisters: "No one present except our family and old General

Pierce," a relative of Jane's wrote, adding that Jane had no "grooms-
men and bridesmaids and did not wait to be congratulated after the
ceremony."

Whatever Jane's feelings about her husband, she never seemed to
come to terms with his choice of careers. She accompanied him to
Washington immediately after their marriage but begged off from
the social engagements, saying she did not feel well enough to
participate. During Franklin's second year in Congress, Jane's pregnancy gave her a reason to stay with relatives in Massachusetts.
When that son died three days after his birth in February 1836, Jane
withdrew more and more from any kind of public role. She insisted
that Franklin sell their house in Hillsborough, New Hampshire,
while she remained in Lowell and submitted to leeching, the currently popular medical treatment.

When Franklin Pierce's political reputation grew and he won election to the United States Senate, Jane reluctantly returned to Washington, but she made no attempt to hide her displeasure with the
capital and rarely ventured out of the boardinghouse where they
lived. After giving birth to two more boys, one in 1839 when she was
thirty-four and another in 1841, she became even more convinced
that Washington would ruin her children as well as her husband. She
thought the social scene encouraged Franklin to drink excessively,
and she saw politics as a demeaning career that damaged the entire
family. In 1842, when Franklin's Senate term ended, Jane prevailed
on him to move back to New Hampshire. To placate her, he refused
an attorney generalship in the Polk administration, but the war with
Mexico was another matter. He enlisted, achieved the status of local
hero, and when the fighting ended, resumed his political career.

By 1852, when Franklin Pierce became a candidate for president,
Jane's abhorrence of everything about the capital and politics was
well established. When she heard that the Democrats had nominated him, she fainted. The messenger who brought the news to the
Pierces while they were out riding in their carriage had thought to
please by pronouncing her the next "Presidentess." Jane fervently

prayed for her husband's defeat because she could not bring herself to consider the alternative—his victory and her return to Washington, this time to the White House. If she had felt uncomfortable as a congressman's wife, she would surely suffer in the considerably more conspicuous and demanding role of First Lady.

The death of their young son Bennie in a train accident in front of their eyes in January 1853 was a traumatic event for Jane and Franklin, and the public accorded Jane enormous sympathy and wide latitude in refusing to undertake official responsibilities as First Lady. To Jane, who had doted on Bennie, the tragedy represented retribution for her husband's excessive political ambition, and the old hatred that she had always felt for Washington and politics revived. Even though her family urged her to be strong, Jane chose not to attend her husband's inauguration. They understood that all through her marriage Jane had found excuses for avoiding unpleasant tasks, and they could only hope that national prominence would help her face up to her responsibilities. One cousin explained that Jane had always been depressed and now that she had her grief to hide behind, she might become a source of anxiety for her husband just when he most needed strength and consolation.

Although his grief may have equaled that of his wife, Franklin Pierce received little of the public sympathy offered her. Bennie had planned to hear his father's inaugural speech, and Franklin was achingly aware of his absence as he stood before the crowds on a cold March 4 in 1853. Sarah Agnes Pryor, wife of a newspaper editor, described Franklin Pierce as "the youngest and handsomest President we had ever elected, but so sad." When he began his speech with a reference to Bennie's death, the audience was shocked: "The public does not tolerate the intrusion of a man's personal joys and griefs into his official life," Pryor observed, and some in the crowd pronounced Franklin's move a ploy to gain sympathy while others thought it an unseemly exposé of his private life. In any case, it was unacceptable. Men could not expect to be popular if they revealed their suffering and grief, Pryor warned.

In Franklin's wife, however, grief was condoned and accepted as sufficient reason for avoiding official duties. Her widowed aunt stayed with her and became "virtually the lady of the White House," according to one guest. The aunt shared Jane's seclusion and little was expected of either woman. After the first few months when Jane saw no visitors and "seemed to be bowed to the earth," she appeared at some public receptions but could not throw off her grief. Washingtonians dismissed her as an invalid and pronounced the President's House a gloomy place for the entire Pierce administration.

HARRIET LANE

JAMES BUCHANAN, the only bachelor president (1857–1861), would continue the tradition of installing young hostesses at the President's House by calling on his twenty-seven-year-old niece, Harriet Lane. At his inauguration, the press hailed her as the "Democratic Queen," and in many ways she performed like a member of royalty. A United States cutter was named for her; necklines went down in response to her fashion lead; and she became the first White House occupant to be credited with having had a song, "Listen to the Mockingbird," dedicated to her.

As a result of her popularity, Harriet was offered many gifts, and although the president cautioned her not to accept the costly ones, she could not resist. One frequently repeated story had it that a wealthy young admirer of Harriet's had picked up some pebbles, fashioned them into a bracelet for her, and then increased the value of his gift by adding a few diamonds. Harriet very much wanted to keep the bracelet but she realized that her uncle would object if he knew the true worth. She waited until she found him in a particularly good mood and then asked if she could keep some "pebbles" she had been given. Buchanan replied offhandedly that she could. Later when she told the story, she would remind her listeners, "Diamonds are pebbles, you know."

Such stories of Harriet's girlish innocence and her insistence on having her own way caused the president some embarrassment, but the press and the public tended to indulge the ingénue at the "head of female society." Although campaigning for male relatives had not yet become acceptable for a "lady" in the 1850s, Harriet Lane met with an important Pennsylvania Democrat to promote her uncle's candidacy. Her youth, and perhaps her unmarried state, evidently rendered the meeting politically acceptable, and the Pennsylvanian pronounced himself much taken with her. One contemporary judged Harriet the perfect combination of "deference and grace."

Behind the innocent charm, Harriet Lane showed evidence of considerable exposure to Washington politics and to foreign courts. Buchanan, then a United States senator from Pennsylvania, had assumed her guardianship at the death of her mother (his sister) when Harriet was ten years old. He had sent his niece to the best Washington school, and later, when he served in James Polk's cabinet, he arranged for her to visit the White House. When he was appointed envoy to Great Britain in 1853, he took Harriet with him to London. Among her English admirers were Queen Victoria, who had accorded her the rank of minister's wife, and an elderly, titled gentleman who proposed marriage. Harriet rejected that offer and returned to the United States with her uncle, who, after many years in public office, finally won the presidency in 1856. By then, Harriet was prepared to leave her own mark on Washington. One Southern congressman's wife saw in Harriet's White House management the "highest degree of elegance." It was sometimes said that the capital had never been gayer than in the years of Harriet Lane, even if the possibility of civil war was on many people's minds.

Harriet Lane was still a schoolgirl in Washington when Dolley Madison rounded out her long career as reigning social figure, but the lesson of the older woman was not lost on the younger. Harriet spared no effort in trying to complement her uncle's political success. "She was always courteous, always in place, silent whenever it was possible to be silent, watchful and careful," one contemporary wrote of Harriet, in what might be considered a prescription for womanly success in the middle of the nineteenth century, adding that she made no enemies and never involved herself in any controversial issue.

A more serious side to the publicly frivolous Harriet showed up in her reaction to requests she received. People who felt they lacked representation elsewhere sometimes appealed to her for help, and her papers indicate that she tried to comply. Indians who turned to her for assistance showed their gratitude by naming many of their daughters "Harriet." She intervened to get jobs for friends and interspersed artists with politicians at White House dinners to give more importance to cultural subjects. Her genuine interest in art is attested to by the fact that she later provided that her own art collection, begun during the years she lived with her uncle, go to the Corcoran Gallery of Art. Eventually, after funds became available in 1920 and other donations of considerably more worth were added to it, it became the basis of the National Collection of Fine Arts at the Smithsonian.

Harriet Lane's prominence and popularity led to rumors that she influenced the president, and according to one careful student of the correspondence between her and her uncle, people believed that he listened to her. Sarah Agnes Pryor, a writer who frequently commented on Washington figures, described Harriet as her uncle's "confidante in all matters political and personal." She possessed political astuteness, Pryor noted, a trait of considerable value during the last months of the Buchanan administration when John

Brown raided Harpers Ferry and war between the states seemed likelier than ever before.

For herself, Harriet Lane did not choose a political life. After leaving the White House, she married a banker, Henry Johnston, and had two sons. After he and both the boys died, she devoted the remainder of her life—until 1903—to charitable work.

Those later years were overshadowed in the public's mind by the time she spent in Washington where she served as a transitional figure in the history of White House chatelaines. Although her age fits her into the string of youthful hostesses, her record indicates that she played a more substantial role. Her remarkable popularity, her experiment with campaigning, her response to individuals who sought access to the president through her, her mixing of artists and politicians at social functions, and her use of her position to promote American art all make her sound very much like a First Lady of the twentieth century.

Harriet Lane's success as First Lady may have tempted Mary Todd Lincoln, who succeeded her in the White House in 1861, to take a prominent role in the capital's social life. Mary certainly had no intention of turning over the spotlight to another woman to serve as White House hostess, although more than one volunteered. Her tragic stay at 1600 Pennsylvania Avenue remains, however, an exceptional case and will be considered in the next chapter.

ELIZA McCARDLE JOHNSON; MARTHA JOHNSON PATTERSON

WHEN MARY LINCOLN left Washington after her husband's assassination in April 1865, the newly inaugurated vice-president,

Andrew Johnson, assumed the presidency. Under the circumstances, it is understandable that Eliza McCardle Johnson, Andrew's wife, did not want a conspicuous role as First Lady. Mary Lincoln had endured four years of almost unremitting criticism, and Eliza's husband had not exactly paved the way for her to enjoy a more favorable reception.

Andrew Johnson had distinguished himself at his vice-presidential inauguration on March 4, 1865, by lurching forward to take his oath and slurring the lines of a long, rambling discourse. Word spread quickly through the audience that he was drunk. Eliza had not been on hand to nurse him through a bad cold, and when on the day of the ceremony he had fortified himself with alcohol, the dose had proven too strong. Abraham Lincoln defended his running mate by volunteering that "Andy ain't no drunkard," but Mary Lincoln was thoroughly annoyed. When the president was shot shortly over a month later, Andrew's performance was still fresh in people's minds, and they had not forgotten it when his family came to join him in Washington in June.

The fragile, blue-eyed Eliza Johnson had other reasons for delaying her arrival in the capital. She had visited the city only once before 1865, but she understood how short she fell of possessing the social skills needed. Grief and poor health sapped her energy. She had tuberculosis before the Civil War; family tragedies, including the deaths of a son and a son-in-law, had further weakened her. To add to her problems, her husband's political career had included few chances for her to develop self-confidence.

Eliza Johnson had not always lagged so far behind her husband, but like many political wives, she had watched the man she tutored in writing and arithmetic outdistance her. Andrew had been a young, poorly educated tailor when she first saw him and it was partly her teaching and help that allowed him to move ahead. They had married while still in their teens, and as soon as he had mastered the three "r's" and put his tailoring business on a prosperous route, he arranged to have himself appointed a trustee of the local academy. He was, one wag had it, a self-made man, inclined to give too much credit to his maker. Certainly he gave little credit to his wife. While he progressed through a string of elective offices—state representative, U.S. congressman, governor of Tennessee, and finally U.S. senator—Eliza followed the example of many other political wives by staying home and setting her sights narrowly on her family, raising five children.

Unlike Mary Lincoln, who had stubbornly claimed a prominent place in the capital's social life, Eliza Johnson insisted on remaining out of sight. Her invisibility was so complete that after four years in the capital, newspapers described her existence as "almost a myth." She appeared briefly at only one dinner (but left after starting to cough), and her only other recorded social activity was a children's party in December 1868, when she greeted her young guests by announcing that she was "an invalid."

Her invisibility should not be taken for inactivity. One report that Eliza's influence over her husband was "boundless" no doubt exaggerated the case, but she did continue to keep remarkably informed during her life, reading many newspapers and magazines. During the White House years, she clipped articles she thought he should see, shrewdly separating the good news, which she gave him at the end of each day, from the bad, which she saved for the next morning.

Martha Johnson Patterson, who substituted for her mother at the president's table on official occasions, could rely on the country's preference for youth to protect her from criticism. The Johnson daughter immediately disarmed potential detractors by announcing, "We are plain folks from Tennessee, called here by a national calamity. I hope not too much will be expected of us." Then to lend credence to her claim, she covered the worn White House carpets with simple muslin and installed two Jersey cows on the lawn to provide fresh milk and butter. In an older woman, such decisions might have prompted ridicule or charges of bumpkin roughness, but in a younger woman, they apparently seemed refreshing. Margaret heard her sister and herself praised as assets to their father, so "frank and unostentatious" that they had gained the respect of all who visited.

In 1868, the Johnson family found themselves in the unwelcome glare of the first presidential impeachment trial in American history. The House of Representatives, in a show of their own strength and their disapproval of the president's handling of a defeated South, had charged him with high crimes and misdemeanors. For three months, while the Senate tried the case, people flocked to witness the proceedings as though it were a carnival show rather than a national ordeal. Kate Chase, whose father presided as chief justice, appeared each day to watch his performance, while others competed for tickets to see her, one of the city's most popular young belles.

The Johnson women remained in the White House—the president's daughters keeping up a regular social schedule and Eliza staying upstairs and out of sight. Each evening, a steward, delegated to attend the proceedings, reported on the day's events. Except for that contact, the Johnsons feigned disinterest in the trial. When acquittal came (by the margin of a single vote), Eliza insisted that she had correctly predicted her husband's vindication.

Several of the accounts of Eliza Johnson's life raise questions about whether or not she was physically able to assume a more active public role in the White House. Her grandchildren evidently enjoyed her company, and according to one witness they ran to her room as soon as they finished their lessons—hardly evidence that she was incapacitated. Often described as fragile or frail but never uncommunicative or disabled, she remained central to the family's life in the White House. After leaving Washington, she outlived her husband, and when he died in 1875, she appeared healthy enough to have herself appointed his executrix under bond set at $200,000.

Any conclusions about Eliza Johnson, however, are bound to be speculative because so little information remains. Her prospective biographer, Margaret Blanton, abandoned the project after years of work because she thought the subject impossible to know. Except for Eliza's loyalty to her husband, which was unquestioned, nothing was clear. "In the end I did not know," Blanton wrote, "whether she loved Andrew or hated him."

Blanton did not definitely conclude that Eliza Johnson withdrew behind explanations of illness to avoid unwanted social duties, but she did judge the entire Johnson family "not very clever and put in a position to which they were unequal." If that is true and Eliza remained a frontier woman, pushed by circumstances far beyond her accustomed setting, then it is not surprising that she looked for an escape and a way to avoid criticism. The country's acceptance of youthful substitutes for First Ladies provided a way out.

Nineteenth-century America encouraged women to describe themselves as sick and frail, and the languishing woman, who fainted frequently, epitomized femininity. This tolerance—indeed solicitous sympathy—for women's withdrawal into illness and grief gave presidents' wives a convenient exit from what had become onerous, often unpleasant responsibilities. Women bored by the hostess role that so many of their predecessors had taken now had another choice—they could take to their beds and install a young ingénue in their place, confident that any social lapses of the substitute would be tolerated and charged to inexperience. For the most part, mid-nineteenth-century America witnessed few mature or strong First Ladies. Some exceptions—Sarah Polk, Mary Lincoln, and Julia Grant—broke the pattern, and they will be considered next.

Three Exceptionally Strong First Ladies

MOST OF THE WIVES of the presidents in the middle of the nineteenth century preferred anonymity rather than exploring new possibilities in the job. However, there are some prominent exceptions to this historical pattern that should be considered.

Sarah Childress Polk (1845–1849) eschewed domestic details so that she could maintain a close working relationship with her husband. Mary Todd Lincoln (1861–1865) left observers unsure about whether or not she had any influence on important decisions, so that merchants, intent on catering to her, permitted her to run up enormous bills. The activities of Julia Dent Grant (1869–1877) and her children received enough attention to qualify the Grants as the first "star" family in the White House. The three women totalled only a bit more than sixteen years in the White House, but they stand out in sharp contrast to the First Ladies who preceded them.

All three had especially good educations for women of their time and place. The schooling itself was not so important, but it may have encouraged the women and those whom they encountered to give special weight to their judgments. Sarah Polk and Mary Lincoln had a long time to prepare for the White House. Their husbands had spent their entire adult lives in politics, and Mary Lincoln had never concealed her lifelong ambition to reach the top. That infatuation with the limelight and an acceptance of the careers their husbands had chosen characterize all three women. Moreover, since Sarah Polk, Mary Lincoln, and Julia Grant were all in their forties when their husbands took on the presidency, these women may simply have had more energy than their older counterparts as First Lady.

SARAH CHILDRESS POLK

AT FORTY-ONE, Sarah Childress Polk was almost as young at her husband's inauguration as Dolley Madison had been when she became First Lady. After James Polk had delivered his inaugural speech, Sarah had accepted the Bible used in the ceremony, tucked away a souvenir fan with its pictures of the first ten presidents, and ridden up Pennsylvania Avenue with her friends. The custom had not yet developed for the president's wife to accompany him to the White House, but in Sarah's case it would have been appropriate since she had played an important part in the career that took him there.

That Sarah Polk figured prominently in James's rise to power is less difficult to prove than the reasons, but from the beginning of their marriage she showed a mind of her own. On their wedding trip, following the nuptials on New Year's Day, 1824, Sarah impressed her husband's relatives as showing more of a mind of her own "than was fitting in one woman." She might have been expected to defer to James, who was eight years her senior and a graduate of the University of North Carolina, but she showed little evidence of doing so.

Partly pampered and partly pushed into self-confidence, Sarah Childress Polk had grown up in very comfortable circumstances. Her parents, prosperous Tennessee planters and tavern keepers, had provided particularly good schooling for their children. In Sarah's case that meant beginning with a tutor at home, then continuing at a Nashville girls' school before enrolling at age thirteen in the best girls' school in the South. Salem Female Academy in North Carolina, founded by Moravians who put great importance on girls' education, eventually drew students from all over the Eastern Seaboard. When its reputation reached Tennessee, Sarah and her younger sister rode two hundred miles on horseback to enroll. In addition to the usual academic subjects, the girls had to improve their needlepoint, practice the piano, and assist in cleaning the dormitory—all part of preparing them for assuming wifely responsibilities in adulthood. Sarah's stay at this exceptional school ended after less than a year when her father died and she was called home, but it is clear from her later statements and decisions that the academic part of Salem's program interested her far more than the domestic part.

From the very beginning of her marriage, Sarah Polk considered household tasks a peripheral part of being a wife, and if forced to choose between domestic chores and spending time with her husband, she almost always chose the latter. During the first year of James's term in Congress she remained in Tennessee, but the next session she accompanied him to Washington. In the style of the time, the Polks boarded—so Sarah had few housekeeping duties. James reportedly supported his wife's view of her role, because she explained that she had volunteered to stay in Tennessee and take care of the house but that he had chided her, "Why? If it burns down, we can live without it."

With that kind of endorsement, Sarah evidently felt comfortable fitting herself into her husband's career. Whenever she could help him, she was there. Her skills as a hostess took on new importance as James became a powerful figure in the capital. Under Andrew Jackson's protection, he was chosen Chairman of the House Committee on Foreign Relations and then Speaker of the House of Representatives in 1835. Rather than objecting to the inconvenience of dividing her life between two places, Sarah concentrated on the advantages of seeing the world beyond Tennessee. A detour to New York City or a stop in Pennsylvania to make political calls interested her as much as it did James. Physical danger in the form of overturned carriages and swollen streams failed to deter her.

When her presence in Washington might have complicated matters for James, as during the Peggy Eaton episode, she remained in Tennessee, offering vague explanations about wanting to economize. Her real motive was no doubt more political. John Eaton was a favorite of President Jackson, but the rumors that Peggy Eaton had had an affair with John while she was still married to another man upset many of Eaton's colleagues and prompted their wives to refuse to socialize with Peggy. Not until John Eaton left the cabinet in 1831 did the matter resolve itself and even then, harsh words, exchanged in anger, continued to echo and affect political careers.

Sarah Polk is sometimes credited with participating in her husband's career almost by default because she had no children. Congressmen's wives frequently complained about the difficulties of boarding a family in the capital; and if Sarah had been responsible for young children, she might have resisted moving them back and forth between Tennessee and Washington. But she remained childless throughout her twenty-five-year marriage. Unlike Rachel Jackson, who was evidently attracted to young people and surrounded herself with nieces and nephews to compensate for the children she never had, Sarah showed little feeling of loss in the letters she wrote.

They show, instead, overwhelming concern with her husband's health and his political career. Because the Polks were not often separated, their correspondence is not so voluminous as that of John and Abigail Adams. Many of the letters were written during campaigns, since the mores of her time did not permit a candidate's wife to campaign openly, and while James was out electioneering,

Sarah had to content herself with reporting to him on local political maneuverings. She frequently began her letters with "nothing to report," but then always managed to find something. When the newspapers criticized James, with one editorial pouring out "a vial of wrath" against him, she passed the word along but predicted that the attack had "too much of a flourish" to continue for long. After the *Knoxville Argus* forecast an increased Democratic vote all over the state, "even in the strong Whig counties," Sarah wrote gleefully to James, "The Whigs are dispirited. Good. Democrats are in ecstasy."

While her husband went out looking for votes, Sarah worked quietly at home promoting harmony so as to get Democrats elected. She did not always achieve the results she wanted, and once, after summoning politicos for a conference, she complained to James that she had accomplished little because many of the important men were out of town and "I have not much to operate on." She almost always included in her letters to James an admonition that he pay attention to his health. "It is only the hope that you can live through the campaign that gives me a prospect of enjoyment," she wrote in 1843 when he was running again for governor. "Let me beg and pray that you will take care of yourself and do not become too much excited."

If Sarah regretted missing out on the excitement of the campaign trips, she kept up a good front and refused to crumble in self-pity. Temporarily disheartened by the lack of good news, she wrote James, "Do not think that I am down in the cellar for as soon as I am done writing I am going to dress and go out visiting." Only when compelled to play an entirely social role did she find herself completely out of sorts, and when she had to assume the part of the solicitous hostess for his visiting relatives, she was really angry.

In Washington, Sarah cultivated friendships with the city's strongest, most opinionated women, including Marcia Van Ness, the founder of the Orphan Asylum; Floride Calhoun, the outspoken wife of the South Carolina senator; and Josephine Seaton, a writer and wife of a newspaper editor. Even women whose husbands opposed James politically became Sarah's loyal friends. When the Polks announced that they would return to Tennessee in 1839 so that James could run for governor, Josephine Seaton volunteered that she did not mind seeing James go—he was her husband's political rival—but that she would miss Sarah.

In addition to a network of achieving women, Sarah maintained friendships with several important men. Andrew Jackson, who facilitated her husband's career; Franklin Pierce, who boarded near the Polks; and Supreme Court Justice Joseph Story all became her staunch supporters. In 1839, Justice Story published a farewell poem to Sarah, very unusual recognition for a living woman, particularly a congressman's wife:

> For I have listened to thy voice, and watched thy playful mind,
> Truth in its noblest sense thy choice, Yet gentle, graceful, kind.

Her roster of friends indicates that Sarah Polk was one of the few nineteenth-century First Ladies to develop her own supporters— people who valued her abilities and judgment apart from her husband's. In that respect, she foreshadows a later development that saw its culmination in the campaign buttons, "Betty's husband for President."

Sarah claimed to have predicted her husband's winning the presidential election well before it happened in 1844, although historians have frequently singled this out as the first victory of a "dark horse." She had been exchanging letters with supporters who named James as "the best man" for the job, and she appeared eager to see him nominated. State politics had begun to bore her, and she had tired of making do on a governor's meager $2,000-a-year salary, although she received additional income from her Mississippi plantation.

The prospect of becoming First Lady carried all sorts of new possibilities, and Sarah meant to be more than a hostess. When someone threatened to support the opponent, Henry Clay, because his wife made good butter and knew how to look after a house, Sarah Polk reportedly countered, "If I get to the White House, I expect to live on $25,000 a year and I will neither keep house nor make butter." Such a public disclaimer of domesticity was exceedingly rare in the nineteenth century; even in 1984, when the Democratic candidate for vice-president, Geraldine Ferraro, was asked if she could bake a muffin, she defended herself, saying, "I sure can."

Keeping a clean house and making good butter appeared far less important to Sarah Polk than catering to voters. When news first reached the Polks of the 1844 victory, well-wishers flocked to their house and a friend of the family suggested it might be wise to keep them outside rather than let them dirty up the carpets. Sarah insisted they come in and the next day reported with satisfaction that the only marks they had left were those of respect.

The affability that cloaked Sarah Polk's remarkable political interest satisfied observers who expected women to be merely pretty, social creatures. Had she broken the rules and dressed eccentrically or entertained inappropriately, she might have been criticized, but she did not. In appearance she reportedly combined the coloring and charm of a Spanish lady with the determination and strength of her frontier ancestors. Although few of her admirers thought her beautiful, most described her as "elegant" and "queenly." Henry Dilwood Gilpin, a good friend of Martin Van Buren's, reported he had been much impressed with Sarah. He thought her attractive, affable, and self-possessed. "If I am not mistaken," Gilpin wrote, "she has both sagacity and decision that will make her a good counsellor in some emergencies."

Vice-president-elect George Dallas wrote his wife just before the 1845 inauguration that Sarah dressed "too showy for my taste," but he had been won over to her completely. Dallas added fuel to rumors that the First Lady had the president under her thumb when he wrote, "She is certainly mistress of herself and I suspect of somebody else also."

Sarah's many years of working alongside her husband had increased speculation that she controlled him. While still in her twenties, she had distinguished herself from other congressmen's wives by the forcefulness with which she stated her opinions. Senator Levi Woodbury had written his family in 1828 that only one of his fellow legislators appeared more under his wife's domination than did James Polk. Rudolph Bunner, a representative from upstate New York, reached a similar conclusion.

In response to comments of this sort, Sarah explained that she was simply assisting her husband in order to protect his health. He had never been strong, and she recalled that she had once reprimanded him for keeping late hours. In reply, he had handed her a stack of papers to read for him. Thus began what became standard practice in their relationship—she marked those portions she thought deserving of his attention, folded the papers so that he would not miss the important parts, and passed them back to him.

For two thinking persons to have agreed on everything would have been unusual, and James admitted that he and Sarah sometimes clashed. When the issue of a national bank divided the country, Congressman Polk stood firmly against it. On one of their many trips to Washington, he had asked his wife for money and she had turned first one trunk and then another inside out in the search. "Don't you see how troublesome it is to carry around gold and silver?" she chided him. "This is enough to show you how useful banks are."

A strict Presbyterian, Sarah Polk had no use for dancing or the theater. She never attended a horse race, and although she liked music and resumed piano lessons as an adult, she thought music on Sunday inappropriate. James, who held less definite views on such matters, deferred to her. On their victory trip to Washington in early 1845, well-wishers came aboard their boat to play some festive tunes, but since it was a Sunday, Sarah insisted that the music stop. Someone turned to her husband to countermand her but James Polk replied, "She handles all domestic matters and she considers this domestic." At the inaugural balls, dancing ceased when Sarah

Polk entered the room, and she forebade such entertainment at the White House. Although some critics thought her rigid, many people admired her sincerity, and friends who did not want to be forced into attending church with her on Sunday morning learned to keep their distance that day.

Reading had been a habit of Sarah's since youth and in Washington she continued to order many books. An Englishwoman visiting the White House found Sarah busy with several volumes, including one whose author was coming to dinner that evening. "I could not be so unkind," Sarah explained, "as to appear wholly ignorant and unmindful of the author's gift."

Sarah's intellectuality complemented the Polk administration's emphasis on hard work. James and Sarah had stayed at Coleman's Hotel in Washington five days before making a courtesy call at the White House, and when the Tylers gave a big final party (for which the candles reportedly cost $350), the Polks stayed away. President Polk boasted that in his first year in office he rarely took an afternoon or evening off; and when he greeted guests every Tuesday and Friday, he did so as part of his job.

All strong-minded people earn some enemies, and Sarah Polk was no exception. Anyone who criticized her husband raised Sarah's wrath, and she did not always conceal her displeasure. When Martin Van Buren's son, who held many unorthodox views, took issue with President Polk, Sarah banished him from the guest lists. When James had his secretary issue an invitation anyway, she burned it. "I was amused," James Polk noted in his diary, but he gave no hint of overruling her.

But Sarah rarely offended or took issue with anyone. Jessie Benton Frémont, then the young wife of the explorer John Frémont who later ran for president, pronounced Sarah a perfect model: "an admirable, erect, attentive, quietly gracious," woman who "really did her part well." Charles Sumner, the Massachusetts senator, wrote a friend, "Her sweetness of manner won me entirely."

Such apparently winning charm evidently excused Sarah from

excessive attention to household management. An able staff took care of most of the domestic arrangements while she concentrated on more important matters. Food held little interest for her and she sometimes became so intent on discussions with her guests that she neglected to eat. Rather than spending much energy on redecorating the mansion, she announced that whatever was good enough for the Tylers would do very well for her. She did install gas lights but in her very practical way insisted on retaining a chandelier of candles, and when the gas system failed during a dinner party, she earned her guests' applause by calling for the candles.

James Polk is sometimes singled out as a particularly strong president because he accomplished in one term all four goals he had set for himself—reduction of the tariff, restoration of the independent Treasury, acquisition of California, and settlement of the boundary dispute in Oregon. Based on this record, the Polk administration raises questions about how the forcefulness or success of the chief executive influences the public's judgment of the spouse. Will Americans more likely tolerate strong women if they move alongside decisive men? Can a wife stave off criticism by keeping a less prominent role for herself if her husband is viewed as a relatively ineffectual president?

Sarah Polk's record suggests no simple connection exists between a wife's public image and that of her husband. The most outspoken and politically involved wife since Abigail Adams, Sarah received a universally good press from both sides of the fence. Capital social arbiters who sized up her "feminine charms" could hardly fault her, and the more intellectually inclined, who wanted a thinking woman in the White House, apparently approved of her, too. Because she had the self-confidence to relegate much of her job as hostess to an insignificant chore—but not neglect it—she achieved remarkable success. The most prominent student of the Polk administration, Charles Sellers, pronounced Sarah "increasingly indispensable" to her husband as "secretary, political counselor, nurse and emotional resource." It was, Sellers wrote, the combination of her "long experience in official circles and her social grace" that qualified her "superbly" to be an outstanding First Lady.

It is difficult to know what Sarah Polk thought about women's rights issues although she was living in the White House during the famous Seneca Falls convention in July, 1848. Led by the pious Quaker from Philadelphia, Lucretia Mott, and the younger, more outspoken Elizabeth Cady Stanton, women gathered in that small upstate New York town to outline their hopes for better education, more voice in decisions about their children, greater access to jobs, and the right to vote.

Sarah Polk did not attend the Seneca Falls meeting, although one student of the Polk administration has concluded that she did encourage her husband to address the group. Perhaps she feared being included in the ridicule that was heaped on suffragists at the time. Instead, Sarah spent the summer going over plans to build a new house for her and her husband's retirement in Tennessee and traveling to New York to select the furnishings. Portraits made of Sarah Polk at the time show little evidence that she associated with women's rights proponents who advocated less constraining clothing and simpler hairstyles. Sarah chose to appear in elaborate, low-cut dresses, with her hair always carefully arranged.

James Polk died in June 1849, three months after his presidency ended, and Sarah survived him by forty-two years. Although her name was briefly linked with that of bachelor president James Buchanan, she never remarried. At first her Mississippi plantation took much of her time; but in January 1860, as the Civil War approached, she sold her land and slaves for $30,000. Although Sarah explained that her husband would never have approved of secession, she could not conceal her strong sympathies for the South, with the result that her Polk Place in Tennessee remained neutral territory for the duration of the hostilities. Leaders from both sides visited her there and when the local historical society needed a safe place for depositing its holdings, it chose Sarah's residence.

Very popular when she left Washington in 1849, Sarah Polk had inspired a national publication, *Peterson's Magazine,* to take the un-precedented step of paying tribute to her in a poem that ended, "You are modest, yet all a queen should be." Most magazines up to that time had chosen their heroines from classical examples or from lists of women long dead. The singling out of Sarah Polk for such a gesture indicates that she had attained unusual prominence.

Her popularity endured long after she left the capital. In 1881, when Congress debated giving a pension to Abraham Lincoln's widow, one man made his crucial vote dependent on including Sarah Polk. On the state level, the Tennessee legislature planned annual pilgrimages to her house, and newspaper reporters contin-ued to seek her opinions on political matters. The *Mt. Vernon Banner* reported that in her seventy-ninth year, she retained a "complexion as clear, face as smooth and eyes as bright as most ladies of 50." In the election of 1884, she made comparisons to the one that had sent her husband to the White House forty years earlier. When she died in August 1891, an article in *American Magazine* described her mind as "undimmed to the end."

Sarah Polk stands out in a period when most wives of public figures stayed home and out of sight. That she had excellent health, an inquiring and trained mind, a supportive husband, and no chil-dren all increased her ability to participate in her husband's career. Reminiscent in many ways of Abigail Adams, Sarah Polk has re-mained lesser known, perhaps because she lacked some of Abigail's wit and sophistication. Both women considered themselves full partners in their husbands' political careers, opinions that their husbands shared. Yet neither woman showed much interest in re-forms for women generally. It is interesting to speculate how they, with all opportunities being equal, would have done as presidents. Their interest in politics was genuine; and perhaps that explains, better than anything else, why they distinguished themselves at a time when most presidents' wives were absent, ill, or inactive during their husbands' administrations.

MARY TODD LINCOLN

COMPARED TO Sarah Polk, Mary Todd Lincoln's national prominence is on an entirely different level, more in the infamous category than the famous, more the result of her enemies' work than her admirers. Mary Lincoln's life included elements of unusual ambition and great personal tragedy, possibly explaining why she became one of the most written-about women in American history. That she provoked unusual antagonisms and raised powerful defenses rendered her story all the more intriguing. It is no wonder that fact and fiction became so intertwined in accounts of her life that it is difficult to separate the two. Unfortunately this woman who stubbornly insisted on staying in the limelight, even when criticism mounted, did not always record her motivation. Speculation about that must come from her associates.

A matronly mother of three by the time her husband became president, Mary Lincoln already had some experience with Washington. She had lived there during the winter of 1847–1848 when her husband served in Congress, but unhappy with the prospect of staying in a boardinghouse with her two young sons, she had returned to Illinois. Those few months had exposed her to the entrenched Washingtonians, but by 1861 she appeared to have forgotten how they operated. When her husband won the presidency, she prepared to return to the capital. Had she known the outcome, she might have reconsidered.

Even with her professed powers of premonition, she never predicted how miserable she would become in the next twenty years as she witnessed the deaths of her husband and two of her sons, found herself maligned on two continents, and was finally declared legally insane. A woman of many contradictions, Mary Lincoln may have stirred up controversy because of her enigmatic nature. Her husband called her his "child wife" and "mother"—neither term entirely inappropriate. He pampered her as a spoiled youngster, humored her when she veered towards fanaticism, yet showed her enormous tenderness and affection. Although she had attended the best schools in Kentucky, indeed in the entire West, she dabbled in spiritualism throughout her life and persisted in believing in her own supernatural powers as well as those of others. Considerably better educated and socially more sophisticated than the man she married, she had become, by the time he was elected president, so unreliable and impetuous that he could not trust her judgment on any significant matter.

Part of the explanation for her contradictory nature no doubt lies in the particular circumstances of her childhood, which combined material comforts with considerable insecurity. When Mary was almost seven, her mother died in giving birth to a seventh child, and a little more than a year later, her father remarried. The new wife, Betsy Humphreys, came from a social stratum above that of the Todds and she did not hesitate to point that out. One of her favorite maxims was that it took seven generations to make a lady, and Betsy indicated by her tone that in her family the requisite time had elapsed. Betsy Humphreys Todd gave birth to eight children of her own, who, added to her stepchildren, made a brood of fifteen, too many for any one of them to claim much individual attention.

To distinguish herself from the rest, Mary competed in every possible way, becoming an ingenious prankster, an excellent student, a superb horsewoman, and a respectable seamstress. Her good looks came naturally. But behind the beauty and ingenuity, her contemporaries observed a very moody young lady, "much like an April day, sunning all over with laughter one moment, the next

crying as though her heart would break." She was frequently compared to her mercurial father, Robert Todd, much given to buying
expensive clothes one day, then regretting his extravagance the
next.

But Todd, a leading businessman in Lexington, provided for every need of his large family and sent all his children, including the
girls, to the best schools in the area. When she was eight, Mary
entered the local academy, and at fourteen she enrolled in a boarding school outside Lexington. Taught French and social skills by a
Paris-born couple, Mary got tested when she went home for the
weekends. Her step-grandmother Humphreys, one of Kentucky's
grande dames, read French philosophers in the original and tutored
the young women of her family in the social graces. To round out
her very full education, Mary had the conversation of her father's
friends, including the already famous Henry Clay. Young Mary
Todd described herself as being much taken with the famous congressman and a "dedicated Whig."

That early interest in politics may help explain why Mary moved
to Springfield, Illinois when she was twenty-one to live with her
sister. The older Todd daughter had married the son of the former
territorial governor, and she counted many politicians among her
friends and acquaintances. Mary's quick wit and beauty attracted
several of Springfield's eligible young men, and according to two of
her biographers, she was courted by two men who would run
against each other in the 1860 presidential election.

If that is true—and there is considerable doubt that it is because
Mary's politics would hardly have put her in both their circles—then
the short Stephen Douglas might have proven a more suitable
match for her than the lanky Abraham Lincoln. Mary's brother-in-
law had described Abraham as too "rough," and Mary sometimes
joked about his lack of social graces. One story, perhaps as apocryphal as so many of the Lincoln stories were, said that Abe had
introduced himself to Mary by saying he wanted to dance with her
"in the worst way" and then, she said, he did, "in the very worst."

Whatever their reasons, Abraham and Mary were married in 1842, and their early years together were unremarkable. He built both an Illinois law practice and a national reputation, and she gave birth to four sons, including one who died at age four. The Lincolns prospered in the 1850s, partly due to Mary's small inheritances from her father and grandfather and to her reasonable management of the household. She often recalled these as the best times of her life, although people who knew her differed in evaluating her behavior. Some said that she kept up with what was happening in the country, frequently sharing her ideas with her husband; but others, less charitable toward her, saw her even then as a jealous, manipulative woman with few intellectual interests.

Everyone agreed that she never lost her ambition to live in the White House—a prospect that increased in possibility when the Republicans, at their second convention in 1860, selected Illinois's favorite son as their candidate. The Northern and Southern states had by then become so divided over the issue of slavery and its extension into new areas that the Democratic convention could not agree on one candidate, with the result that the Northern branch chose Stephen Douglas while the Southerners went with John Breckinridge. To complicate matters, a fourth group, under the Constitutional Union banner, named John Bell, a Tennesseean who won not only his own state but also neighboring Kentucky and Virginia. When the results were in, Abraham Lincoln claimed victory, but with only 40 percent of the popular vote cast, his was a dubious victory. Uncertainty increased when it became apparent that the Southerners' pique was not temporary. They refused to accept the results of the election, and additional states seceded from the Union. The capital grew somber as the indications of civil war multiplied.

Mary Lincoln stood squarely in the middle of the storm. Although she professed complete loyalty to the Union cause, several of her relatives enlisted on the side of the "rebels," as Mary and most Northerners referred to those who favored formation of the Confederacy. She presented an easy target for people who questioned how a woman could be dedicated to winning a war when her brothers were fighting for the enemy. As stories proliferated about spies in high places, the president's wife was named, sometimes by people whose statements could not be dismissed lightly. Thurlow Weed, a prominent New York supporter of Abraham Lincoln, reportedly announced that Mary had been banished from Washington because she was a "traitor." That was, of course, untrue, but it indicates the kind of rumors that circulated.

Nor were the stories of Mary Lincoln's treachery confined to her lifetime. One poignant account of her husband's defense of her was originally printed in a Washington newspaper in 1905, then repeated many times even after it had been demonstrated to be untrue. According to the original source, an unnamed senator had recalled how President Lincoln had taken the unprecedented action of going before a Senate committee to defend Mary. Without mentioning her by name, the president had sworn that no "member of my family holds treasonable communication with the enemy." According to the senator's apocryphal account, the committee was so moved that it immediately and without discussion "dropped all considerations of the rumors that the wife of the President was betraying the Union."

Even without a civil war, Mary's personal insecurities would have made her stay in Washington difficult. She understood that her education and social skill stood her well in the West, in Kentucky and Illinois, where she had acquired them but might not satisfy the "cave dwellers," the judgmental residents of Washington. "The very fact of having grown up in the West subjects me to more searching observation," she explained to her seamstress, as though trying to justify why she spent so much money and effort on clothes. Mary had stopped in New York on her way to Washington to purchase yardage for sixteen outfits, and she never let the seamstress catch up before placing more orders.

Part of Mary Todd Lincoln's poor reputation may very well have

Martha Dandridge Custis Washington

Abigail Smith Adams

Dolley Payne Todd Madison

Elizabeth Kortwright Monroe

Louisa Johnson Adams

Rachel Donelson Robards Jackson

Angelica Singleton Van Buren

Anna Symmes Harrison

Letitia Christian Tyler

Priscilla Cooper Tyler

Julia Gardiner Tyler

resulted from the bad luck she had to arrive in the capital just as the public's appetite for information about the White House grew. Her extravagant spending provided reporters with copy they could not pass up, and even the most intimate details of her life became the subject of public rumor. Speculations that she might be pregnant produced a cryptic denial, published in the "Personal" column of a national magazine, *Leslie's Weekly*, on October 10, 1863: "The reports that Mrs. Lincoln was in an interesting condition are untrue."

But in the early months of the Lincoln presidency, when the full horror of what would follow had not become clear, national magazines flattered Mary Lincoln. *Leslie's Weekly* applauded her "exquisite taste" in redecorating the mansion, in entertaining, and in choosing her clothes. "No European court or capital can compare with the President's circle and the society of Washington this winter in the freshness and beauty of its women," *Leslie's Weekly* reported. The First Lady was described as "second in no respect, displaying the exquisitely moulded shoulders and arms of our fair 'Republican Queen,' absolutely dazzling."

Very quickly the reports changed. Hundreds of thousands of men took up arms for either the blue or the gray. Battlefield casualties climbed, and Mary Lincoln had her own personal grief in addition to concern for her relatives who were fighting for the "rebels." In February 1862, her eleven-year-old son, Will, died at the White House. Mary purchased costly mourning clothes and special mourning jewelry. Families who had lost sons and husbands in the war were dismayed by her extravagance, and they began to raise questions about the sincerity of her grief. How could she mourn her son and yet direct so much attention to spending money? But she had shown signs before of spending money as though that could help her forget her problems.

Stories began to spread that Mary threw tantrums to get her way, and because several of the accounts originated with her best friends, they could hardly be discounted. Julia Taft, a teenager who spent a great deal of time at the White House because her two younger brothers shared a tutor with the Lincoln boys, told how the First Lady had appropriated a part of another woman's hat for herself. At a concert one evening, Mary Lincoln had eyed the bonnet of Julia's mother and then asked for the ribbons from it. Mary explained that the fashionable French milliner whom both women patronized had been unable to find more of the black and white satin ribbon he had used on Mrs. Taft's hat and Mary wanted that ribbon for herself. In the end Mary got the ribbon, the milliner replaced Mrs. Taft's ties with some of a different color, and Julia concluded that "Mrs. Lincoln wanted what she wanted when she wanted it and no substitute! And as far as we know she always had it, including a President of the United States."

Other stories had the First Lady threatening merchants who refused to humor her and deliver some item she demanded although it had already been bought by somebody else. Mary Lincoln's dressmaker, who was devoted to her employer, described how the president's wife would kick and scream, sometimes lying on the floor, when costumes were not delivered on time or in quite the condition that she expected. Julia Grant, wife of the general who commanded the Union troops after 1863, related other examples of Mary's irrational behavior. On one occasion Julia calmed Mary, who insisted that another officer's wife was maneuvering to catch Abraham's interest. Mary became "annoyed" and could not "control her wrath," Julia reported, although there were no grounds for jealousy.

These stories, added to those about her spending and the rumors of her Southern loyalties, reached a peak during the reelection campaign in 1864, causing Mary considerable worry. She had neglected to share the extent of her extravagance with her husband and now she desperately needed him to win so she would not have to pay up. Merchants had extended credit, sometimes requesting her intercession with the president in return, and Mary had no illusions about how quickly her credit would be cut off if her husband lost the election. Reassured by the victory of November 1864, she quickly resumed her buying spree and spent in the first three months of 1865 several thousand dollars on nonessentials such as jewelry and silverware. She admitted to a friend that her unpaid clothing bills amounted at that time to $27,000—more than her husband earned in a year—but she actually owed much more.

Mary might have deflected some of the criticism by retreating to her room upstairs, as so many of her predecessors had done, but she refused all offers to substitute for her as hostess. Kate Chase, daughter of the secretary of the treasury, coveted the White House for her father and would have relished a social leadership role for herself in the Lincoln administration. Other members of the cabinet volunteered to help, too, and when Prince Napoleon came for a visit, Secretary of State Seward offered to host a major event. But Mary Lincoln, proud of the French she had learned in Kentucky, insisted she could handle the arrangements herself; and at the end of the evening when "mostly French was spoken," she reported with some pride that the prince had turned to her and remarked with some surprise, "Paris is not all the world."

If Mary Lincoln had diverted her attention from parties and clothes (subjects that appeared frivolous to many war-sufferers) and concentrated on appearing supportive and protective of her husband, she might have disarmed her critics. Instead, she badgered him more than she helped. According to one White House employee, she interrupted the president's work at the slightest whim, and invited favor-seekers to meals without the president's knowledge. Then, when he appeared "sad and harrassed," she lobbied openly for whatever the guest had come to ask. According to one of Mary's relatives, who had accompanied her to Washington, Mary was constantly being flattered by people who wanted to gain access to the president, and Abe's announcement that "Women have no influence in this administration" did little to stop them. With so many rumors of power on the distaff side of the White House, it is not surprising that Mary received an unusual gift from an anonymous donor. It made its point more clearly than any words could—it was a bonnet with the president's photograph attached to each of the strings.

Charges that a First Lady influenced her husband were nothing novel—they went all the way back to the first Adams administration. But Mary Lincoln's brand of self-centered manipulation appealed to no one. People who championed strong women and respected their opinions had found heroines in the partisan Abigail Adams and the astute Sarah Polk, but Mary Lincoln's influence was negative— petty, unpredictable, and self-serving.

Some of Mary's critics blamed her selfishness for exposing the president to danger, including that at Ford's Theater on April 14, 1865. The president had been aware of the possibility of personal harm during his entire first term, and special guards had been assigned to protect him. Mary insisted, however, that her husband needed relaxation, too, and she sometimes arranged for him to ride around the capital with her. On the last day of his life, they had gone out driving and she later said that she had rarely witnessed her husband so content as on that afternoon. General Lee had just surrendered the armies and ended the long war. Taking this move as initiating a new, more tranquil period for themselves personally, the Lincolns resolved to put behind them their grief over their son Will's death and move on to better times.

That evening Abraham accompanied his wife to the theater and she was seated beside him when the assassin struck. Mary, who never attended funerals of any member of her family, did not go to this one and delegated all the arrangements to her son Robert. Five weeks later, she rallied enough to pack and leave the White House, thus beginning a long, tortured pilgrimage to find a place to spend the rest of her life. She was forty-seven years old.

Of the two sons still living (of the four she had borne), Mary felt closer to Tad, the youngest, than to Robert, then at Harvard Law School. Tad required special attention because of learning problems and a speech impediment that made him difficult to understand. Although generally cheerful, he could sometimes be hard to manage, throwing tantrums until his mother had to have him removed from the room. She had been indulgent with him, indeed with all the boys, taking as her motto "Let the children have fun," but now she determined to substitute strictness and to enroll Tad in a school in Germany. Her motive held more than a little self-interest —she had never traveled in Europe and believed she could live there more economically than in the United States.

Money so occupied Mary Lincoln's thoughts after 1865 that it may well have been the most important consideration in her move to Europe. Although her husband's estate left about $35,000 to her and to each of her sons, she thought the amount inadequate. Congress had traditionally paid a year's salary to the widow of any president who died in office, but Abraham Lincoln had been the first to be assassinated and Mary thought the wife of a martyr deserved more. Others agreed that the different circumstances somehow required a larger compensation for the family.

In a controversy that lasted until her death and beyond, Congress divided over the country's obligation to presidents' widows. As long as she lived, Mary Lincoln stayed at the center of the discussion, fueling it with exaggerations of her poverty. She arranged to auction her old clothes and jewelry in a New York hotel, and although she acted under an assumed name, word leaked out, increasing the suspicion that she was either poorer than anyone realized or slightly crazy.

The final blow in the long string of misfortunes that hammered away at Mary's natural instability came from her husband's old law partner, William Herndon. While the men worked together in the 1850s, Mary and Herndon made no secret of their dislike for each other. He had compared her dancing to that of a serpent, but her disapproval of him went beyond such tasteless but harmless comments. Herndon lacked the polish that Mary Lincoln required in her husband's associates, and she excluded him from her dinner parties. He retaliated by attributing Abraham's moodiness to pressures caused by Mary's unreasonableness.

After Abraham Lincoln's assassination in 1865, Herndon began a biography and requested interviews with anyone who had known the president. In the process of taking down notes, he gave currency to many stories that were patently false or enormously exaggerated. Although he did not publish his book until much later, his speeches on the subject received newspaper coverage, and his claims gained publicity in the works of other authors.

By far the most sensational of the Herndon material argued that Abraham Lincoln had never loved anyone but Ann Rutledge, a young woman who died before he met Mary. This was the first time that Mary Lincoln had heard the story, and although she had plenty of reason to doubt its truth, she was unprepared emotionally to deal with its implications. As headlines carried the news across the country, she became more and more distraught.

Herndon's evidence was shaky at best. Abraham knew Ann Rutledge but only as the young daughter of the boardinghouse keeper where he stayed. At the time the future president met her, Ann was already engaged to be married and gave no indication of breaking off the agreement when Abraham appeared on the scene. But evidence that the martyred president had never loved Mary appealed to people who wanted to believe the worst, and the Rutledge connection gained currency.

By going to Europe, Mary hoped to get away from the stories. She enrolled Tad in a Frankfurt school and went to take the waters at fashionable spas, never neglecting to follow news accounts of what was happening in the United States, particularly attempts in Congress to get her more money. Two other presidents' widows figured in the picture but each from a slightly different angle. Julia Tyler negotiated from a disadvantaged position since her husband had sided with the South in the Civil War; and Sarah Polk, who lived quietly in apparent comfort in Nashville, seemed in no great need.

After learning that Congress had granted her a pension of $3,000, Mary returned in the spring of 1871 to Illinois. She thought it a niggardly sum but had decided to try living in her own country again. A few months later all her resolution fell away when Tad, her youngest son, died at eighteen. Of all her sorrows, she later said, this cut the deepest.

On all sides, Mary felt besieged. She continued to worry about money, although what she had was ample for her needs, and she was humiliated by the stories about her husband and Ann Rutledge. She felt estranged from her one remaining son, the rather cold and distant Robert, who had a promising government career. His marriage to the daughter of a prominent judge had not pleased Mary and the fact that the young couple named their daughter for her hardly evened things out.

By early 1875, Robert asked for a court decision on his mother's sanity. He knew she carried her life savings sewed into her clothes, and when suspicious-looking characters began calling on her, he feared she would lose everything. In May 1875, Mary Todd Lincoln sat quietly in an Illinois court and heard her son and old friends describe her erratic behavior. Some talked of her heavy spending and others of her dabblings in spiritualism, a popular pastime involving supposed communication with dead relatives. The judge listened and then committed her to the care of Robert, who promptly arranged for her to enter Bellevue. A private mental institution near Chicago, Bellevue catered to "a select class of lady patients of quiet and unexceptionable habits." Mary, one of twenty patients, had freedom to wander about the grounds. Doctors prescribed very little medication, and she had a private room and her own attendant.

But confinement under the best of circumstances did not appeal to Mary Lincoln, and she became less cooperative as time passed. Hospital records show that she would order one dish for breakfast, then change her mind and refuse to eat it; she requested a carriage and then would not get in it. Such "lying and deceit should be put down to insanity," a hospital attendant reported with considerable overstatement.

Evidence pieced together later shows that Mary spent a good deal of her time plotting how to regain her freedom. When Robert came for one of his weekly visits, she discussed her wish to live with her sister, and when he left, she asked to accompany him into town in order to mail a letter. Hospital attendants, who agreed to the trip, later learned that she mailed several letters, including one to a former congressman and another to an attorney, asking for their assistance in securing her release. Both the congressman and the attorney came for visits. The latter, Myra Bradwell, the first woman to be admitted to the bar in Illinois, pronounced Mary Lincoln "no more insane than I am."

Mary's older sister, with whom she had lived when she first arrived in Springfield as a young woman, was becoming less convinced that Mary belonged in an institution. The attendant publicity was certainly unpleasant. Joining forces, the sister, lawyer Bradwell, and Mary requested a new hearing. Without alerting hospital attendants, Bradwell arranged for a newspaper reporter to interview Mary, and after a two-hour talk, the reporter concluded that Mary showed no sign of mental weakness. The efforts of the three women led to Mary's release in September, 1875.

Still looking for a place to settle, Mary returned to Europe and made her headquarters in Pau, France, until a bad fall partially paralyzed her. Saddened and broken, she returned to America on the same ship that carried the famous actress Sarah Bernhardt. In terms as dramatic as the parts she played on stage, Bernhardt later described how she had saved Mary Lincoln from falling down a flight of stairs. The two women introduced themselves, and after they had talked, Bernhardt realized that she had done the one thing for Mary Lincoln that she should not have done—saved her life. But not for long. Mary returned to her sister's house in Springfield, the same house where she had married, and she died there in 1882.

Except for her good education and remarkable spunk, Mary Todd Lincoln had everything against her. Geography made her suspect, both socially and politically. The competitiveness and insecurity she had shown as a young girl matured into a self-defeating combination. The loss of three sons and the assassination of her husband in front of her eyes broke her.

It is ironic that Mary Todd Lincoln would become so much discussed, more books and plays being written about her than any other First Lady of the nineteenth century, because in all important ways she was a failure. After the early years of her marriage (when she may have helped Abraham develop socially and may have improved his financial situation by her inheritances), she proved a hindrance to him. Historians have generally dismissed her as unbalanced; and a century after her death, a highly respected scholar, Henry Steele Commager, described her as "a half-crazy woman."

Yet for all her flaws, Mary Lincoln showed considerable determination throughout her life, particularly in her refusal to accept anonymity in Washington and later, in engineering her release from the mental institution. She had a good excuse, especially after the death of her son in 1862, to plead grief as a reason to avoid social life in the capital; or she could have fallen back on her recurring headaches and refused any public role. Only her stubbornness lifted her out of the obscurity that surrounds most nineteenth-century presidents' wives. In a time when women had few constructive outlets for their energy and talents, they sometimes selected destructive ones, directing their strong wills to insignificant, even damaging actions. Given other choices, Mary Lincoln might have behaved differently.

JULIA DENT GRANT

J ULIA DENT GRANT, the third woman to emerge from a long string of generally undistinguished First Ladies during the middle of the nineteenth century, profited from the optimism that surrounded her husband's first inauguration in 1869. The Federal City, as people still called the capital, was cold and dark that day; but the rain held off and thousands of people got the chance to see the man they trusted to initiate "a reign of loyalty and truth and patriotism." To signal their determination to put both the Civil War and the bungled Johnson administration that followed it behind them, supporters had traveled many miles and paid high prices for seats to witness the Grant inauguration. About the new president's wife the crowd knew very little, but in the next eight years they would hear a good deal. Julia Dent Grant had never been one to stay in the background.

Born in 1826 to relatively wealthy Missouri slaveholders who already had three sons, Julia had enjoyed more than her share of her parents' attention. Even after the birth of another daughter, Julia Dent remained her father's favorite. A cheerful, good-natured youngster, she matured into a self-assured young woman who chose to marry against strong parental objection. Ulysses Grant showed little promise of success, and Julia's father thought she could do better—an opinion that did not change quickly. Ulysses performed well enough in the army as long as he was fighting against Mexico, but later assignments to Panama and then to a lonely outpost at Fort Vancouver, Washington, went less well. Rumor had it that his excessive drinking led to his resignation from the army. He tried selling real estate and farming before going to work in his father's Illinois harness shop. Although Julia later brushed aside hints that these had been trying times, as she tried to cope with her erratic husband and the four children born to them in twelve years, friends admitted she had been frequently unhappy.

If the Civil War had not rescued Ulysses from obscurity, he might well have ended up a stooped, soft-spoken, sloppy store clerk, who never excelled in anything. At West Point, he had been a mediocre student—riding was his best subject. But the war brought out new strengths in the middle-aged Ulysses and he managed to get himself appointed head of the Twenty-first Illinois Volunteers. Then in one battle after another he showed he could be both ruthless and tenacious. His insistence on the enemy's "unconditional surrender" earned him the nickname "butcher," and provided a new explanation for his initials "U.S."

By the time the victorious general Ulysses Grant met Robert E. Lee at war's end at Appomattox, he had become a national figure and soon there was talk of nominating him for president. He won in the 1868 election, just two months after Mary Lincoln, who had vowed to leave the country if "that butcher" ever became president, had sailed for Europe.

The Grant family appeared particularly healthy and appealing occupants of the White House after the tragedies associated with the Lincolns and the difficulties encountered by the Andrew Johnsons. The two older sons, Frederick and Ulysses, Jr., spent most of the first years of their father's tenure away at college, but teenager Nellie and mischievous Jesse, the baby of the family, made up for the absence. Nellie's participation added a youthful touch to official parties that had tended to become stiff and predictable.

Twelve-year-old Jesse Grant, whom his mother described as "never at a loss for an answer," kept several reporters busy with his antics and his gossip about other family members, especially his two grandfathers who often stayed at the White House. Frederick Dent,

Julia's father, and Jesse Grant, Ulysses's father, did not get along, according to young Jesse, and sometimes they would refuse to communicate with each other except through Julia. In the presence of the elder Grant, Frederick Dent would instruct Julia to "take better care of that old gentleman. He is feeble and deaf as a post and yet you permit him to wander all over Washington alone." Overhearing the remark as he had been meant to do, Grandfather Grant would retort to young Jesse, "Did you hear him? I hope I shall not live to become as old and infirm as your Grandfather Dent."

Accounts of such harmless family squabbles entertained a public that had become accustomed to a more somber White House. Actually, part of the attention to the presidential family resulted from changes in journalism. Inexpensive newspapers, more available after 1830, helped enlarge the reading public. Women had finally caught up with men in literacy by the middle of the nineteenth century and increased their purchases of newspapers and books accordingly. Editors, always alert for a new audience, changed the focus of their columns to attract this new market. Details of women's lives were very popular, and if the subject happened to live in the White House, so much the better.

Partly because of the new market, more women reporters began working the capital, and they slanted their stories to interest women. Emily Edson Briggs, wife of a clerk in the House of Representatives, took advantage of her proximity to important sources of information to start a column for the *Philadelphia Press*. Using the pen name "Olivia," Briggs relayed capital gossip, informing readers who had never seen General Grant's wife that she appeared "fair, fat, and forty, much like any other sensible woman would who had been lifted from the ranks of the people to such an exalted position." Rather than stoop to real nastiness, Briggs preferred to quote others on Julia Grant's appearance, and she reported on one occasion that a "little upstart woman who sat near me had the impudence to say Mrs. Grant looked horrid." When Julia Grant did not take the seat assigned to her at a public ceremony, Emily Briggs's readers learned all about the gaffe.

Fascination with the private side of famous peoples' lives became so much a part of late-nineteenth-century American journalism that a word was imported from England to cover the phenomenon. Jenkins, the slang name conferred on the staff reporter of court news and social events for an English newspaper, was converted in the United States to "Jenkinsism," meaning a preoccupation with or exaggerated attention to such subjects.

Once *Godey's Lady's Book,* the leading women's magazine, recognized the general interest in the White House occupants, it introduced a regular monthly column on the subject. Beginning in 1873, a fictional "Aunt Mehitable" (pseudonym for Harriet Hazelton) relayed the social trivia of Washington life to anyone who wanted to read it, writing about who among the senators' wives made the best appearance, how the Washington women dressed and curled their hair—even the condition of their teeth. In her columns, "Aunt Mehitable" would judge the president's teenaged daughter, Nellie Grant, "just moderately good lookin'," and as for Mrs. Grant, she "ain't half as good lookin' as the pictures we see of her." Julia Grant had closed out the sunlight and used gas chandeliers for her afternoon receptions, it was reported, "because she knowed she wasn't very handsome an' gaslight would make her look better."

"Aunt Mehitable" referred to an eye condition of the president's wife that would have remained little known had she arrived in the capital a few decades earlier. Julia Grant, whose White House tenure coincided with a remarkable increase in the number of Washington cameras, understood that she would not be flattered by the results. Her mildly crossed eyes did not lend themselves to becoming pictures and she had considered having surgery to correct the condition. Ulysses vetoed the plan, however, saying that he loved her the way she was. Julia, good-natured and confident about her appearance as about most things, reacted to photographers by cheerfully obliging them, with the result that many pictures of her survive—but most of them show her in profile, concealing the inter-section of her gaze.

Unlike the criticism that was leveled at Mary Lincoln only a few years earlier, extravagant spending by the Grants would increase their attractiveness with the public. In what came to be called the Gilded Age, large price tags were less objectionable than they had been during the Lincoln war years, and no one seemed to care what Julia bought. No expense appeared in bad taste, no shine too bright. The newly rich vied with each other for the title of bigger spender, with the prize placed squarely on quantity of purchase rather than quality. In such an atmosphere, the White House hostess could hardly overspend, and an approving nation watched as Julia served dinners of twenty-nine courses, accompanied by high-priced French wines.

In May 1874, when eighteen-year-old Nellie Grant wed the young and wealthy British nephew of the famous actress Fanny Kemble, the event was the center of national attention. The first White House wedding since that of President Tyler's daughter thirty-two years earlier, this one was a bonanza for reporters looking for a big story. *Harper's Bazaar* described the East Room as transformed into "a perfect bower of bloom." The bride's dress was reported to have cost thousands of dollars (one paper gave the figure of $5,000). While a wedding breakfast for five hundred was served inside the White House, crowds lined the streets outside in hopes of catching a glimpse of the couple or of some of the famous guests.

When the newlyweds left Washington the next day on the first leg of their European honeymoon, the entire Grant family accompanied them to New York, thus extending the festivities. Newspapers could not print copies fast enough, as the *New York Graphic* explained one day after the wedding, "It's of no use. We are utterly unable to meet the demand for today's issue."

Julia Grant had to rely on such social events for gaining attention because she showed little political prowess. By her own admission,

Julia once came out both for and against a particular piece of legisla-tion. She explained that she had been in New York on a shopping trip when she was approached by both proponents and critics of the bill, wanting her to influence the president in their behalf. Since she knew nothing about the bill at that time, she cheerfully implied agreement with both sides.

Back in Washington, she confronted Ulysses and asked that he explain the bill and its possible effects. When he had finished, she urged him to veto it. "I always flattered myself," she wrote, "that I had rendered my husband and the country a very great service in advising the President to veto the all-important Finance Bill that was almost convulsing the country, but I find I had more than one rival in that honor. To tell the truth, I think the President knew his duty quite well and would have fulfilled his duty in any case."

Ulysses made no secret of the fact that he liked the women around him dependent, and Julia usually humored him by appearing docile and agreeable. She never quite hid, however, a stubborn, willful streak. She once signaled her independence by refusing to sign the necessary papers for the sale of their Washington house. As presi-dent-elect, Ulysses had arranged the sale without consulting his wife, and to underscore her objection, she refused to go along. Ulysses was thus forced to back out of the deal with no other expla-nation than that his wife would not cooperate. The next time he located a prospective buyer, he discussed the offer with Julia, and this time she reported that she cheerfully signed, having made her point.

Julia Grant prolonged her tenure in the public eye by accompany-ing her husband on a trip around the world after his second term ended in 1877. (She would have preferred a third term in the White House but Ulysses did not consult her on the matter.) In the twenty-eight-month journey, Julia was treated more like a reigning mon-arch than like the wife of an ex-president, and she thrived on the attention she received. The Grants dined with royalty at Windsor Castle, breakfasted with "London literati," and drank with English workingmen. After more banquets and honors on the continent, they sailed for the Far East. Governments along the way competed for title of biggest giver, the Japanese distinguishing themselves only slightly more than the others by offering the ex-president the furnishings of an entire room.

The Grants returned to settle in New York, and Ulysses set about writing his memoirs. He was already ill with a spreading throat cancer, and just days after he had completed the work, he died. He had feared he would not finish in time and had sketched in the important parts first, knowing he could go back and fill in the details if time permitted. What later became a standard exercise for ex-presidents—the writing and selling of their memoirs for large sums —began with Ulysses Grant, and it did not spring so much from his own ego as from a desire to provide an income for his family.

The book earned half a million dollars in royalties, so that Julia was encouraged to write her own autobiography—the first by an ex-president's wife. Memoirs of Abigail Adams and Dolley Madison had already been published but heirs had spliced them together out of the women's letters. Unfortunately, Julia's work failed to interest a publisher until nearly three quarters of a century after her death, and it was not published until 1975.

Less than one tenth of her book deals with Julia's eight years as First Lady, and in those few pages, she concentrates on describing her social accomplishments and defending Ulysses. His own autobiography had ignored rumors about his malfeasance in office, and Julia determined to set the record straight. Several of her relatives took jobs on the public payroll but that hardly constituted corruption. "There was that dreadful Black Friday," she admitted, referring to a scheme drafted by the financiers Jim Fisk and Jay Gould early in the Grant administration to "corner" the New York gold market and make themselves millions richer. They enlisted the help of President Grant's brother-in-law and believed—incorrectly as it turned out—that they had secured the president's assurance that the federal treasury would cooperate and not release gold. On

"Black Friday" in September 1869, the plot reached its culmination. While businessmen watched helplessly, Gould and Fisk bid gold prices up and out of reach. Then the federal treasury moved in and filled the vacuum by releasing its funds. Questions remained about the president's complicity. Had he intended to participate or been misread?

Julia's account of her husband's role predictably concurred with that of historians who later decided Ulysses was naive and a poor judge of character but not dishonest. As for her own part, she explained, "The papers seemed to say I knew something of the scheme but I did not." The president had instructed her to add in a letter she was sending to his sister: that it would be wise to have nothing to do with Fisk and Gould because Ulysses "will do his duty to the country and the trusts in his keeping." Thus Julia added, for what it was worth, her own account of her husband's honesty.

Ulysses Grant's two terms as president were also marred by reports that members of his family and some of his closest advisers were involved in plots to defraud the government; and in each case Julia's account portrays her husband as naive and misunderstood rather than dishonest. The Whiskey Ring involved Orville E. Babcock, the president's secretary. Contrived as a kickback system in which federal taxes on alcohol production were not collected if distillers paid off the inspectors, the scheme would have enriched the Republican Party and Babcock. Julia explained that Babcock had always been "civil and obliging and never officious," and she urged the president to assist him at his trial. When Babcock was acquitted in the courtroom, but not in the public's mind, Julia encouraged the president to replace him at the White House.

In the case of the cabinet member William Belknap, Julia extended the same tolerance for poor judgment and bad luck that she had offered her husband. Belknap had entered into agreements with prospective traders in the Indian Territories but the agreements appeared to line Belknap's pockets more than they provided needed items to the Territories. When evidence mounted against him, Belknap went to the president and resigned, thus protecting himself from a worse fate. He was impeached but the Senate would not convict since members believed his resignation removed him from their jurisdiction. In spite of a great deal of concrete evidence to the contrary, Julia accepted Belknap's plea of innocence and she continued to see the Belknaps socially.

Julia reported that she was hurt by the fact that her husband rarely informed her of important decisions, but the press and public showed her more attention. She recalled how she had been "followed by a crowd of idle, curious loungers, which was anything but pleasant." When she requested that the White House grounds be shut off to the public so that she and her children would have some privacy, she observed a "ripple of comment" about the Grants "getting too exclusive." The objections had little effect on her, however, and Julia got her way. Later she looked back on the White House years and remembered, "The children and I had that beautiful lawn for eight years, and I assure you we enjoyed it."

Julia Grant represents an important turning point in the succession of presidents' wives because she marked the beginning of a new phase in which the First Lady would eventually become a national leader, widely recognized, frequently criticized, and often emulated. As though to mark the changed role of the president's wife, the journalist "Olivia" called Julia Grant "first lady of the land," one of the first documented appearances of that term in a newspaper. Julia's energetic clan and her own vivacious personality appealed to reporters who were increasingly focusing their attention on Washington. But the media played only one part in the change. Julia's cross-country travel, her long journey around the world, and her memoir writing all hint at the kind of activities that would become more common for presidents' wives who followed her. Like Sarah Polk and Mary Lincoln, she expended considerable energy on a public role for herself, and thus helped set the stage for First Ladies who came later.

The Limited Promise
of the
"New Woman"
1877–1901

Although the image of the First Lady as nothing other than the nation's chief wife, head hostess, and leading fashion plate seemed firmly in place under Julia Grant, history had shown that an individual woman might, if she chose, do more in that role. Lucy Hayes (1877–1881) appeared to be just such a woman. The first college graduate to preside over the White House, she was widely heralded as introducing the era of a "new woman." An even more intellectually inclined Lucretia Garfield followed. After James Garfield was assassinated, a widower, Chester Arthur, took over the presidency, and he was succeeded by Grover Cleveland, a bachelor. If the nation could ever be diverted from its need for a purely social creature "at the head of female society," the decade after 1877 was surely the time to try to divert it.

Changes in Women's Lives

Events outside the executive mansion also indicated change. The generation of women who came of age in the late 1870s were less inclined than their mothers to marry, or at least to see marriage as their only choice. More and more colleges and universities, including some medical and theological schools, had opened their doors to women, and several states permitted women to practice law. Even the justices of the United States Supreme Court finally capitulated in 1879 and admitted a woman to practice before them.

Much of the impetus for change had come out of the Civil War, which, although a national tragedy, had encouraged many women to give their first speech, organize their first club, or take their initial trip out of home territory.

The large number of woman-run organizations formed after the war indicates the extent to which women were redefining their lives to reach beyond their own families. Sorosis, a woman's club founded in 1868, announced in its charter an intention to help women by encouraging them to meet with other women and engage in discussion—not only to help themselves but to improve the world.

Hundreds of other clubs followed. Some, such as the National Council of Jewish Women and the National Association of Colored Women's Clubs, had ethnic bases, while others, such as the PTA and the Sunshine Club, reached out to a broader membership. Unlike the local organizations of pre–Civil War days, these new organizations were national in scope, with branches in many states. One of the largest, the Women's Christian Temperance Union, was formed in 1874 just before Lucy Hayes entered the White House.

Because support for women's right to vote was still weak, Victoria Woodhull's campaign for president in 1872 was more principled than practical, but women did register other political gains at just about this time. Some won local elections and others gained appointive positions in government. The suffrage movement gathered force, and even some anti-suffragists argued that working women deserved better wages.

The woman who became involved in these kinds of endeavors— running an organization, carving out a career for herself, or speaking out on public issues—was vaguely referred to as a "new woman." Eventually that phrase came to have many meanings, including the woman who dressed daringly, or the one who flaunted her nonconformity by taking up residence in a bohemian enclave. But in references to Lucy Hayes and other presidents' wives of the late nineteenth century, "new woman" meant a serious woman concerned with substantive matters such as reform rather than with empty party-giving. It meant having opinions and an identity of one's own.

LUCY WEBB HAYES

LUCY WEBB HAYES came from an Ohio family that had a long history of enthusiastically pursuing many of the reforms of their time. Her parents, moved by the evangelical fervor that swept America in the 1830s and 1840s, had joined the Methodist church. Drawn into the abolitionist camp, Lucy's father, a doctor, went to

Kentucky to arrange for the manumission of some slaves he had inherited, but he became ill with cholera and died there.

Lucy's mother, dependent on the generosity of her family for her support and that of her three small children, nonetheless made no concessions to her reduced circumstances and dedicated the rest of her life to seeing that her two sons and Lucy received the best education available. When Lucy's brothers enrolled at Ohio Wesleyan, a Methodist college, she became the school's first woman student. Later, when the Webb boys chose medical school in Cincinnati, the family moved again and Lucy enrolled at Wesleyan Female College.

During her early years, Lucy had been exposed not only to abolitionists and reformers in education and religion, but also to the arguments of the emerging feminist movement in which two of her aunts participated. In college, she had confronted the question of whether or not women's intellectual abilities equalled men's and had concluded, "Woman's mind is as strong as man's—equal in all things and his superior in some." After her marriage to Rutherford B. Hayes in 1852, her exposure to feminism continued when his older sister, Fanny, took Lucy to hear famous speakers on the subject. One of Lucy Stone's lectures, on improving women's wages, so moved Lucy Webb Hayes that she wrote to her husband defending "violent methods" if necessary to achieve change.

Lucy had already tempered her youthful enthusiasm for reform well before she became First Lady. As soon as Rutherford entered politics, she transferred her own energies there. Lucy had some experience with election campaigns because her uncle had served in the state legislature, and now she turned attention from what might have become a feminist crusade and directed it toward her husband's career and to the victories of other Republicans. In 1856, she had attended a rally in support of John Frémont for president, and she wrote her mother at that time that she hoped he would win. When Frémont's defeat became clear, Rutherford informed his Uncle Birchard that Lucy "takes it to heart a good deal. She still clings to the hope that the next election will bring it all right."

By the late 1850s, Lucy's world pretty much centered on her husband's career and her family. She gave birth to eight children in twenty years, but in reacting to the often competing demands of being a good mother or being a valuable wife, it appears that she chose to make herself an extension of Rutherford. He suggested that she would have liked to have enlisted on the Union side in the Civil War but had to content herself with sending him and then joining him whenever possible. Rutherford wrote his uncle that Lucy "wishes she had been in Fort Sumter with a garrison of women." Sometimes she left her young children with relatives and other times she took them along to their father's army camp. In June 1863, during one of her visits, the youngest Hayes son died. Although Lucy described that time as the "bitterest hour" of her life, she shipped the boy's body back to Ohio for burial while she remained at her husband's side.

During the war years Lucy became a great favorite with her husband's comrades and she began then to achieve what eventually became an almost legendary reputation for kindness and simplicity. One story had it that several of the soldiers had decided to embarrass a new recruit by convincing him to take his mending to the "sewing lady" down at the colonel's cabin. Shirts in hand, the youth knocked at Hayes's cabin door, and when he announced his purpose, Lucy Hayes got out her needle. When he returned to the others, they were waiting for their laugh but learned, to their disappointment, that he had accomplished his mission. When the other soldiers pointed out that the "sewing lady" was the colonel's wife, he stuck to his initial judgment that whoever she was she had treated him kindly. Years later when she was living in the White House, a Civil War veteran came to be photographed and, so that he would have appropriate insignia on his uniform, First Lady Lucy Hayes sewed it on for him.

Close behind the stories of Lucy's kindness were those illustrating her dedication to her husband's welfare. During one wartime separation she had received a telegram informing her that he had been wounded near Washington, D.C. Although she lacked specific details on his whereabouts, she left her three children, including one she had been nursing, and set off to find Rutherford. Her search took five days, but when she located him, she took charge of his care and then escorted him and several of his comrades back to Ohio to recuperate.

By the time the Civil War ended, Rutherford B. Hayes had been elected to represent his Ohio district in the U.S. House of Representatives, and Lucy left her children with relatives in Ohio so she could join her husband in Washington. Her strong abolitionist views had led her to favor a punishing reconstruction policy for the South, and she became an avid observer of congressional debates on the subject. When she returned to Ohio, Rutherford wrote that he missed seeing her "checkered shawl" in the gallery, and she replied that he should send her more details of the debates. He had already informed his mother that "Lucy finds politics very pleasant in all respects."

With the elevation of her husband to the Ohio governorship in 1868, Lucy assumed a more active role. Although her children were still young (the last to survive was born in 1871), she traveled around the state with her husband to visit prisons and mental hospitals. When the Democratic legislature refused to appropriate money to start a home for children orphaned by the war, Lucy worked with others to collect voluntary contributions. Then, when the home had been started, she lobbied friends in the legislature to have the state assume financial responsibility for its operation. Lucy appeared to be occupied on many fronts, and Rutherford wrote his brother-in-law, "Lucy employs herself about the soldiers' orphans, about the decoration of soldiers' graves and about the deaf and dumb pupils at the Reform Farm for boys."

Each time Rutherford registered a political success, Lucy's excitement grew, although she recognized that her enthusiasm was not shared by her children. "Your ignorance of politics is not a grave offense," she once consoled her son. "You could not expect to know and enjoy politics as I do."

As soon as the 1876 presidential campaign began, reporters zeroed in on the sober Lucy Hayes and contrasted her with the fun-loving Julia Grant, whom she meant to replace. Some accounts still concentrated on appearances and the *New York Herald* described Lucy as "singularly youthful" and "a most attractive and lovable woman." But as the campaign went on, the *National Union* speculated in its column "Gossip About Women": "Mrs. Hayes is said to be a student of politics and to talk intelligently" on the subject. Few people could recall similar claims for a prospective First Lady since Sarah Polk moved into the White House in 1845.

The results of the 1876 election could hardly be called a victory for anyone since the count was so contested that a commission had to decide who had won, but on March 5, 1877, simply dressed Lucy stood in a prominent place at Rutherford's public inauguration. In this first appearance in her new role, she signaled that she would neither compete with fashion models nor disappear—as many of her predecessors had done. Public approval was overwhelming in the next few months, and even the politically unfriendly *Philadelphia Times* reported, "Mrs. Hayes deserves the thanks of every true woman for the stand she has taken against extravagance in dress." Six months later the same paper reported that the White House showed "a refreshing absence of pretension and formality." Employees at the executive mansion underlined these glowing reports with their own compliments, noting that Lucy remembered each employee with an individually selected Christmas gift and invited employees to the family's Thanksgiving table.

The saintly image was not effortlessly achieved. Although the Hayeses spent freely from their own considerable personal fortune, Lucy fostered a reputation for being economy-minded. She carefully preserved her clothing receipts to prove her frugality, and when Congress refused appropriate funds for refurbishing the executive mansion, she searched attic and cellar for old pieces of furniture to put back into service. She relegated the billiard table to the basement and used the space it had occupied for a conservatory to produce the fresh flowers that she liked to dispense to sick friends, lonely orphans, and journalists who wrote kind things about her. One White House steward, who had served every president since Abraham Lincoln, reported that Lucy Hayes brought a "new atmosphere" to the executive mansion.

This was not exactly the change that the phrase "new woman" promised. Rather than exemplifying strength and independence, Lucy's model stressed demureness and solicitous attention to those around her. Instead of emphasizing her college education, she operated entirely within the definition of "wife" as that word had been used since colonial days when it was, as a matter of course, combined with "good" to mean a woman "obedient to her husband, loving to her children, kind to her neighbors, and dutiful to her servants." If Lucy Hayes failed to portray exactly the innocent youthfulness that had been so favored in the White House in the 1830s and 1840s, it was a difference of style, not substance. Hers was only a matronly version of the "goodness" of Emily Donelson and Angelica Van Buren who had so charmed Jacksonian America.

Lucy Hayes, the same woman who in the early 1850s had defended "violent" measures to achieve equal pay for women, now worked very hard for no pay at all. She oversaw large receptions, and on nights when she had nothing scheduled, she received callers. Perhaps she considered her overwhelming popularity adequate recompense. Hers became the most familiar woman's face in America. Advertisers used her picture, without her approval, to promote household products, and popular magazines carried photographs of her, often with her children or flowers or animals. Longfellow, Whittier, and Oliver Wendell Holmes toasted her in words. Ben Perley Poore, a famous Washington reporter at the time, judged that she had become more influential than any president's wife since Dolley Madison.

Even her husband, who suffered from charges of having attained the office unfairly and heard himself taunted as "His Fraudulency," admitted that Lucy had become extremely popular: "It is very gratifying to see," he wrote in his diary in May 1879, "the heartiness and warmth of friendship for Lucy." If he had not entirely decided what guaranteed approval for a president, he at least recognized the value of a popular wife.

Some Americans, including Washington's more sophisticated set, found the Hayeses impossibly dull, and they singled out Lucy as a tight-lipped moralizer. The family's decisions to attend the unfashionable Foundry Methodist Church, hold prayer meetings each morning, and sing hymns with their friends on Sunday evening were generally attributed to her influence. Lucy's storytelling and mimicry may have delighted her family, but the diplomatic corps and more traveled Washingtonians were not amused.

Henry Adams's novel *Democracy,* written at the end of the Hayes administration, drew an unflattering picture of "the President's wife" who remained unnamed but whose likeness to Lucy was clear. Midwestern in origin and rigid in her views, the First Lady in *Democracy* lashed out at anyone who did not share her opinions. She insisted that the clothes then being worn in the capital were a disgrace and that "in her town in Indiana, a young woman who was seen on the street in such clothes wouldn't be spoken to." When a woman guest in the story mildly criticized the president, his wife became furious and vowed, "See if I don't reform you yet, you jade!"

There were also many people who would object to the Hayeses' ban on alcohol. The Hayes presidency coincided with a powerful surge in temperance sentiment and both he and Lucy realized that refusing to serve alcohol in the White House could win votes without causing any personal inconvenience. Lucy had the example of her parents, who had pledged never to touch alcohol, and both she and Rutherford found repulsive the drunkenness they sometimes witnessed at Washington parties.

The suspicion that political expedience, as well as personal preference, figured in Lucy Hayes's ban on alcohol in the White House emerges from evidence of several kinds. Lucy actually served wine at her first White House dinner, honoring two Russian dukes, and then responded to the outburst of criticism by changing her course. Her failure to participate in the Women's Christian Temperance Union, the most important voice in urging a ban on liquor, is even more revealing. Lucy Hayes never joined the WCTU, an omission that cannot be explained on the grounds that she steered clear of all such organizations since she accepted a national office in the Women's Home Missionary Society. Lucy's biographer, Emily Apt Geer, concluded that although Lucy did not drink alcohol, she was "not adamant" about abstinence in others. The WCTU's reputation for militance displeased Lucy, and Rutherford encouraged her to keep a distance from the WCTU president, Frances Willard.

Whether or not alcohol was served in spite of the ban remains uncertain. The reporter Ben Perley Poore insisted that state dinners included a course, called "Life Saving Station" by those in the know, that provided alcohol to anyone who requested it "with the strongest mixture going to those needing it most." President Hayes countered that the joke was on the tellers. He had given orders, he said, that flavoring be added to the punch and some people had mistaken the extract for the real thing.

Whether it was Lucy or the president who stood more firmly behind the ban remains unclear but she clearly took the blame. To taunts about her "dry dinners" and nicknames of "Lemonade Lucy," she replied in terms particularly revealing about how she viewed her role: "It is true I shall violate a precedent; but I shall not violate the Constitution, which is all that, through my husband, I have taken the oath to obey."

Because temperance was an immensely popular cause in the 1870s, Lucy gained many friends for her stand. When she accompanied her husband on a seventy-one-day trip to California, temperance supporters flocked to her train to obtain her autograph and cheer her on. The crowds became so thick at one point that her youngest son, traveling with her, mingled with others and got his mother to sign his album several times before she noticed him. At one stop, women held up a silk banner imprinted with the biblical quotation, "She hath done what she could."

Except for her well-publicized refusal to serve liquor, Lucy Hayes remained silent on every important issue, including suffrage for women. The stand she had taken earlier when she spoke out on the equality of the sexes did not lead her to conclude that women should vote. When Susan B. Anthony and Elizabeth Stanton came to discuss the issue with the president, he received them alone, and Lucy appeared only at the conclusion of the interview for the housewifely duty of showing the visitors around the mansion. The Citizens' Suffrage Association of Philadelphia appealed to Lucy and even her Aunt Phebe McKell urged her to speak out for woman's suffrage after she had become First Lady, but to no effect. Lucy either did not see voting as an appropriate activity for women or she perceived it (correctly) as a politically unpopular cause. Perhaps she agreed with Rutherford, who had written before he became president his thoughts on women voting: "My point is that the proper discharge of the functions of maternity is inconsistent with the like discharge of the duties of citizenship."

The president's wife had always been seen as an avenue to the president, but the Hayes administration marked a new level of appeals for her help. Lucy's travel across the continent and the appearance of her picture in advertisements and magazines made her one of the most famous women in America, and people who lacked advocates elsewhere looked to her. One member of the Church of Jesus Christ of Latter-day Saints couched her request in woman-to-woman terms when she wrote "Mrs. President Hayes," asking that she help defend plural marriage or polygamy.

Such entreaties, along with those of the suffragists and the leaders of the temperance movement (which had become dominated by women in the late nineteenth century), show that something new had happened to the role of First Lady, as the president's wife was now being called. Women throughout the country approached her as their special representative. Those who saw themselves as traditional homemakers would seek her endorsement of their view, while those who sought a more active role in public affairs would want to make her their champion. The old conflicts were still present. Some Americans would expect the president's wife to represent the taste of the majority while others wanted to see in her the epitome of sophistication and high culture. Never an easy job to fill, the role of the president's wife now became even more complex.

The interest in describing the role was just beginning when Lucy Hayes left the White House. In the 1881 edition of *Ladies of the White House,* Laura Holloway divided her subjects into three groups. From Martha Washington to Louisa Adams, they had been strong women, Holloway wrote, "appropriate to the needs of a young country," but those who followed (1829–1877) had reigned as "social queens, nothing more." Lucy Hayes initiated the third period: "her strong, healthful influence gives the world assurances of what the next century's women will be."

Holloway's enthusiastic support of Lucy Hayes has not stood the test of time, and history has tended to write her off as narrow-minded "Lemonade Lucy." Whatever her failures—and since so many sought her help, she was bound to disappoint some of them— Lucy Hayes did mark an important change. She played the part of First Lady as an adult role, rather than in the childlike mode of some of her predecessors, and her popularity shows that for many Americans of her time she was the ideal First Lady.

LUCRETIA RUDOLPH GARFIELD

LUCRETIA RUDOLPH GARFIELD, who followed her sister Ohioan, Lucy Hayes, into the White House in 1881, provides another, far more poignant example of a political wife who learned to fit her own ambitions into her husband's career. The Garfield presidency was during a period of history that took its name from Queen Victoria, when strong pressures pushed wives to conform to accepted standards and heavy sanctions awaited those who did not. Dress reformers, "free love" advocates, and even suffragists found themselves the object of reproach and ridicule, and even a tentative word favoring reform was interpreted as taking an extreme position. Lucretia's diaries, although not nearly so complete as those of her husband, show real evidence of an intellectually alert, capable young woman whose increasing docility paralleled James Garfield's political success.

The woman who became the wife of the twentieth president of the United States had attended Ohio's Eclectic Institute (later renamed Hiram College), a school her parents and other members of the Disciples of Christ Church had helped found. James Garfield also began his studies there in the early 1850s but he quickly transferred to the considerably more prestigious Williams College in Massachusetts, where his good looks and charm earned him immediate popularity. His prowess in debate attracted many women friends and even he seemed unsure why he continued an almost dutiful courtship to a serious and shy Lucretia Rudolph back in Ohio.

James's first mention of Lucretia in his diary indicates that her abilities first attracted him. While both were still at the Eclectic Institute, they had been selected to speak at a school ceremony, and James judged his own performance poor; but Miss Rudolph's speech, he wrote, was "full of good, practical, sound commonsense and elegantly and eloquently expressed."

About a year later, after he had broken off a romance with another woman, James's thoughts turned again to Lucretia, whom he alternately praised and criticized. She had, he admitted, "a well balanced mind, not of the deepest and most extensive kind but logical and precise." Yet he could not deny that he found her dull and he concluded that either she concealed her gaiety or did "not possess it." Her views on women's rights alarmed him: "There are some of her notions concerning the relation between the sexes which, if I understand, I do not like."

Until James and Lucretia married in 1858, their courtship never followed a smooth line. In fact, at one point James seemed ready to terminate their romance—until Lucretia showed him her diary, where she had expressed her strong feelings about him, thus convincing him she had "depths of affection that I had never before known that she possessed." After he returned to school at Williams, her correspondence became full-blown love letters in which she wrote of "walking in the warm sunlight of your love" and he responded that he looked forward to the time when "I will have you in my arms again."

James Garfield confessed at one point in the courtship that he did not feel about Lucretia as he thought a bridegroom should but then abruptly, in the fall of 1858, when Lucretia was twenty-six and employed as a teacher, he told her to proceed with plans for their simple marriage rites. She had her own doubts and right up to the time of the ceremony worried about losing the autonomy she had enjoyed—earning her own money and making her own decisions. Just weeks before the wedding, Lucretia warned James, "My heart is not yet schooled to an entire submission to that destiny which will make me the wife of one who marries me." She determined to try her best, even though her "heart almost broke," she wrote, "with the cruel thought that our marriage is based upon the cold, stern word duty."

In the first years of her marriage, Lucretia continued to live almost as a single woman. She kept her teaching job, and since she and James boarded with another family, she had few housekeeping chores. Her husband's election to the state legislature a year after their marriage meant that he was frequently absent from home, and when the Civil War started, he enlisted. James made very clear that he considered their marriage a mistake, and although Lucretia accepted much of the blame, she thought him "a little hard." While his letters were often brusque and judgmental, hers repeatedly promised to attempt to conform to his demands and become the submissive helper he required: "I am going to try harder than ever before to be the best little wife possible," Lucretia wrote in March 1860, and then she vowed to avoid those subjects that struck "such a terror" in him.

On their fourth wedding anniversary James coolly appraised their time together as unsatisfactory but concluded that both partners deserved credit for trying. Lucretia, who had become aware of his attentions to a New York widow and confronted him on the matter, learned in late 1862 that James wished to continue with his wife only a "business correspondence." After four and one-half years of marriage, Lucretia calculated that she and James had spent less than five months together. They both understood that the separation was partly voluntary and that theirs was a troubled union.

If something had not affected the course of this marriage, it is unlikely that James Garfield's political career would have proceeded as it did, but Lucretia became increasingly docile in the 1860s and her husband's attitude toward the family changed. In part the alteration may have resulted from grief. Within a few months of each other, two of their children died—their first daughter at age three and then, only weeks later, an infant. In 1867 Lucretia and James went to Europe, a kind of second honeymoon, and soon after their return she convinced him that they should move the family, now numbering three children, to Washington. The house they built at Thirteen and I Streets became their residence for much of the year.

Two more children were born to the Garfields, and James began to take greater interest in his older sons' education, drilling them in Latin and Greek and urging Lucretia to brush up on her knowledge of languages so that she could help too. He did not lose interest in other women and even had to make a special trip to New York to retrieve compromising letters he had sent to a woman friend there, but more and more of his time centered on family activities. In 1873, after fifteen years of marriage, he wrote to his wife, "The tyranny of our love is sweet. We waited long for his coming but he has come to stay."

Whatever James Garfield meant in that letter, his actions did not show that he considered his wife an important part of his social life in the capital. Between 1872 and 1874, his diary records that he accepted dozens of invitations, only three of which involved Lucretia. The Garfields rarely invited people to their home, and Lucretia understood that Washingtonians found her dull. One man wrote his daughter after an evening with the Ohio congressman and his wife that they were probably "very good people—but a plainer, stiffer set of village people I never met."

By the time James Garfield won the Republican party's nomination for president in 1880, Lucretia had become a seasoned political wife in the nineteenth-century meaning of the term. Newspapers extolled the Garfields' exemplary family life, and Republican party literature bragged that its candidate, born in a log cabin, had made a "fortunate marriage to a farmer's daughter, who was refined, intelligent, affectionate." "She shared his thirst for knowledge and his ambition for culture," the Republican party emphasized, but she was no bluestocking, and her domestic tastes and talents would fit her equally to preside over the home of a poor college president and that of a famous statesman. In that brief but telling description of

Lucretia Garfield, nothing remained of the young bride who had described herself twenty-two years earlier as in no mood for "submission."

During the brief time that Lucretia Garfield served as First Lady, she kept a White House diary which shows that she could deal firmly with critics. A newspaper correspondent who came to complain about some of the president's advisers got nowhere with Lucretia. "I made her understand," Lucretia wrote in her diary, "the President knew not only the men around him but also knows what he is about." When a writer on etiquette insisted on a "special appointment" with the president's wife, Lucretia treated her severely, and later, after the two women had talked, Lucretia decided that she had been seen as "wax" in the woman's hands. "This is only the beginning," Lucretia complained in her diary, "of the petty criticism which might worry me, if I would let it."

The former schoolteacher who had liked having her own money stopped short of advocating the vote for women, and her husband phrased his own disapproval in rather strong terms. He insisted that political differences between husband and wife would lead to divorce: "The suffrage movement is atheistic in a great measure and it must logically result in the utter annihilation of marriage and family."

Although Lucretia Garfield appeared to share her husband's view of suffrage, she showed a great deal more understanding than he of the particular problems of women, and she sometimes tempered the pettiness and moralizing that characterized his thinking. The contrast between the two is obvious in an exchange of letters concerning the conduct of a Maine senator. A rumor circulated in Washington in 1875 to the effect that James G. Blaine, a Republican contender for the presidency, had many years earlier become a father only six months after his wedding date. "How does this story strike you?" James Garfield wrote his wife. "If it is true, should it have weight with the people in the Presidential campaign?"

Lucretia replied that she had previously heard something similar but she had not given the story much importance. "If it is true, it ought not to affect the voters very much unless it should have been considered more honorable by the majority to have abandoned the woman—seduced. My opinion of Mr. Blaine would be rather heightened than otherwise by the truth of such a story for it would show him not entirely selfish and heartless."

Lucretia Garfield, ill with malaria and absent from the capital, had only a few weeks in the White House before her husband was shot on July 2, 1881. Most of her record as First Lady comes from the weeks she kept vigil at her husband's side until his death nearly three months after the assassination attack. The entire country monitored the president's condition through frequent medical bulletins and newspaper accounts which made a stoic martyr of Lucretia. "The wife of the President is the bravest woman in the universe," one newspaper reported.

On September 19, 1881, when James Garfield succumbed to the infection that gathered around the bullet lodged in his spine, he became the second president to be killed by an assassin, and this less than twenty years after the first. Talk of senseless "martyrdom" encouraged an outpouring of sympathy to the widow and children, whose pictures had become familiar to people all over the country. School youngsters, summoned to special memorial programs, heard how the president's daughter, "poor Mollie Garfield," let "a tear roll down her cheek." Congregations listened as ministers chronicled how James Garfield's family had figured in his meteoric rise from poor boy to president. Individual, unsolicited contributions to Lucretia and her children eventually amounted to more than $360,000, or about seven times the chief executive's annual salary.

For the first time in history, the presidential widow participated in her husband's public memorial services. William Henry Harrison, Zachary Taylor, and Abraham Lincoln had all died in office, but in the style of the time, their widows deemed the public ceremonies too trying to attend. Lucretia Garfield assumed a prominent part in the funeral and made a point of letting the crowds see her, even insisting that the curtains be left open in her railroad car, much as Jacqueline Kennedy, eighty-two years later, kept on a bloodstained suit so the people "can see what they have done."

Not yet fifty years old at the time her husband was murdered, Lucretia lived another thirty-six years, dedicating most of that time to his memory. She supervised the preservation of his papers, one of the most extensive and complete of any set left by a president, and although she had plenty of opportunity to destroy documents illustrating the troubled phase of her marriage, she never did so. Not until the 1960s, more than forty years after her death, did her family consent to placing those revealing letters between Lucretia and James Garfield in the presidential collection. That correspondence reveals a very different woman from the one described in her husband's diary or in accounts published during her lifetime. The letters show an intelligent, capable woman who reluctantly relinquished her own autonomy in favor of her husband's career. She had not started out that way, but she became, as one of her contemporaries pointed out was frequently the case with politicians' wives, a "quiet and noncommittal little moon revolving around a great luminary."

MARY ARTHUR McELROY

CHESTER ARTHUR, the widower who became president at the death of James Garfield in 1881, had almost an entire term to serve. His one daughter was much too young to take on any social responsibilities and his teen-aged son was not old enough to take a wife.

President Arthur could have relegated much of the First Lady work to a staff, leaving for himself final decisions on matters that had political implications. He had always shown considerable interest in living well (having brought along with him from New York his own chef and valet, the latter a "first" for the White House) and could have been expected to want to implement some of his own ideas about entertaining.

Although he personally oversaw redecoration of the White House, Chester Arthur imported his sister, Mary McElroy, to act as his official hostess. He occasionally hosted dinners for men who were either single or had not brought their families to Washington, but for the formal events, he relied on his sister to even out the numbers so that guests could go to the table in twos, like animals entering Noah's ark. Then in her forties and the mother of four, McElroy had followed her schooling at the progressive Emma Willard's with a completely conventional marriage. The daughter of a minister, she had married a minister, and when her brother moved to the White House, she temporarily left her own family to help him during the capital's social season.

The choice of Mary McElroy, a serious mature woman, as substitute hostess in the White House, was characteristic of the trend toward stronger models of femininity in late-nineteenth-century America. The old emphasis on youth had not entirely disappeared but the most admired woman was now taller, more rounded, and more imposing than the shy, innocent, emaciated maiden so fashionable a few decades earlier. Advertisements pictured stout women, often "of a certain age" to tout their household appliances and beauty aids. The bustle, with its emphasis on a large posterior, returned, and the preferred dress fabrics were weighty and ornate, so heavy that only a large woman could manage them easily. England's Queen Victoria, whose name came to apply to much of the furniture and clothing of her time, was in her seventh decade by 1880 and the solidness and rectitude that she exemplified seemed embodied best in a mature woman. This new vogue was underlined

ROSE CLEVELAND 135

by the kind of woman who served as "First Lady" in the White House during the 1880s.

ROSE CLEVELAND

As though to reaffirm the country's new preference for older, more mature women, Chester Arthur's successor, the bachelor Grover Cleveland, enlisted his sister as White House hostess in 1885. Rose Cleveland, the most intellectual woman to preside over the White House up to that time, had graduated from the Houghton Academy and then gone to head an institute in Indiana. She had read widely, studied several languages, including Greek, and had completed a book-length manuscript on George Eliot. Her reputation as a lecturer on women's rights was well established. Yet her entire adult life had been shaped around the needs of her mother and her brother, and when he summoned her to Washington, she dutifully abandoned her own career to assist him in his.

The new respect for seriousness in models of femininity did not extend to scholarly types—at least not in the press's treatment of Rose Cleveland. In spite of her many intellectual achievements, reporters preferred to concentrate on what she wore. Her "Spanish lace over black silk" and "rose colored silk" both made the first page of a major newspaper, while a review of her book was relegated to the inside section and treated with condescension. The *New York Times* congratulated Rose on her achievement and noted that although her book would not please everyone, "its heart beats warm and womanly."

Rose Cleveland's boredom with her White House social obligations, although not explicitly stated, can be inferred from her confession that she occupied herself in reception lines by silently conjugating difficult Greek verbs. When her brother announced that he would marry, Rose left Washington in 1886 and resumed her own life. She edited a literary magazine in Chicago for a while and taught history in New York City before moving to Italy, where she died in 1918 while caring for people stricken in an influenza epidemic.

FRANCES FOLSOM CLEVELAND

ROSE CLEVELAND relinquished her role of White House hostess in June 1886, when her brother married twenty-one-year-old Frances Folsom. Speculation about his marital plans had surrounded Grover Cleveland since his inauguration and several suggestions had been offered about the ideal First Lady. Various candidates' names appeared in print, and reporters appraised each White House guest list for a potential bride. By the time more positive evidence leaked to the press in May 1886, many readers refused to take it seriously, believing this just another unsubstantiated bit of gossip.

But the bachelor Cleveland really did mean to marry and he had chosen the young daughter of his former law partner. The president had known Frances Folsom since she was born. He had bought her first baby carriage, and according to accounts of his fellow club members, had led "chubby Frankie" around by the hand when she was a youngster. After her father's death, when she was eleven,

Grover became in effect, although not in law, her guardian and played a role in her upbringing. As governor of New York, he invited her and her mother to be his guests in Albany and later they came to the White House. Anyone observing Grover's attentiveness to Frances over the years might have guessed at his intentions had not the twenty-seven-year difference in their ages made marriage seem unlikely. Gossip centered more on Frances's mother as the subject of the courtship than on the daughter.

His marriage on June 2, 1886—the first of a president in the White House—encouraged ingenious attempts to witness the ceremony. The New York baker engaged to produce the bride's cake reportedly received many offers of free assistance, and John Philip Sousa, scheduled to conduct the wedding march, turned down a bribe to plant a reporter among his musicians. Failure to crack White House security did not deter the press from reporting the event anyway, and magazines carried widely varying descriptions of what happened. *Harper's* and *Leslie's Weekly,* two of the most popular periodicals, produced dissimilar sketches of the bride's dress.

After the ceremony, the president and his bride escaped from the White House through a basement door and made off for a private honeymoon at a cottage in nearby Deer Park, Maryland. Only personal servants accompanied them, but reporters camped out in the bushes near the honeymoon cottage. Four days after the ceremony, the *New York Herald* announced in big headlines that the bride and groom were "No Longer Secluded" but had emerged to chat with villagers. The president fumed that some of the news people relied on spyglasses to gather their material, and he lodged a formal complaint to the press, but to no avail—Americans were enchanted with the young bride in the White House.

Nothing in either the appearance of Frances or in her actions resembled the ingénue stance of Julia Tyler, the only preceding president's bride. Frances was all seriousness. A graduate of Wells College in 1885, she was taller than average and full-figured, and she carried herself with such authority and confidence that she might have been mistaken for a much older woman. Advertisers who freely appropriated her picture to sell their own products portrayed her as a mature individual. Flimsy, virginal white dresses had been the typical costume of young women in antebellum America, but the vogue now was the matronly shape, even for twenty-one-year-old Frances Cleveland.

Quickly becoming one of the most popular First Ladies of the century, Frances saw women imitate her hair style and line up by the thousands to catch a glimpse of her at White House receptions. Presidents' wives would hear her singled out for years to come, alongside Dolley Madison, as one to imitate. Grover had attempted to divert some of the attention from Frances and provide a refuge for them both by setting up a second Washington home. The possibility of the president's dividing his time between an official residence and a private one had been debated since the earliest days of the republic, but the Clevelands were the first to work out the details very successfully. At the time of his marriage, Grover informed his sister, "I shall buy or rent a house near here where I can be away from this cursed, constant grind." "Red Top," as reporters dubbed the house, offered the Clevelands a retreat, with a magnificent view of the Potomac, and except during the busiest part of the White House social season, they could live there and arrange for the president to commute to his office.

Newspapers and magazines published many pictures of Frances. Possibilities for commercialization were not ignored, and unauthorized photographs and sketches of her began to appear in advertisements. A perfume manufacturer publicized a note of appreciation alongside a photograph of her, giving the impression that she personally endorsed that fragrance.

To put a stop to such practices, a bill was introduced in the House of Representatives in March 1888, making the unauthorized use of the "likeness or representation of any female living or dead, who is or was the wife, mother, daughter or sister of any citizen of the United States" a crime subject to fines of up to $5,000. The bill's sponsor made clear that he was seeking to protect current First Lady Frances Cleveland, one of the few women in America then famous enough to encourage use of her likeness in testimonial advertising. Although the measure never passed, its introduction suggests a whole new phase in press attention to presidents' wives.

Frances Cleveland received many requests that she champion one reform or another, but she refused to associate her name with any cause. An advocate of temperance (she had toasted her own marriage with mineral water), she would not impose her beliefs on others and blithely served wine at all White House functions. Temperance advocates could hardly reprove her since she reportedly had her own wineglasses removed at the start of the meal. Although her receptions were frequently described as elegant, she offset possible charges of elitism by scheduling regular events for Saturday afternoon so that working women could attend.

The image of Frances as a sweet, gracious lady contrasted sharply with her husband's reputation as boorish and morally corrupt. During his first campaign for the presidency in 1884, rumors had spread when he acknowledged that he supported a child whose mother he had never married. During the reelection campaign of 1888, stories circulated that the president physically abused his young wife. When a Worcester, Massachusetts, woman wrote asking Frances Cleveland if the reports were true, the First Lady felt obliged to issue a disclaimer unique in American history. These were "wicked and heartless lies" aimed at Grover, Frances wrote, and "I can wish the women of our country no greater blessing than that their homes and lives may be as happy and their husbands may be as kind, attentive, considerate and affectionate as mine."

The voters may have taken her word on that matter but many of them faulted Grover in other areas. His attempt to make a lower tariff the central issue of the 1888 presidential campaign backfired; Grover had not been generous with veterans' pensions; and as the first Democratic president since the Civil War, he was vulnerable to charges of having treated Southerners too kindly. When the votes came in, the incumbent lost to Benjamin Harrison in the electoral college, although not in the popular vote.

Frances packed up to leave the White House but she instructed the servants to take good care of all the furnishings because she expected to be back in exactly four years. When history proved her right and the Clevelands returned to Washington in 1893, they brought a young daughter with them, and again rented a separate residence to protect the family from excessive attention.

It was during this second term that a second daughter, Esther, was born to the Clevelands—the first to be born to a president in the White House. By the time the Clevelands left Washington to settle in Princeton, New Jersey, they had a third daughter, and later they had two sons. Grover Cleveland did not live, however, to see them all mature, because he died in 1908 at age 71.

Five years later his widow remarried, thus testing for the first time the perquisites that had been assigned to presidents' widows. It had never been quite clear whether the franking privilege and the pension, both generally accorded all former First Ladies who requested them, constituted a reward for services each had rendered or represented some sort of recompense for her husband's work. Frances Cleveland had not sought a pension after Grover's death, but she continued to avail herself of the franking privilege, even after her remarriage, adding only a final surname "Preston" to her signature of "Frances Cleveland." Before she died in 1947, she had amassed a string of firsts—the first to marry a president in the White House (the Tylers had married in New York City), the first presidential wife to serve two noncontinuous terms, and the first presidential widow to remarry after her husband's death. Perhaps because she was a young bride, the public tolerated her doing what several of her predecessors had unsuccessfully attempted—keeping a distance between the president's private residence and the White House.

What stands out most about Frances Cleveland, however, is the extent to which she underscores a change in style for First Ladies. Coming almost exactly forty years after Julia Tyler, Frances differed significantly from her predecessor. Rather than sitting on a raised platform to receive her guests in imitation of royalty as Julia Tyler had done, Frances was the model of simplicity and maturity, even though she was still in her twenties.

CAROLINE SCOTT HARRISON

CAROLINE SCOTT HARRISON, who served as First Lady from 1889 to 1892, was a serious-minded woman—a seriousness associated with domesticity rather than with scholarship, public action, or a career of her own. In her youth, she had shown exceptional talent in both music and art, and after graduating from the Oxford Female Institute in Ohio, she had taught music in Kentucky. After her marriage to the young law student Benjamin Harrison in 1853 (when she was twenty and he was nineteen), those interests gradually lost out to the demands of her husband's career. She enlisted in the appropriate women's organizations, and after her husband's election to the United States Senate, she dutifully moved the entire family to a rented suite in Washington. Although her mother had described Caroline in her young years as showing no interest at all in domestic chores, she was singled out by contemporaries as the best housekeeper the White House had ever known and characterized by her biographer as "by nature strongly domestic."

Every administration refurbished the White House but Caroline Harrison wanted to make major structural changes, a course long overdue for a building whose cornerstone had been laid almost a century earlier and not rebuilt since 1818. Architects went to work on plans and came up with two. The first outlined minor alterations, and the second, which the First Lady favored, projected a whole new look, including the addition of a large office wing on one side and a "historic wing" on the other, with conservatories for plants and flowers stretching across the grounds to give the enclave the look of a European palace.

Congress drew back from supporting such luxury and the Harrisons had to settle for much less. Caroline ordered the vermin exterminated, the floors repaired, and the furniture fixed. After she had arranged in the spring of 1891 to have electricity installed, she began a renovation program to replace the open fireplaces and spits that had been used for cooking. In modernizing the President's House, the First Lady was following, rather than setting, the national style. Electric appliances were being heralded as introducing a new age and some people even hinted at an eventual "servantless kitchen." "Perfectly controllable cooking," easy laundry, and effortless cleaning were all in the near future, one home economist argued, for wives who mastered the elements of scientific management, and every good wife should do just that.

In the face of such high praise for domesticity, politicians' wives did well to emphasize their homemaking abilities. *Good Housekeeping* singled out Pennsylvania Governor Pennypacker's wife for admiring notice because she was "most domestic in her tastes and habits." The wife of Iowa's governor was described as "perfect" because she directed all her attention to domestic chores. In the most conspicuous position of all stood the president's wife, and although one Washington journalist discounted as "absurd the stories that Mrs. Harrison spends half her time in the kitchen, actually taking part in the preparation of the food," she did take great interest in every detail and "the servants adore her." Her domestic interests were further emphasized when she designed the cornstalk-and-flower border for the china used during her husband's administration and then began the White House collection of china patterns that had been chosen by the preceding presidents and their families.

Caroline Harrison became ill with tuberculosis during the last year of her husband's term, and she died just weeks before the 1892 election. The death of Letitia Tyler, the only preceding First Lady to die in the White House, had occurred half a century earlier, but accounts of the two women's lives varied little. Both had directed their energies to family concerns, and only a hint of the "new woman" breaks that pattern in the latter's record. At the time of the founding of the Johns Hopkins Medical School in 1890, Caroline Harrison agreed to help in fundraising on the condition that women be admitted to study on the same basis as men. It is ironic that she should be remembered for two such different achievements—starting the White House china collection and helping make one of the country's major medical schools coeducational. Only she could have said which of the two she considered the more appropriate memorial, but it is a sign of her times that her contemporaries gave considerably more attention to the plates.

IDA SAXTON McKINLEY

Soon after Caroline Harrison's death, her husband lost the presidential election to Grover Cleveland and Frances Cleveland returned to the White House. By the time that administration ended in 1897, some important changes were under way. National magazines had begun to give considerable coverage to wives of presidential candidates—something unheard of in the early part of the century.

Reporters who covered the capital typically praised sweetness and docility over independence, and in no case is this better illustrated than in a comparison of Ida Saxton McKinley, wife of the successful Republican candidate for president in 1896 and 1900, and Mary Baird Bryan, wife of the Democratic loser. Ida McKinley, who was frail and sick, insisted on all the attention that Mary Lincoln had wanted, but received little of the criticism. Meanwhile, Mary Bryan, who attended the same law school as her husband and was known to research, write (and type) his speeches, gained little favorable comment for her efforts.

By all accounts Ida had been a vigorous young woman whose physical and mental condition deteriorated rapidly in the first years of her marriage. In just three years' time, she had lost her mother, with whom she had been very close, and two young daughters. She never recovered her strength or came out of the depression that followed these tragedies.

Although accurate medical opinion on Ida McKinley is difficult to find, there is every indication that her illness was very real. After the delivery of her second child, she may have suffered from phlebitis, making unassisted walking difficult, and she also had seizures, resembling epilepsy (although the name for the disease, still so misunderstood in the nineteenth century, does not appear in newspaper coverage of her). Even in the McKinley household, the nature of Ida's illness remained outside the bounds of acceptable discussion. Her niece, who spent considerable time with Ida, remarked after her death that she had first heard "epilepsy" in connection with her aunt in a political campaign and she had assumed it was part of the opponents' plot to discredit William McKinley.

The grief and limitations Ida experienced in her adult years represented a big change from her youth. In Canton, Ohio, where she grew up, her family had been prominent for two generations and one of her grandfathers had started the town's major newspaper. Nurturing bigger ideas for her schooling than Canton could satisfy, Ida enrolled first in an academy in Delhi, New York, then in a Cleveland academy before finishing at Brook Hill Seminary outside

Philadelphia. To round out her education, she went off to Europe with her sister on an eight-month tour. The teacher who chaperoned the girls later complained that she had found Ida so obstreperous that she had contemplated abandoning her charges and going off on her own.

Back in Canton, Ida continued in her independent ways by going to work in her father's bank at a time when middle-class young women eschewed paid labor. By some accounts Ida even managed a branch, but whatever her official title, she had taken it not out of necessity but because she wanted a job. Young William McKinley, new in town and from much less advantaged circumstances than hers, appealed to Ida so much that she vowed to marry him. Her parents made an imposing Canton house their wedding present, and in January 1871 the couple appeared to be started on a fairy-tale marriage—that is, until the deaths of both their children and the onset of Ida's illness.

While the loss of her daughters appears to have precipitated Ida into depression and disability, her husband rushed into politics, making his first run for Congress in 1876. For the rest of their marriage, as he progressed through several terms in the legislature, to the governorship of Ohio and finally the presidency, Ida developed a reputation as one of the most demanding invalids in American history. Unlike many of her predecessors who had relied on their poor health to excuse them from unwanted official tasks, she insisted on a central position for herself at every public event. She frequently summoned her husband from important meetings in order to ask his opinion on ribbons for a new dress or some other trivial matter. During his governorship, the McKinleys lived in a hotel across from his office in Columbus and each morning when he went to work, he turned and waved to Ida from the street. Then precisely at three in the afternoon, he stopped whatever he was doing to signal her again and wait for her to respond with a swish of white lace.

In the White House, Ida continued to insist on occupying center stage even though she was too ill to be more than just physically present. Each time the president left Washington, Ida was at his side, waiting to be escorted out on the train platform to acknowledge crowds at every stop. Wherever she went in Washington, a special exit route had to be prepared in advance so that she could be removed quickly in case she had one of her seizures.

The seating arrangement at formal dinners was adjusted so that the president could always sit near her. At the slightest sign of one of her attacks, he would take a white handkerchief that he carried especially for this purpose and throw it over her face. William Howard Taft, a guest on one occasion, reported hearing a hissing sound while he was talking to the president, and before anyone knew what had happened, the president had shrouded his wife's face from view. While William McKinley continued his conversation as though nothing unusual had happened, Ida remained rigid in her chair and then when the seizure had passed, she removed the handkerchief and resumed her conversation.

William McKinley's solicitous attention to his wife earned him the reputation of a saint. A brochure in 1895, later expanded into a kind of publicity release, predicted that he would go down in American history among the country's greatest heroes. "It was an example," *Century* magazine wrote effusively after his death, "which even sin respects and the criminal can admire." According to *Century*, knowledge of the president's dedication to his wife extended "beyond our geographical boundaries and reached even the people and the courts of Europe."

Others thought William McKinley went too far. They pointed out that for twenty years he had renounced almost all pleasures, except work, in order to nurse his wife. The one diversion he still permitted himself—smoking several cigars a day—had to be enjoyed away from home because Ida did not care for the odor. William made no attempt to control Ida's outbursts of bad manners, and she frequently snapped back at people. One White House guest was amazed when Ida pointed a finger at a startled woman and accused her of wanting to take Ida's place.

Popular magazines included many formal, posed pictures of Ida McKinley in the 1890s but failed to prepare people for how ill she seemed in the flesh. Rows of delicate, expensive lace and lots of diamonds, her favorite jewel, gave her a doll-like appearance. One congressman's wife, meeting Ida for the first time, described her color as "ghastly. . . . Her poor relaxed hands, holding some pitiful knitting, rested on her lap as if too weak to lift their weight of diamond rings, and her pretty gray hair is cut short as if she had had typhoid fever."

Ida's one demonstration of strength and stamina came after her husband's assassination in the summer of 1901. She had accompanied the president to Buffalo but had not gone with him to the exposition where he was shot as he stood greeting admirers. As the dying president was being carried away, his thoughts ran to his wife and he warned that the news should be given to her carefully. Escorted to his bedside, Ida amazed everyone by appearing much stronger than she had been for some time. At first she begged to die with him, then composed herself and accompanied his body back to Canton, Ohio, for burial. Before her death six years later, she oversaw the building of his mausoleum and planned for the dedication of his monument.

The century ended and time "turned over" in 1900 with very few changes in the role of First Lady. Several First Ladies of the late nineteenth century had attended college, but their degrees were in the typical "women's" fields of art and teaching. Even those who had shown a hint of independence in their youth seemed to mature into models of domestic acquiescence. A small minority of the country might appeal to them to speak out on women's issues but a majority still held for the homey hostess. The nation's Head Housekeeper might present a more serious, mature image but she was not really a "New Woman."

The Office of
First Lady:
A Twentieth-Century
Development

As THE TWENTIETH CENTURY began, sickly, ineffectual Ida Mc-
Kinley still sat in the White House, but before many more administrations were over, evidence would show that the role of First Lady
was changing. Gradually, presidents' wives began to hire separate
staffs of their own, take part in policy and personnel decisions, and
lead important reform movements. Although still unpaid, the job
was quasi-institutionalized. Edith Wilson (1915–1921), Woodrow's
second wife, received most of the publicity associated with this shift
in the role of First Lady and heard herself criticized for exercising
"petticoat government," but she should be seen as part of a trend
rather than an anomaly. Each First Lady between 1901 and 1921,
even the most insecure, left her mark.

It is no accident that a new and stronger role for the president's
wife coincides with the United States' growing importance in the
world and the executive branch's ascendancy over the legislature.
Theodore Roosevelt (1901–1909), William Howard Taft (1909–
1913), and Woodrow Wilson (1913–1921) all possessed much
greater knowledge and experience in the field of foreign affairs than
had most of their immediate predecessors. Press coverage of chief

executives increased dramatically during these years, and some of the new attention focused on the president's family. When Theodore Roosevelt described the presidency as a "bully pulpit," he might have also noted the increased opportunities for a First Lady.

EDITH CAROW ROOSEVELT

EDITH CAROW ROOSEVELT traced her American roots all the way back to the 1630s, through a line of illustrious men and women that included the prominent Puritan Jonathan Edwards. She grew up in New York City in the same Union Square neighborhood where the Roosevelts lived, and Corinne, Theodore's sister, became Edith's best friend.

Theodore's relationship with Edith is less clear. Although he was three years older than she, they moved in the same circles, and before he enrolled in Harvard the two may have reached an agreement to marry. Edith later explained that Theodore had proposed but that she had refused, presumably influenced by her family's opinion that she was too young to accept. In any case, Theodore's path in Cambridge intersected with that of an exceptionally beautiful young woman, Alice Lee, the daughter of a socially prominent Boston family, and as soon as he graduated, he married her. Four years later she died of a kidney disease on the same day that Theodore's mother died of typhoid fever. He was inconsolable and left his New York State Assembly seat for a period of reflection and strenuous exercise on a North Dakota ranch. Rejuvenated, he returned to run (unsuccessfully) for mayor of New York City in 1886.

A few weeks later, in an unheralded ceremony, he married Edith Carow in London.

In addition to Theodore's daughter, Alice, product of his first marriage, Edith raised five children born to her and Theodore. Frequently she implied that she considered her husband a sixth. While he roughhoused with them and encouraged them in all kinds of shenanigans, she remained aloof, neither participating nor intervening. Once, while she was preparing to return to their Sagamore Hill home on Long Island, someone suggested that she wait until Theodore could accompany her, but she laughingly dismissed the offer, saying that she already had her hands full.

Whether hurt by being second choice or because of some other inclination, Edith showed an almost complete detachment from everything around her, an attitude described by one historian as almost "Oriental." She was one of those rare women with such a strong sense of her own self that neither a large family nor a conspicuous place in the country's capital could disconcert her or shake her certainty that she knew what was appropriate.

This exceptional confidence helped Edith Roosevelt initiate changes in the executive mansion that a more insecure woman would have hesitated to risk. In slightly less than eight years, she solved the old problem of how to separate the president's personal residence from his official home, developed a new model for dealing with the insatiable demand for information about the president's family, removed herself from decisions about official entertaining by turning to professional caterers, and hired a secretary to handle her official correspondence, thus institutionalizing the job in a way that had not been done before.

Part of Edith's managerial ability resulted from years of running a large household and overseeing its transfer from one city to another. In the fifteen years between her marriage to Theodore and his ascendancy to the presidency, he had progressed rapidly through several important offices, including president of the New York City Police Board (1896–1897), assistant secretary of the Navy in Washington (1897–1898), and governor of New York State (1899–1901). Although the governorship had lasted only two years, it provided Edith, just as it did Theodore, with valuable experience in administration. The family's house on Long Island became an extension of the governor's mansion, with political associates and foreign dignitaries visiting the Roosevelts there.

Edith opposed Theodore's run for vice-president in 1900, just as she had previously objected to his attempts to win other elective offices, because she understood that the financial drain would be considerable. When the Republican ticket won and then William McKinley was assassinated only months later, she had to face the prospect of moving her family to Washington. At his inauguration in 1901, Theodore was the youngest yet to take that oath of office. Edith, who had just turned forty, had to solve the problem of how to spread a president's salary to cover the costs of her brood of six and yet meet all the obligations of her husband's job.

The rambunctious children reinforced the image of a vibrant, energetic man in the White House. Ranging in age from debutante Alice down to four-year-old Quentin, they had already gained national attention for their antics in the New York governor's mansion. On one occasion, widely and gleefully reported in magazines, they caused an official party to end abruptly when the windows of the reception room were opened and smells unmistakenly those of a barnyard wafted in from the children's basement menagerie.

The White House provided new opportunities for their imaginative minds, and no corner remained long unexplored. The children slid down bannisters, tried their stilts in the Red Room, and repeatedly startled dinner guests by introducing pets at unexpected moments. Jacob Riis, the famous journalist, reported that he had been breakfasting with the Roosevelts when the president apologized for not being able to show him the children's kangaroo rat. Young Kermit Roosevelt immediately obliged by taking the rat from his pocket and demonstrating how it could hop, first on two legs and then on three, across the dining room table.

Such a young and active family acted like a magnet for the curious, and Edith resolved to handle the publicity more successfully than her predecessors had managed. Frances Cleveland had assumed that she could bar reporters from the White House lives of her children, but she found that the lack of access resulted in wild rumors that they were deformed or ill. An older and wiser Edith Roosevelt, aware that she could not deny the public's curiosity, decided to satisfy it on her terms.

Raised in a society that dictated that a lady's name should appear in print only at her birth, her marriage, and her death, she had to cope with being a First Lady whose activities the public wanted to see in print every day. By supplying posed photographs of herself and her children, she solved most of the problem. *McClure's, Harper's Bazaar, Harper's Weekly,* and *Review of Reviews* all ran pictures of the Roosevelt family but gave little information. Edith appeared on the cover of the *Ladies' Home Journal* and alongside articles that featured her husband but had nothing to do with her. When the time came for Alice Roosevelt's wedding to Nicholas Longworth and for Edith's daughter's debut, photographers and reporters were included in the preparations so that the uncontrolled snooping that had marred the Cleveland wedding would not be repeated.

Anyone who thought the formal, posed photographs of the White House family represented increased access was wrong because Edith Roosevelt instituted changes to increase, not lessen, the distance between herself and the public. In Albany, she had learned that a bouquet of flowers, firmly held, relieved her of the duty of shaking hands in a reception line, and she continued this practice in Washington. After Theodore obligingly greeted 8,538 people on New Year's Day, 1909, one writer in a national magazine asked readers if anyone could blame Edith for clutching her bouquet of orchids.

Extensive renovation of the mansion during the summer of 1902 made possible a greater division between the family's quarters and those set aside for official events. While the Roosevelts stayed at another house on Lafayette Square, the architectural firm of Mc-Kim, Mead and White supervised the enlarging of the White House. The conservatories came down and were replaced by an office wing. Many First Ladies had wanted a separate residence for the family, at a distance from the official duties of the president. Edith Roosevelt settled for one house but engineered a clearer division between its two functions. The family's quarters were upstairs and off-limits to the president's staff and to people invited to the public areas down below.

In many ways, Edith acted as top commander. The secretary she hired, Belle Hagner, oversaw many details, and one of the other aides reported he was "simply astonished" at Hagner's executive ability. She managed the White House so well, the aide said, that she became the "chief factor" there. To control the information that went out concerning official entertaining, Edith enjoined her children not to talk to reporters but arranged for Hagner to release details. All presidents have attempted to some extent to control the reports concerning their administrations, but Edith showed that presidents' wives could learn from the same book. Her stepdaughter Alice explained how Edith was not above "managing" the news. She would wear the same dress several times but instruct reporters to describe it as "green" one evening and "blue" the next.

In a further move to establish command over Washington social life, Edith scheduled weekly meetings with the wives of cabinet members. On Tuesdays, while their husbands conferred on one side of the White House, the women met on the other. Archibald Butt, an aide to the president, reported that the women did nothing more than take tea and compare crochet patterns, but Helen Taft, wife of the secretary of war, attended and supplied a different version when she explained that this was no "social affair."

Indeed, they were planning conferences engineered by Edith to set the limits on entertaining and help keep expenses down. Even with a presidential salary of $50,000 and an equivalent allowance for running the household, she needed to economize. Simply cutting

costs would not accomplish her purpose. She could not risk having
the president's parties judged inferior to those of cabinet members.
The other wives would naturally be tempted, she understood, to
compete among themselves unless she set boundaries for them all.
By announcing just what she planned to serve or wear or how she
would decorate or entertain at a particular reception or dinner, she
restrained exuberant hostesses and reassured the insecure ones
who feared falling behind. Rumor had it that she also used the
gatherings of cabinet wives to issue ultimata on behavior and that on
one occasion she warned a married woman to break off her romantic
involvement with a foreign diplomat or else find herself banned
from the capital's social events.

The institutionalization of the job of First Lady is underlined by
Edith's delegating to specialists the responsibility of preparing food
for official dinners, rather than burdening herself with small details.
Though the caterers were expensive, charging $7.50 per person per
guest (when the average woman clerk did not earn that amount in a
week), the arrangement shielded Edith from some public criticism
and saved her a great deal of work. To assure that her own contribution and that of other First Ladies would not be forgotten, she
continued the presidential china collection begun by Caroline Harrison, and she initiated a portrait gallery so that all presidents'
wives, "myself included," she said, could have memorials. Haphaz-
ard and incomplete before Edith Roosevelt, the series gained regular additions after her tenure because every administration arranged for an official portrait of the wife, as well as the president, to
stay behind when residence in the White House ended.

When Edith Roosevelt vacated the White House after nearly eight
years, in 1909, opinion was almost unanimous in her favor. Archibald Butt judged that she left the job "without making a mistake."
Columnists marveled at her stamina, and a leading women's magazine, in an article entitled, "Why Mrs. Roosevelt Has Not Broken
Down," attributed her good health to exercise. That was far less
important, however, than the shield of self-confidence that seemed

to insulate her against criticism that had worried some other presidents' wives. When a famous woman was quoted in a national magazine as saying Edith Roosevelt "dresses on 300 dollars a year and looks it," Edith proudly clipped the column for her scrapbook.

Her most celebrated brush with public opinion resulted from a disagreement over her right to remove a piece of furniture from the White House, and she wisely abandoned her fight rather than pursue it. The question arose when she left the White House and wanted to take with her a small settee that she had purchased for $40 during the refurbishing of the mansion. It had come to symbolize for her the years in Washington and she wanted to have it reproduced, at her own expense, and take the original back to her Long Island home. Word leaked out and the press treated the settee as though it were a national treasure that the First Lady was trying to purloin. Edith surrendered, saying that she would not have the settee even if it were given to her because of the unpleasant associations it now carried for her.

Edith Roosevelt never went beyond classes at New York's Comstock School, but the erudite setting in which she was raised provided a complete education. If she failed to flaunt this, as her husband sometimes did his intellectual prowess, it was because of a difference in their styles. Theodore confessed that Edith's education was really much broader than his own and that he often got credit for her ideas. "She is better read," Theodore once told a friend, admitting that he valued her judgment and feared she had a good-natured contempt for his knowledge of literature.

Edith's shrewdness extended to politics, and she told a friend she could not understand why, in 1904, Theodore made a premature public promise not to run again in 1908. Her strong streak of practicality and good sense helped moderate her husband's view of the world and his chances in it, and she was one of the few people who did not hesitate to set him straight. When Theodore ventured into crowds, evidently oblivious to possible physical danger, she kept tabs on his guards and encouraged them to disregard his requests for less surveillance. His plans to wear a fancy colonel's uniform on a post-presidential tour of Europe received a veto from Edith, who pointed out that he would be ridiculed by his countrymen. When he toyed with the idea of trying for an unprecedented third term in 1912, she advised him, "Put it out of your mind. You will never be President again."

Political differences with the Democratic Roosevelts enticed Edith to take an uncharacteristically public role in the presidential campaign that pitted Franklin Roosevelt against Republican Herbert Hoover. Though Franklin's wife, Eleanor, was Theodore Roosevelt's niece, she had campaigned against Theodore, Jr. in the New York State election in 1928. Edith, therefore, felt justified in speaking out against Eleanor's husband in the 1932 election. Her endorsement of Herbert Hoover made the front pages of the country's newspapers in August 1932, and her appearance at a large Madison Square Garden Republican rally in October received similar notice.

Edith could not always control contacts between the two branches of Roosevelts, as her daughter-in-law pointed out. In the Philippines in 1933, Theodore, Jr. was asked by a reporter why his younger brother was yachting with Franklin Roosevelt back in New York when it was well known that the two sides of the family were political foes. Theodore, Jr. hesitated, uncertain how to answer, but Edith spoke up from across the room: "Because his mother wasn't there."

For the most part she lived quietly the years between her husband's death in 1919 and her own death in 1948. Rather than write the memoirs of her marriage or of her years in the White House, she teamed up with her son Kermit to produce a volume on her illustrious ancestors. When her children decided to publish a book on travel, *American Backlogs*, she contributed a chapter in which she wrote, "Women who marry pass their best and happiest years in giving life and fostering it." She then added tellingly that some women can become very "irked" by the "shackles" their families place on them. By diplomatically refusing to cite which of the shackles she connected with her job as First Lady, Edith Roosevelt added a final enigmatic note to a remarkably successful tenure in the White House. Like many presidents' wives who preceded her and others who would follow, she decided that the job required a little distance between herself and everybody else. Few of the others had her self-confidence to make that work.

HELEN HERRON TAFT

HELEN HERRON TAFT, who succeeded Edith Roosevelt in 1909 when William Howard Taft became president, lacked Edith's quiet control but greatly outdistanced her in personal ambition. Born in southern Ohio in 1861, Helen (known as "Nellie" to family and close friends) had determined very early to escape that region, not only because of a desire for adventure but because of the narrow limits she perceived for herself if she remained there.

Being a woman complicated the escape, she realized, and she fretted over her lack of options. At age eighteen she wrote in her diary that she doubted she would ever marry, and at twenty-two, she explained why: "I have thought that a woman should be independent and not regard matrimony as the only thing to be desired in life." Helen tried teaching, one of the few jobs open to middle-class women like herself and one that many used to leave home, but she found that an imperfect solution. "I do not dislike teaching when the boys behave themselves," she wrote, implying that much of the time they did not. Her mother, more content with the routine of life in southern Ohio, counseled her daughter not to attempt too much. Helen knew she had musical talent but not of the magnitude to justify planning a career around it, and church work did not appeal. Depressed by the lack of alternatives, she admitted that she cried a lot.

With the purposefulness that marked her entire adult life, Helen Herron enlisted the help of two of her friends to start a Sunday afternoon "salon" where "specifically invited" young people could "engage in what we considered brilliant discussion of topics intellectual and economic." Showing an unusual ability to predict who in Cincinnati would eventually achieve most success, Helen invited the two Taft brothers: William Howard, who would later become the first man to serve as both his country's president and chief justice, and his younger brother Horace, who founded the Taft School in Connecticut.

The young attorney, whom she called Will Taft, was soon squiring Helen to Cincinnati social gatherings, including the then popular "German" dancing party. His letters literally begged for her attention and approval, and when she complained that he did not put high enough value on her opinions, he tried to reassure her that he knew no one who gave more weight to her opinions than he did. Bouquets of flowers arrived at Helen's house with Will's cards, some of them asking forgiveness for "inconsiderate words and conduct" and others declaring, often in German, his love for her.

Years of insecurity about her appearance and social skill made Helen Herron wary of all compliments, no matter how genuine, and she demanded reassurances. Her diary shows ample evidence of self-criticism, and she repeatedly judged that she had behaved like "a goose" or failed to invent a witty rejoinder. When she accused Will of "reasoning" himself into loving her, he replied patiently in his careful script that he was genuinely attracted to her "high character" and to her "sweet womanly qualities."

Helen Herron refused Will Taft's proposal for marriage at least twice before accepting in 1886 when she was twenty-five. A three-month European honeymoon, with a $1,000 price tag, was her idea, although he worried they could ill afford it and finally rebelled when she filled their itinerary with too many visits to the opera.

Back in Cincinnati, William practiced law and Helen attempted to settle into quiet wifedom. She gave birth to three children and helped start the city's Orchestra Association but made no secret of her unwillingness to continue such a monotonous life indefinitely. William's appointment to solicitor general in 1890 and to a federal circuit judgeship in 1892 raised the dreaded prospect that she might pass her entire adult life as the unnoticed wife of an unimportant judge.

For an ambitious woman who had decided to pursue a vicarious career through her husband, the need to intervene in his decisions was obvious. In the case of Helen and William Taft, the choice to enter elective politics appears more hers than his. Her father and maternal grandfather had both served in Congress, and unlike her husband, who preferred the law, she enjoyed the excitement of a campaign. The prospect of putting herself forward as the candidate apparently held no interest for her, although William laughingly predicted early in their marriage that if they ever got to Washington, it would be because of an appointment for her. Even after he had won election to the presidency, he wrote that he felt a little uncomfortable in the new office but "as my wife is the politician, she will be able to meet all the issues and perhaps we can keep a stiff upper lip."

Women of Helen Taft's generation exercised few political rights on their own. In the four states that had provided for female suffrage before 1910, popular prejudice against women in high office was almost as great a barrier as were discriminatory laws. The lower echelon offices that women sometimes captured, such as justice of the peace or sheriff, did not appeal to Helen Taft. When she was seventeen, she had gone with her parents to visit the Hayses, their Republican friends in the White House, and Helen had stayed for a few days. She later admitted that she had been impressed and that she had set her sights at that time on becoming First Lady.

An opportunity to move closer to her dream came in 1900 when President William McKinley selected William Taft to head a commission to the Philippines. Even the nominee was surprised by the offer and said the president might just as well have told him "to take a flying machine." When her husband hesitated, unsure about what the job entailed, Helen urged him to accept, although her ideas were no clearer than his. "It was an invitation from the big world," she later wrote, "and I was willing to accept it at once and investigate its possible complications afterwards." While some of her friends and relatives worried about unknown diseases and other dangers for the Taft children, she packed them up and moved them halfway around the world. Her only regret in leaving Cincinnati, she later wrote, was relinquishing the reins of the city's Orchestra Association.

The Philippine assignment, which lasted four years and eventually led to governorship of the islands, marked an important step for both William and Helen Taft. He gained administrative experience, and she learned to manage a large staff of servants who, she frequently pointed out, did not always follow her orders but appeared more valuable to her after she no longer had their services. When she published her autobiography in 1914, she used more than half of its 395 pages to describe the four years she spent in the Philippines and only a fraction to discuss an equivalent length of residence in the White House.

As the consort of the Philippines governor, Helen lived more luxuriously than she ever had before or would afterward, but her insistence on perfection in every detail resulted in a nervous exhaustion that sent her to Europe for rest. In 1904 when the invitation came from Washington for William to return to the United States to enter the cabinet, she worried privately how they could live on a secretary of war's salary. President Roosevelt's chiding her that Edith "never minded not having champagne" did little to cheer her up.

William Howard Taft accepted the offer to become secretary of war, and Helen faced up to a different set of wifely duties when she returned to Washington. Cabinet wives still engaged in the leaving of cards, and Helen was expected to call on the spouses of other cabinet members and set aside one day each week to receive them at her home. It all added up to a routine she described as "monotonous stress." Holding less than first rank annoyed Helen, who clearly had become accustomed to the deference accorded the top of the foreign community in the Philippines, and even the prospect of accompanying her husband on official missions abroad did not make up for the loss.

Helen bided her time in Washington as patiently as she could, always ready to speak up when she thought she could advance her husband's ascent to the presidency. While the Tafts were still in the Philippines, President Roosevelt had held up the possibility of a Supreme Court appointment for William Taft, but both Helen and William's mother urged him to refuse. By 1906 when another vacancy on the court revived the prospect of putting the scholarly William Taft on the country's highest court, Helen was back in Washington and could speak more directly on the subject. Who scheduled the resulting meeting between her and President Roosevelt remains unclear, but afterward the president wrote to William Taft that, following a talk with Helen, he understood why the court appointment was not desired.

In 1908 when William was nominated for President on the Republican ticket, Helen finally saw victory in sight. William appeared less enthusiastic. "I didn't think I was going to be foolish enough to run for the presidency," he jested on one occasion, but he went ahead to win in November, defeating the Democrat nominee William Jennings Bryan. Preparing for the inauguration, Helen sent off dresses to the Philippines to be embroidered, and she confidently outlined her plans for the White House. "I had been a member of Washington's official family for five years," she later wrote, "and I knew as well as need be the various phases of the position I was about to assume."

On the day of the inauguration, Helen Taft signaled publicly her intention to play an important role in her husband's administration —she took the unprecedented step of riding back to the White House with him. Theodore Roosevelt had decided to leave Washington immediately after the ceremony and so could not accompany his successor. Helen was determined that she, rather than some insignificant member of the inaugural committee, should claim the vacant place of honor. The solution was worked out almost a week before the inauguration but kept a secret, and Helen had to rush down from her seat in the gallery before her husband had finished his speech to make sure she arrived ahead of all usurpers. Her innovation did not go unobserved. Ike Hoover, a White House steward, noted "severe criticism" of Helen's adding a new ceremonial role to those already accepted for First Ladies. She felt obliged to defend herself: "Of course there was objection," she wrote, "but I had my way and in spite of protests took my place at my husband's side."

Only the servants and a few friends were on hand to greet the Tafts when they arrived at the White House, but their accounts emphasized that the new president and his wife reacted very differently. Helen remembered that as soon as her eyes lit on the presidential seal, she immediately thought, "and now that meant my husband." William was more sanguine, and according to separate accounts of two of the servants, he threw himself into a chair and said, "I'm President now and tired of being kicked around."

William Howard Taft's discomfort in high political office and Helen's zeal to achieve perfection in her role had an effect on both their lives, more disastrous for her than for him. His weight, always on the rise when he was feeling dissatisfied with himself, rose to 340 pounds, the highest in his life, and necessitated the installation of a new bathtub. Helen, then forty-seven years old, suffered a stroke two months after the inauguration, impairing her speech so severely that she had to work for the next year to relearn how to form sounds. Newspapers described Helen as suffering from a "nervous breakdown" which kept her away from the White House during the summer of 1909. For several months after she returned to Washington in October, she made only token appearances that did not require her to speak.

Missing the social events constituted the least of Helen's regrets —she could rely on her sisters or her college-aged daughter to substitute for her—but her illness necessitated her absence from important decisions of her husband's administration. Judith Icke Anderson, a Taft biographer, admitted to assuming "speculative privilege" when she pointed to the irony of the situation. It was Helen Taft, not her husband, who proved unable to handle the stress, losing her power of speech just when he needed her most. Anderson concluded that Helen's absence gave William a chance to be "his own man" and that he acquitted himself remarkably well. Although he feared that historians would judge his a "humdrum" administration, he believed he had performed well enough. When the split within the Republican party promised to end his presidency after only one term, he wrote to his wife that he was content to retire because he had done his best. He urged her to be proud of what they had done together: "I think you and I can look back with some pleasure in having done something for the benefit of the public weal."

President Taft's inclusion of his wife's accomplishment along with his own is not remarkable. Well before he took on the country's highest political office, national magazines had spoken openly of her influence on her husband. In its March 1909 issue, the *Ladies Home Journal* informed its readers that the new First Lady had a touch of domesticity and a healthy respect for the arts but was most remarkable because of the mentor role she played for her husband. Her "intense ambition" had helped propel him into the job and she remained his "close confidante." "Had it not been for his wife," the *Journal* readers learned, "Mr. Taft would never have entered the Presidential race." In the beginning of his term, she sat in on important discussions, justifying her presence by claiming to keep him awake. She accompanied him on political forays and golf outings. One acquaintance characterized their relationship as resembling that of "two men who are intimate chums." Helen's insistence that she had stopped participating in her husband's career when he became President rings a little false in light of so many statements to the contrary.

Helen lost little time in taking charge at the White House. Unlike Edith Roosevelt, she did not care for the company of women and she dispensed with the meetings of cabinet wives. If given the choice, and as First Lady she was given her choice on many things, she preferred staying close to the center of power rather than being shunted off on a peripheral social mission. She had frequently complained that on campaign trips her husband was "taken in charge and escorted everywhere with honor while I am usually sent with a lot of uninteresting women through some side street to wait for him at some tea or luncheon."

While Edith Roosevelt had proceeded as confident administrator, keeping herself aloof from the details of White House management, Helen involved herself in every tiny matter. She insisted that her vigilance could save money. The Roosevelts had attempted economizing but had judged it inappropriate to try saving anything from the president's salary or living allowances. Helen Taft harbored no such reservations. Since the chief executive's salary had just been increased from $50,000 to $75,000, she resolved to budget carefully so that $25,000 could go into the family's personal bank account. Like most of the objectives she set for herself, she succeeded in this one and accumulated $100,000 during the four-year term. Her zeal during the first two years alone resulted in an $80,000 nest egg which the president bragged to his aide was a "pretty good sum."

New economies were effected by revolutionizing the running of the White House. A housekeeper replaced the steward because Helen decided that no man, no matter how competent, could do the job adequately. Elizabeth Jaffray, the woman hired, insisted that she had not set out to obtain the White House job, but she had been "swept into the position" by Helen Taft. Later, Jaffray had further opportunities to witness the First Lady's commanding presence when orders came down for comparison shopping to economize.

The celebration of their silver wedding anniversary in 1911 gave the Tafts another opportunity to appreciate a material gain. Helen dispatched invitations to four or five thousand people (she could not recall the exact number), and although some of her friends thought gifts inappropriate, she saw no reason to discourage generosity. The response was overwhelming. One White House employee confessed that he had not known so much silver existed in the world. The head of U.S. Steel, Judge Elbert Gary, who hardly knew the president, sent a silver tureen reputedly two hundred years old and worth $8,000. A congressman's wife described the rather bizarre party scene in which one guest, Alice Roosevelt Longworth, took center stage in her "electric blue suit, flesh colored stockings and gold slippers," while the other guests quietly inquired among themselves as to how much each had "put up" for a gift. The president attempted to head off criticism by ordering that none of the gifts go on display, but Helen showed much less embarrassment and treated the presents as money in the bank: later she attempted to have the Taft monogram erased on one piece so that she could recycle the silver as a gift for someone else.

While Edith Roosevelt's influence on her husband had been quiet and private, Helen Taft's was publicly documented. Early in their marriage he had called her his "dearest and best critic," and he thanked her for pushing him to do more. Although she did not include cabinet meetings in those she attended (as Rosalynn Carter would later do), she stayed close by the president's side whenever political discussions occurred in social settings. One aide reported that Helen supplied her husband with names and numbers he forgot, and during parties, whenever some important person took the president aside to talk, Helen would join them as soon as she realized the situation. She made no secret of her differences with the president and announced that she would serve wine at White House dinners although "Mr. Taft does not drink."

Personnel decisions interested her particularly and she frequently based her judgments on subjective or irrelevant considerations. One visitor overheard her as she disagreed with her husband on an important nomination, saying she found the individual in question "perfectly awful and his family are even worse." She engineered the recall of an American ambassador to France even though Theodore Roosevelt judged the man extremely capable. His downfall resulted from his having slighted Helen on her honeymoon in London more than twenty years earlier. Easygoing William Taft confided to his friends that he would have forgotten the whole matter and let the man remain at his post but Helen proved less forgiving.

Like other First Ladies before her, Helen Taft refused to take a public stand in favor of woman's suffrage or other reforms for women. In 1912, President Taft appointed Julia Lathrop to head the newly formed Children's Bureau, but there is no evidence that Helen influenced this first appointment of a woman to such a post. She made no additions to the First Lady's staff, but by abolishing the cabinet wives' meeting and inserting herself in more substantive discussions, she showed her disapproval of a limited "women's sphere."

Helen Taft's stint as First Lady ended after only one term. The stroke she suffered within weeks of the inauguration had rendered her far less effective than she had planned, and her one permanent contribution to the capital was a cosmetic one, although not insignificant. During the years she spent in the Orient, she had become fond of Japanese cherry trees and she saw no reason why they could not survive in Washington's climate. She arranged for the planting of several thousand, thus providing for one of the capital's biggest tourist attractions, the annual spring blossoms.

After William Howard Taft lost the 1912 presidential election to Woodrow Wilson, the Tafts moved to New Haven, where William taught classes at Yale Law School. In 1921 the Tafts would return to

Washington when he was appointed chief justice of the United
States. Even after his death in 1930, Helen Taft remained in the
capital. When she died in 1943, she was buried beside him in Arlington National Cemetery, the only First Lady to be interred there.

ELLEN AXSON WILSON

THE DEGREE to which a more substantive, less purely social role
for the president's wife was becoming common rather than exceptional is apparent in the brief tenure of Woodrow Wilson's first wife,
Ellen Axson Wilson. Although she lived little more than a year in the
White House (1913–1914) and was seriously ill much of that time,
she took a prominent leadership position in housing reform and had
her name attached to the slum clearance bill that Congress passed at
the time of her death. That such a reticent woman, who admitted
she was more interested in painting than in politics, should have
been drawn into a major reform effort suggests that it would be
difficult for any woman in her place to withdraw completely from a
public role.

Woodrow Wilson's presidency (1913–1921) coincided with the
dropping of many barriers against women in politics. In 1912, the
summer his fellow Democrats chose him as their standard-bearer,
Jane Addams, the settlement house founder, stood up at the rebellious Bull Moose Convention to second Theodore Roosevelt's nomination for a third term. In 1917, Jeannette Rankin, a thirty-seven-
year-old former teacher and social worker from Montana, broke
Congress's old tradition of no women members when she took her

seat in the U. S. House of Representatives. In August 1920, near the end of Woodrow Wilson's second term, Tennessee ratified the nineteenth amendment. Overnight millions of American women acquired exactly the same power at the ballot box as their husbands and brothers.

Such an assault on the old male monopoly of politics perplexed Woodrow Wilson, the first president since Andrew Johnson to have been born in the South. Although Woodrow eventually came out in favor of the suffrage amendment, he acted reluctantly, moved less by conviction than by the realization that he could not arrest change. He had, after all, been raised in a Presbyterian manse where he was accustomed to hearing the male head of the household speak not only for the family but also for God, and he did not easily transfer authority to women. Few men outdid Woodrow Wilson in appearing to like women, but rather than treating them as intellectual equals, he expected them to supply his support system: bolster his ego and laugh at his jokes.

Ellen Axson of tiny Rome, Georgia, might not have seemed a likely candidate for Woodrow Wilson's attention. Like Woodrow, she grew up in a Presbyterian manse, and in her case, both grandfathers had also been men of the cloth. Ellen showed little interest, however, in following the examples of her mother and grandmothers. Her father pronounced her as a youngster too "obstreperous and independent" for her own good, and she dreamed of going to New York to study art as her teacher had done. That plan was deferred, however, while Ellen attended a local women's college. Then her mother died, leaving Ellen, the oldest of four children, to help raise the younger ones. Just as she was finally working out the possibility of combining serious art study and family responsibilities, young Woodrow Wilson came through her town and imposed another complication. He renamed her "Eileen," and pursued her with what one historian called "among the greatest love letters in the English language."

Ellen put Woodrow off, pleading first that her family needed her

Sarah Childress Polk

Abigail Powers Fillmore

Jane Appleton Pierce

Gowns of the First Ladies in the Victorian Room, First Ladies Hall, Smithsonian Institution. From left to right: Martha Johnson Patterson, Jane Appleton Pierce, Mary Todd Lincoln, Abigail Fillmore, Bettie Taylor Bliss, Harriet Lane Johnston, Sarah Childress Polk.

Harriet Lane

Mary Todd Lincoln

Eliza McCardle Johnson

Julia Dent Grant

Lucy Webb Hayes

Lucretia Rudolph Garfield

Gowns of the First Ladies in The Blue Room, First
Ladies Hall, Smithsonian Institution. From left to right:
Mary Harrison McKee, Caroline Scott Harrison, Mary
Arthur McElroy, Lucretia Rudolph Garfield, Lucy
Webb Hayes, Julia Dent Grant.

and then pointing out that he could hardly think of supporting a family on his income. Both her excuses ring a little hollow, however, because when Ellen, at age twenty-four, inherited some money of her own after her father's death, she left the brothers and sister and headed north—not to Baltimore where Woodrow had gone to pursue a doctorate in political science, but to a boardinghouse on New York City's West Eleventh Street and art classes nearby.

Like many presidents' wives, Ellen Axson showed a streak of independence in her youth that her husband lacked. While he picked his schools carefully from among the most prestigious (Princeton, University of Virginia, and Johns Hopkins), Ellen went to New York City and enrolled in the infant New York Art Students' League. To fill her time and help her feel more useful, she joined a reading club and volunteered to teach two nights a week in a missionary school.

Since Ellen Axson had evidently already decided to marry Woodrow Wilson, her assertion of independence is remarkable, particularly in light of Woodrow's disapproval. From Baltimore he wrote that he did not like the idea of her going out alone in the evening, although he hastened to add that she had every right to develop her own talents. In any case, he considered this show of independence on Ellen's part a temporary aberration because he was convinced, and assumed she agreed, that a woman found completeness only through marriage and a family. Ellen showed only temporary ambivalence between accepting the excitement of art classes in New York City and the staid life of a professor's wife. She wrote to Woodrow in strangely biblical terms: "I was indeed meant for you—that I may do you good and not evil all the days of my life."

In June 1885, Woodrow completed his course work for the doctorate at Johns Hopkins, and Ellen accepted his calculations that two could live "as cheaply as one and one-half." Since Woodrow's beginning salary at Bryn Mawr was only $1,500, he and his bride had to pay careful attention to finances. They boarded the first year with another family, and Ellen did her part in economizing by putting her painting easel away and traveling into Philadelphia twice a week to take a course in home economics. The next year the Wilsons were able to rent a house of their own and bring Ellen's younger brother and sister to live with them.

The move came none too quickly because Ellen gave birth to two daughters, Margaret and Jessie, within twenty-five months. When she bore a third daughter two years later, Woodrow concealed rather poorly his disappointment—he had written his wife that he was "glad—almost as at the thought of having a boy." The future president now headed a family of four females.

Frances Wright Saunders, in a carefully researched biography of Ellen Axson Wilson, portrays the Wilson marriage as a partnership, with Ellen playing an important, background role in Woodrow's success while, at the same time, pursuing her own interest in art. More than a skilled hostess, she translated German texts for Woodrow and worked out administrative arrangements which he, when he became president of Princeton, offered to the faculty for their acceptance. She traveled on her own and continued to paint and sell her work.

That view of Ellen Wilson fails to give adequate weight to the evidence that shows her repeatedly sacrificing her own time and energy so that Woodrow could have more pleasure and rest. When he received an invitation to travel, she encouraged him to go while she stayed home with the children. He explored the Chicago Exposition in 1893 and then she made the trip later. He journeyed through Europe twice on his own and then she went with one of their daughters. As a student of government and an advocate of the parliamentary system, he was drawn to Britain, but Ellen headed for Italy's art treasures.

Although Ellen knew that one of Woodrow's trips was financed by a wealthy woman who lived near them in Princeton, and that other journeys involved meetings with women, she refused to appear jealous, and she tolerated Woodrow's long relationship with Mary Peck.

Woodrow met Mary Peck in 1907 when he went to Bermuda for a rest, while his wife took her vacation with relatives in Georgia. He then began a correspondence with Mary that did not stop until after Ellen's death and his own remarriage in late 1915. Mary regularly escaped Massachusetts winters and what historians have called an "oppressive" marriage by going to Bermuda, and after she separated from her husband and established a permanent residence in New York City in 1909, Woodrow was, according to his wife's biographer, "constantly in touch" by letter and in person. The wording of their correspondence suggests the confidences did not remain platonic. He wrote that he was "wild" with the thought that she might be able to join him, and she replied that she wished she could be at his side "to fling myself where I would."

Woodrow had not yet run for elective office, and his wife Ellen acted decisively to head off any gossip that might hurt his chances. She treated Mary as a family friend and encouraged her daughters to do the same. When Woodrow journeyed to Massachusetts to visit Mary and her husband, Ellen accompanied him, and later, on a theater trip she took to New York, Ellen made a point of calling on Mary. In appearing not to notice how close her husband had become to Mary, Ellen was, according to her biographer, protecting her husband "and her own ambitions for him." She issued some "astute warnings" and then kept quiet. Woodrow's timing was fortunate for him since his second wife, Edith, was less tolerant of rivals.

Voters may have been unlikely to suspect much in Woodrow's attentions to Mary, because as Theodore Roosevelt said of him, "You cannot cast a man as Romeo who looks and acts so much like an apothecary's clerk." But Ellen Wilson's role in Woodrow's 1912 victory is also important. If she had not made such a point of treating Mary as a family friend, later inviting her to the White House, the political damage from the correspondence between Woodrow and Mary might have been considerably greater.

Ellen Wilson did well to conceal her feelings because she was the subject of close scrutiny. A month after the inauguration, the *Ladies*

Home Journal published two of her landscapes in full-color pages and noted that one painting had been exhibited at the Pennsylvania Academy of Fine Arts and that others had been shown in Chicago and Indianapolis. *Good Housekeeping* and *Current Opinion* carried similar stories. Ellen's domestic interests and abilities were not ignored and there were the usual speculations about tne cost of her wardrobe. She felt moved to defend herself when one newspaper reported that on one of her shopping trips she had bought seven new gowns costing several hundred dollars each. The actual amount spent had been much less, as she proved with the receipts which showed two gowns, one hat, one blouse, two pairs of gloves, and some fabric to repair old clothes—all for a total of $140.84.

The intricate political maneuvering that had appealed to Helen Taft held little interest for Ellen Wilson, but she was not opposed to acting as an intermediary to promote Woodrow's career. He was out of town in March 1911 when William Jennings Bryan, three times nominated to head the Democratic ticket, came to speak at Princeton. Ellen had to make her own decision about what to do. She invited the Bryans to dinner and then wired Woodrow to get back in time. When questioned later about her motives, Ellen replied that she had thought it the kind thing to do, but historians have seen it differently and have emphasized the importance of Bryan's support in Woodrow's attaining the 1912 nomination.

Ellen Wilson's apprehension and initial qualms about becoming First Lady had increased after she arrived in Washington in 1913. Trying to bolster her ego by outfitting herself for the inauguration in the "most wonderful gown" she could find, she nevertheless burst into tears before setting out for the traditional pre-inaugural visit to the White House. Her youngest daughter, observing her mother's discomfort, predicted then that the White House would "kill her."

As First Lady, Ellen Wilson edged toward advocating the vote for women but refused to take a public stand on the issue. Much safer than suffrage as a "cause" for the president's wife was housing, and in the same month as her husband's inauguration, Ellen started her own investigation of Washington's slums. While enlarging the electorate might be controversial, ameliorating housing was more acceptable because the fallout from slums hurt everyone, resulting in epidemics, increased infant mortality, and absenteeism.

Ellen Wilson's first scheduled visit to Washington's slums had to be postponed because of a smallpox outbreak. When she finally saw the dilapidated and filthy housing, she was appalled and became determined to work for congressional appropriations to provide clearance money. After she designated a White House car for touring alleys and arranged a reception so that housing reformers could present their case directly to congressmen, the topic of slum clearance took on a respectability and urgency that it had not previously had. By February 1914, the relevant legislation, known as Ellen Wilson's bill, had been introduced in Congress—the first piece of legislation to be passed with such direct and public assistance from a president's wife.

Meanwhile, in the White House, Ellen's family responsibilities piled on top of official ones when two of the Wilson daughters had White House weddings within six months of each other. Not long after Jessie's big ceremony in November 1913, Ellen's health began to fail. She had spent the previous summer in New Hampshire, but a few weeks back in Washington wiped out all the gains she had made. A kidney disorder, later diagnosed as Bright's disease, debilitated her, and although she seemed to rally at the time of her daughter Eleanor's marriage in May 1914, she soon worsened. By August 1914, it was clear to everyone except her husband that she was dying.

The housing bill that she had championed still lay in congressional committee, where there was unanimity on the abysmal quality of alley residences but little agreement on who should pay for improvements. After word of Ellen Wilson's deteriorating health reached Capitol Hill, the Senate quickly approved the measure so that she could be told before she died.

Until her death on August 6, 1914, Ellen Wilson insisted that her only objective in life had been to make life more comfortable for her husband and daughters, but her record is more complex. Naturally shy, she shooed away photographers and refused to appear on the platform with Woodrow. Yet she was often there to support her husband on public occasions. When he broke tradition and addressed Congress directly, she and her daughters set their own precedent by seating themselves prominently in the gallery to hear him. Only a little of the rebellious young artist from Rome, Georgia, remained in the White House Ellen Wilson, but she permitted her paintings to be exhibited, sometimes under the name, "E. A. Wilson," so as to disguise the origin of the work, and when they sold, she donated the proceeds to charity. Nonpolitical and insecure, she showed that even a very reticent First Lady can make a difference.

EDITH BOLLING GALT WILSON

WOODROW WILSON still had almost three years to serve in the White House when his wife Ellen died. Because his daughters were all busy with their own families or careers, he asked his cousin Helen Bones, who had helped Ellen as social secretary, to assist him in running the White House. It was Helen who invited her friend Edith Bolling Galt to the White House one March afternoon in 1915, thus setting the stage for Woodrow's remarriage.

The first meeting between the president and the attractive, forty-three-year-old widow was entirely accidental, Helen Bones later wrote. She had not reckoned with the possibility that the same rainy weather that forced her inside that day, with her friend Edith in tow, would also terminate the president's golf game. As they all sat down to take tea together, Helen Bones observed the almost immediate attraction between her cousin Woodrow and her friend Edith. After months of gloom, the president finally laughed.

Edith Bolling Galt combined a good measure of exuberant independence with sufficient amounts of the subservience that Woodrow Wilson found essential in all women. A bit more stylish and sophisticated than most of the women Woodrow liked, she was accustomed to ordering her clothes from a top Paris designer and creating a stir when she drove herself around the capital in her own little electric runabout. She boasted that policemen learned to halt traffic at Fifteenth Street so she could maneuver through. At a time when most matrons shunned close association with "business," Edith helped manage her own jewelry store. Yet she resembled other independent women in seeing such activities as somehow unique to herself. Working to increase opportunities for other women evidently held no interest for her. Before meeting Woodrow, she had paid no attention to politics and she admitted that during his victorious 1912 campaign she could not have named the candidates.

The path to Edith Galt's financial independence had been cut by accident, although she should not be deprived of the credit for picking her way across it. In 1896 when she was twenty-four, she had married a cousin of her sister's husband. Older men had always appealed to her, she admitted, and although she did not want to marry anyone, Norman Galt, part-owner of the capital's most prestigious jewelry store, pursued her until he won her. Their one child did not survive infancy, and when Norman Galt died in 1908, Edith was left with considerable personal and financial freedom. While keeping some control over the jewelry business, she made several trips to Europe.

The only president to possess a doctorate at the time of his election, Woodrow Wilson fell in love with a woman whose education was very limited. One of eleven children born to a Virginia judge and his wife, she received most of her instruction at home, then enrolled for two years at Virginia finishing schools. Historian Arthur Link concluded that, even as an adult, her writing was "primitive" and "almost illegible."

Much more relevant to her place in history, however, was the self-confidence that allowed her to act without constant reinforcement from those around her. Years of making her own decisions had prepared her to handle new ones with relative ease, and if she ever felt the inadequacy that had troubled Ellen Wilson, she kept it to herself. While Ellen Wilson had agonized over details, including whether or not to purchase a particular piece of clothing, Edith showed little hint of caring what people thought of her or of the amounts she spent on clothing. She never offered to show her bills to an inquisitive public.

Only two presidents before Wilson had married in office and each had approached courtship differently. John Tyler wed Julia Gardiner before reporters were able to find out, and Grover Cleveland avoided detection of his courtship of Frances Folsom by using the mails. Woodrow Wilson and Edith Galt had to conduct their nine-month courtship in the full glare of curious reporters, at first concealing their meetings under cover of Edith's friendship with Helen Bones and with the Wilson daughters.

Whatever inconvenience the burdens of his office imposed (and they were, no doubt, considerable since much of Europe stood embroiled in World War I), the president's courtship progressed rapidly. When Woodrow vacationed in New Hampshire in June 1915, Edith was there, ostensibly as Helen Bones's guest. But a postcard written during that visit testifies to the fact that Edith's romance with Woodrow had already matured into commitment only two months after their first meeting. Dated June 29, 1915, on the "West Porch," the card conveys the same kind of subservience that Ellen Axson had promised Woodrow thirty years earlier in a similar situation. Edith Galt's pledge had no limits. She would, she wrote, "trust and accept my loved Lord and unite my life with his without doubts or misgivings."

Even after having sworn such devotion, Edith shied away from marriage to the president for two reasons. Her own explanation was that she had lived in the capital too long to have missed the public's fascination with whoever happened to occupy the White House. Early in her acquaintance with Woodrow, she discovered that he shared her disdain for the snooping that had become a part of Washington life and for the vigor with which tourists hounded the president's family, but she knew that the two of them together could not change those habits. Much more important, however, was the matter of allowing an appropriate interval to elapse after Ellen Wilson's death. Woodrow was so in love he refused to acknowledge the consequences, but his advisers warned that a quick remarriage would hurt his chances for reelection in 1916. Such considerations became all the more important when rumors began to circulate that the courtship had begun before Ellen's death.

In spite of all these objections, the marriage took place in Edith's Washington home on December 18, 1915. The third bride of a president in more than a century, she attracted enormous attention. At five feet nine, she wore her fashionable French clothes well, and for a touch of the exotic, she explained to reporters that she could trace her ancestry back through nine generations to Pocahontas and John Rolfe. After months of dreariness, the White House came alive again under her direction as she entertained, sat devotedly at the side of a contented-looking president, and even learned to ride a bicycle. Elizabeth Jaffray, who worked more than seventeen years as the mansion's head housekeeper, judged Edith's first two years there the best of all.

By the time of the 1916 election, Americans had more on their minds than the circumstances of the president's remarriage and whether or not he now slept in a double bed. The war in Europe threatened to involve the United States, and by April 1917, Congress voted to enter officially.

Many women, including those in the president's family, participated on various levels in the war effort. His daughter Margaret, a
concert singer, announced that she would donate all the proceeds
from her singing to the Red Cross, and Eleanor, now married to the
secretary of the Treasury, went six mornings a week to supervise a
Red Cross storeroom. She left at noon only because she was scheduled to preside at meetings of the Women's Liberty Loan Committee.

Edith Wilson outdid them all by converting the White House into
a model of wartime sacrifice. She announced that she would observe
meatless days just like everybody else, and to save the cost of cutting
the lawn, she borrowed a flock of Shropshire sheep from a Virginia
farm. When the time came to shear them, she donated the wool,
totaling ninety-eight pounds, to the forty-eight states for auction-
ing, the proceeds designated for the war effort. In Kansas one zeal-
ous bidder bought two pounds of White House wool for $5,000
each, and the total sold in all the states brought more than $50,000.
With less publicity, the First Lady knitted sweaters for soldiers and
arranged for a White House car to take furloughed men around
Washington. When the time came to christen warships, the only
First Lady to claim Indian ancestry selected Indian names.

At the war's end in November 1918, President Wilson announced
that he would go to Europe to work personally on the details of the
peace agreement. The first American president to engage in such an
international overture, Woodrow gained enormous attention, and
Edith, who accompanied him, also received considerable notice.
Florence Harriman, an American woman who had organized a Red
Cross motor corps in France during the war, was in Versailles and
she reported that Edith "then, as always, was a First Lady to be
proud of." When the Wilsons traveled to Italy after the peace conference, an American army captain compared Edith to the Italian
queen, and *Ladies Home Journal* quoted him as saying, "I don't think
the Italians have got anything on us."

It remained for Edith's return to the United States, however, for her to achieve lasting prominence in the history of presidents' wives. Woodrow had decided to appeal directly to the people for support of his peace plan—a measure necessitated, in part, by the opposition to it in the Senate. On September 26, 1919, while traveling through Pueblo, Colorado, he suffered a paralytic stroke and then returned to Washington. For several weeks his condition remained uncertain, and his doctor refused to say specifically what ailed him or even how severely disabled he was. Rumors spread.

Woodrow's trusted friend and physician, Cary Grayson, had impressed Edith with the importance of keeping all business from the patient but she hardly needed convincing of the seriousness of his affliction. His trembling hands, gray color, and halting speech told her that, and she resolved to spare him all unnecessary stress. If anyone mentioned that Woodrow ought to relinquish his office to his vice-president, the suggestion was quickly discarded, on the grounds that fighting to get back in shape would prove the best medicine. Edith isolated Woodrow from everyone except his doctors, so that even his secretary did not see him for weeks. Any communication that reached the president went first to the president's wife. "So began my stewardship," Edith later wrote, and although she admitted studying "every paper," she insisted that she "never made a single decision regarding the disposition of public affairs."

Observers had no way of knowing who made decisions in the White House, and when she issued memos, signed Edith Galt Wilson, curiosity grew. On papers requiring the president's signature, Woodrow's name bore so little resemblance to what it had looked like before his illness that charges of forgery were raised. Edith explained the discrepancy by saying that the bedridden president lacked a hard surface for writing but that his handwriting improved as soon as she provided him with a board.

Word spread that Edith Wilson was running the government. Housekeeper Jaffray referred to Edith as the "Assistant President," and at a Foreign Relations Committee meeting, one senator

stormed that the country was under a "petticoat government." Requests to the president frequently began "Dear Mrs. Wilson," indi-
cating that the writers recognized her as controlling access to the
president if not actually making all decisions. Popular magazines
reinforced this impression and *Collier's* reported that Edith "came
close to carrying the burden of the First Man."

The cabinet looked for precedents about what to do when a
president became seriously incapacitated but refused to relinquish
the office. In the one case that seemed relevant, James Garfield had
lingered for almost three months in 1881 but the vice-president had
not taken over. The Constitution left unclear who should decide
that a president was no longer able to discharge the powers and
duties of the office. In the vacuum that developed, the president's
wife was permitted to enter center stage. She did not have to risk the
charge that an ambitious politician might have feared of using the
president's illness to advance her own career.

Edith Wilson certainly acted to protect her husband's health and
well-being but evidence mounts on several sides to show that her
influence in her husband's administration has been greatly over-
rated. She had never shown any interest in politics, although in the
romantic early days of their marriage, she had sat alongside him
while he studied official communications. After his death, she refused political involvement, and when Eleanor Roosevelt appealed
to her for a statement in support of a woman candidate, Edith cited
her forty-year record of obliviousness to politics.

Most telling of all, in assessing Edith Wilson's influence, is the
nature of the criticism leveled at her. Her alleged dominance occurred only during Woodrow's illness, from September 1919 until
early 1920. A time of great tumult in the United States, this period
included a miners' strike and a government injunction against mine
leaders, a steel strike, the continuation of the fight over the peace
treaty, and the deportation of aliens. Yet through all these difficulties, the complaint leveled at the White House was a lack of direction, an unwillingness to act—hardly evidence of a powerful leader.

When the attorney general, Mitchell Palmer, began his wholesale attack on people he suspected of being disloyal, the president's secretary futilely begged Edith to see that her husband acted.

Edith had married a man who rarely listened to women on any substantive issue, and only his debilitating stroke placed him in a dependent position so that rumors could thrive about his wife's running the country. Her memoirs describe how during his illness she abandoned ideas that differed with his rather than risk upsetting him. When the fight over the League of Nations became particularly acrimonious, for example, she reported that she had suggested to Woodrow that he compromise rather than hold out for what might be a losing proposition. She quickly reversed herself, however, when he accused her of deserting him. Judith Weaver, a student of the Wilson administration, concluded that Ellen Wilson, had she lived, might have exerted strong influence on a sick president and possibly convinced him to accept Senator Lodge's amendments concerning the League of Nations. Such a judgment reinforces the interpretation of Edith Wilson as nonpolitical, interested only in Woodrow's health and happiness. It is ironic that Edith should have gone down in history as the strong Mrs. Wilson, while Ellen Axson Wilson has been almost forgotten except by researchers who resurrect evidence of her strength and talent.

Edith Bolling Galt Wilson survived her husband by thirty-eight years, and when she died in 1961, she was buried beside the president, a tradition begun by Martha Washington. Every widow who had remarried and become First Lady had chosen burial beside her second husband rather than by her first. Edith had lived only eight of her nearly eighty years as Woodrow's wife, but those few years brought enormous publicity. Two full-length biographies detailed the influence she supposedly exerted in the White House and virtually all accounts of her husband's life assessed her role. She was called "Gatekeeper Extraordinary" and "surrogate President." Yet the consensus is that she described her role as accurately as anyone when she wrote that she simply looked out for her husband's health.

Edith Wilson's prominent tenure as First Lady capped the institutional changes made by Edith Roosevelt, the public and influential participation of Helen Taft, and the acknowledged reform leadership of Ellen Wilson. Together, the four women altered the meaning of the title they held, and what had been unusual before 1900—the contribution of significant work of their own—would become common among presidents' wives in the decades to come.

The Paradoxical
1920s

D URING the 1920s Americans experienced great strides in their personal lives at the same time that the nation took one giant step backward into "normalcy." A country tired of sacrificing for war and weary of high-minded slogans about "making the world safe for democracy" reverted to old ways that emphasized personal comfort and national isolation.

Nowhere is the contradiction of the 1920s more apparent than in the lives of the three First Ladies. Warren Harding's landslide victory over James Cox in 1920 brought into the White House Florence Kling Harding, considerably more conscious of the value of good public relations than any of her predecessors but, at the same time, extremely narrow in her outlook. After Warren Harding's death in 1923, charming Grace Goodhue Coolidge captured the nation's attention. With her dropped waistlines and raised hemlines, she epitomized current flapper style. Not until she left Washington did she reveal her considerably more serious side in the poetry she published. After Calvin Coolidge chose "not to run" in 1928, an erudite, well-traveled Lou Henry Hoover became First Lady, and for all her demurrals about merely "forming a backdrop for Bertie," she gave some remarkably feminist speeches. All three of the presidents' wives who moved into the White House in the 1920s sought to present themselves in ways that reflected contemporary standards without offending those whose views remained less modern. Together they set the stage for many of the innovations for which Eleanor Roosevelt gained credit in the 1930s and 1940s.

FLORENCE KLING DE WOLFE HARDING

F LORENCE KLING DE WOLFE HARDING, at sixty-one, was the oldest woman yet to assume the job of First Lady. She made a point, however, of appearing energetic and youthful, and in the 1920 campaign, she seemed every bit as up-to-date as the twenty-nine-year-old wife of Warren's Democratic opponent, James M. Cox.

The new acceptability of cosmetics assisted Florence considerably in her determination to appear young and vigorous. Married to a man five years her junior, she had grown adept at camouflaging the difference, and even her enemies agreed that she usually succeeded in looking younger than her years. She employed lace inserts and wide velvet ribbons, often studded with a bauble, to cover neck wrinkles. Instead of accepting the comfort of flat shoes, she wedged her feet into the then fashionable pointed toes with toothpick heels. Daily appointments with a hairdresser kept every gray hair marcelled tightly in place, and liberal applications of rouge suggested, at least from a distance, the rosy glow of youth. Her wardrobe of plumed hats and pearl-studded satin gowns could have competed with those of a Hollywood starlet.

By the time she became First Lady, Florence's earlier divorce had been forgotten, and she had been married to Warren Harding, for nearly thirty years—time in which she had shown two powerful traits which her enemies and supporters agreed she excelled in: willfulness and determination. While enrolled in the Cincinnati Conservatory of Music as a young woman, her energies had turned more to play than to the piano, and she had joined in with a hometown group of young people known as the "rough set" because they took up, among other sports, the new fad of roller skating. One of their number, Henry A. De Wolfe, was particularly attractive to her, perhaps because her father detested his heavy drinking and playboy attitude. When Amos Kling, Florence's father, forbade her seeing Henry, she promptly married him and six months later gave birth to a son.

The young couple's attempt to run a roller-skating rink in nearby Galion, Ohio, failed, and Henry quickly tired of the responsibilities attached to being head of a family. Before their son had reached two years of age, Henry deserted Florence, who had little choice but to return to her hometown of Marion, Ohio. The story persisted for years that she had taken her son and slept in an abandoned house the first night back rather than humble herself by appealing to her father for help. Her in-laws supplied some money, Florence gave piano lessons, and eventually her father came to her rescue, but she had learned an important lesson about the costliness of dependence and never allowed herself to become quite so defenseless again. After her divorce, she let her father adopt and raise her son while she set out to try again.

In a city of 4,000 people, an ambitious young piano teacher could not have remained long unaware of the charming, handsome newcomer who had just bought part ownership in one of Marion's newspapers. The publisher, Warren G. Harding, had a sister who studied piano with Florence, and soon music teacher and newspaperman met. Amos Kling's vehement opposition to his daughter's having anything to do with Warren increased his attractiveness immensely.

By the 1880s the Hardings ranked below the Klings in Marion's hierarchy, although a few years earlier that would not have been the case. In 1860 when Florence was born, her family lived in an apartment over their hardware store, but circumstances changed as Amos Kling prospered in real estate and business. By the time Warren began to court Florence Kling, her father was one of the most important men in town. Warren's parents both practiced medicine and his mother later acquired midwife's certification, but their specialty, homeopathy, paid none too well. Warren, however, had prospered during his first few years with the *Marion Star,* and had bought out his partners and built himself a handsome house on one of the town's best streets. Such considerations mattered far less to Amos Kling than the persistent rumor that Warren had Negro ancestry. Marion, Ohio, was not integrated in the 1880s, and racial prejudice was strong. In such a setting, the ancestry of a new young man in town became the subject of much speculation. Some of the locals insisted they detected Negro features in Warren.

Continuing a long tradition, the future First Lady married against strenuous parental objection, and in this particular case, the objection remained so strong that Amos Kling did not speak to his daughter for seven years. The small ceremony at Warren's new house in 1891 united a divorcée, one week short of celebrating her thirty-first birthday, with a promising businessman, then twenty-five. Some of their friends detected a mother-son relationship in the match and they pointed out that Warren had always been very attentive to his mother, taking her fresh flowers every Sunday or, if he could not go, arranging for someone else to make the delivery. Now he transferred that filial devotion to his wife, making her his conscience, bookkeeper, and monitor. For the fun part of his life he evidently went elsewhere—at least two women friends left accounts of the time they spent with Warren, and his poker-playing friends supplied their own recollections of his participation in their games.

Although she came from the same generation that had produced many women who insisted on independence, including First Ladies Helen Taft and Ellen Wilson, Florence Harding was less overtly rebellious. She married local young men whom her father detested but then worked hard to prove him wrong.

Florence devoted herself to Warren's career as though her own reputation were at stake. His mother, Phoebe Dickerson Harding, who was something of a career woman herself, had warned Florence to keep the icebox full and both eyes on Warren. Florence lost no time stopping at the *Star* office to see how the business—and Warren—operated. She remained for fourteen years, first streamlining the bookkeeping system and then organizing a home delivery service to boost circulation. One of the carriers whom she hired ran for president himself later, and he recalled how she had taken over the *Star*. "She was a woman of very narrow mentality and range of interest or understanding," Norman Thomas wrote, "but of strong will and within a certain area, of genuine kindness." He credited her energy and her business sense with making the *Star* successful. According to Thomas, Florence complemented her husband's enormous affability by overseeing the advertising and circulation while Warren supplied the popular, convivial part of the team.

As for the other part of her mother-in-law's advice, Florence dutifully pedaled her bicycle home to cook Warren's dinner, but her domesticity did not extend to maternity. She showed little interest in the son from her first marriage, and by Warren she remained childless, even though one of his women friends reported that he would have very much liked to have a child. He put the blame for their childlessness on Florence and on the "tiny white pills" she took to avoid conceiving.

The control over her own life that had been so conspicuously absent from Florence's first marriage showed up in other ways in her second marriage. She involved herself in each of Warren's campaigns: from state senator he moved to lieutenant governor and then, after losing a bid for governor in 1910, to the United States Senate in 1915. In the early days, she accompanied him on the lecture tour, impressing some of his managers as "meanly accurate in calculating expenses." By the time Florence arrived in Washington, one politically active woman observed in her a "ruthless ambition to become First Lady" as she "constantly worked and made Warren work toward that end." Florence once confided to Norman Thomas's wife that Warren got into a lot of trouble when she was not around so she limited those opportunities whenever possible. During his Senate days, she encouraged him to give his interviews at home so that she could participate, and she kept up with the issues so that eventually Warren's campaign manager pronounced her "one of the best informed women in the country."

When, as the wife of an Ohio senator, Florence first arrived in Washington in 1915, she lacked the celebrity status she might have liked. But she could prepare for success. Alice Roosevelt Longworth who, with her husband Nicholas, socialized with the Hardings in their Senate days, reported that Florence kept a little red book with the names of people she meant to get even with when she got the chance. In the meantime, the handsome senator from Ohio appeared on many guest lists and even Alice included him at her poker table. She waited until he was dead to write, "He was not a bad man, just a slob."

Florence had spent too much time around the newspaper office to remain unaware of the value of good publicity, and she added some dash to her own image by associating with the capital's wealthy, risk-taking social leaders. One of Florence's closest friends became the legendary Evalyn Walsh McLean. The daughter of an Irish immigrant who made his fortune in Colorado mining and then spent the remainder of his life enjoying the money and spoiling his children, Evalyn had married Edward McLean, a man every bit as fun-loving as she. On their European honeymoon, $200,000 proved insufficient to pay the bills. Back in Washington he concentrated on running the *Washington Post,* which he owned, and she engineered a highly publicized social life for them and spent money as though it would never run out. On one shopping trip, conducted comfortably from her chauffeured Rolls Royce, she admitted to paying $5,000 for a St. Bernard dog for her daughter (although the girl had requested a poodle). On another day, Evalyn purchased the famous Hope diamond, reputed to bring tragedy to whoever owned it, and then attempted to negate the curse by having a priest bless the gem.

Such extravagance fascinated small-town Florence Harding, and Evalyn admitted that she grew fond of Florence, who could be haughty and nagging, "her mouth a revelation of discontent." The unusual friendship between the two very different women continued until Florence's death. Evalyn, who rarely admitted to caring what anybody thought about her, confessed she was flattered to have an important politician's wife seek her advice. Florence knew where to place herself when cameras started rolling, but she knew where to draw the line, too, and on one occasion, when she feared being photographed beside a cigarette-smoking Evalyn, she knocked the offending article from her friend's mouth.

The careful housewife's dependence on the flamboyant Evalyn McLean represents one of several inconsistencies in Florence Harding's life. When Warren's name came up for consideration for president in the 1920 campaign, she very much wanted the glory of victory but she feared the disastrous exposures that a national campaign could bring. Warren had already been linked romantically with at least two women, and one of them, a Marion housewife, had frequently vacationed with her husband and the Hardings. Because the woman's husband was in poor health, he removed himself from the scene for long recuperative jaunts to the West Coast, and Florence, who had had one kidney removed in 1905, was often ill. Their absences left their spouses considerable freedom, causing speculation in Marion about what they did in their time together.

Warren Harding's other reported romance involved a much younger woman who had developed a crush on the senator while she was still a high school student and had aroused Florence's suspicions. Nan Britten later published a book about her involvement with Warren Harding and thus became the first (but not the last) to divulge the details of her own sexual liaison with a president. Like her latter-day counterparts, Judith Exner (who publicized her relationship with President John F. Kennedy) and Kay Summersby (who described the time she spent with then-General Dwight Eisenhower during World War II), Britten waited until the other principal was dead before going public.

Britten titled her account *The President's Daughter*, although at the time of her daughter's birth, Warren was still a senator. The book details how Warren helped young Britten move from Marion, Ohio, to New York City to find a job. On trips the two took together, Warren registered her in hotels as his niece. With that record and that visibility, her relationship with Warren could hardly have escaped sharp-eyed Florence or his colleagues, and Florence had good reason to fear the close scrutiny of a national campaign.

Even if fear of exposure of her husband's active extramarital sex life had not deterred Florence, she had other misgivings. While she would have liked to think that matters of life and death did not depend on such things as the stars, she could not free herself from the belief that they did. A medium whom she frequently consulted had predicted that Warren would win the presidency but that disaster would follow: Warren would die in office and Florence, soon afterward. When he won the nomination, Florence was widely quoted as saying she saw only tragedy in his future.

Her own poor health also concerned Florence. Her one remaining kidney frequently became infected, swelling to several times its normal size and causing great pain. She had barely escaped death once when she had chosen to rely on her Marion homeopath rather than on other doctors who had advised surgery, and she understood that her luck might not hold the next time.

In spite of these misgivings, Florence put her best effort into getting Warren nominated and elected. Early in the primary campaign when his determination flagged, she stymied his attempt to drop out by seizing the telephone from him and shouting to his campaign manager on the other end that they were in the race until "hell freezes over." When people came to Marion to assess the candidate, she was unfailingly courteous to all, smiling agreeably when they ran over the hedge and trampled the grass so thoroughly that the yard had to be graveled. On questions of politics she curbed her inclination to speak out and deferred to Warren, even though more than one of her friends thought she found it trying to learn at her age to appear submissive.

Florence held strong ideas about when to use the press and when to keep quiet. When a Wooster College professor published pamphlets outlining Warren's black ancestry, Warren and his campaign advisers were uncertain how to react. The candidate wanted to go public with the explanation he had already given his friends—that the story persisted because of his family's record of giving aid to slaves escaping on the underground railroad. Florence decreed otherwise and ordered a cancellation of the denial that Warren's staff had drafted. Some charges, if treated as unworthy of response, would eventually die down, she reasoned, and no statement on the matter came out.

Warren Harding easily won the 1920 election (garnering 16 million popular votes to James Cox's 9 million), and preparations began for an inaugural celebration to outshine all previous ones. Edward McLean, who headed the inaugural ball committee, planned a party that would combine, his wife wrote, "the liveliness of ten July fourth celebrations with the ending of a victorious war." The Republican National Committee, having a more modest celebration in mind, balked at spending that kind of money and dropped sponsorship of the official inaugural ball so that the McLeans hosted their own party at their Washington home.

The expensive, private initiation of the Harding administration set the tone for what followed, and the Hardings persisted in acting as though they operated above and apart from the rules governing other people. In spite of a constitutional amendment prohibiting the "manufacture, sale or transportation of intoxicating liquors," the Hardings kept a well-stocked bar in the private quarters of the White House. While official "dry" receptions were held downstairs, the president would be upstairs, Alice Roosevelt Longworth reported, surrounded by his friends and all brands of whisky, playing cards, and poker chips, thus presenting an atmosphere more appropriate to a saloon than to the residence of a head of state. The First Lady was left to move between the two worlds, adding a touch of schoolteacher rectitude while keeping the drinks fresh.

In honing a public image as a nonimbiber, Florence reflected typical First Lady behavior, not restricted to the prohibition years. Until Betty Ford's post–White House confession that she was an alcoholic, presidents' wives regularly objected to accounts that they consumed alcoholic beverages and to photos showing them with drink in hand. The temperance movement itself rarely caught their fancy, however, and except for Lucy Hayes, no First Lady became an outspoken advocate of the cause.

To assure the most favorable publicity possible, Florence carefully tended her relationship with reporters—the men became "my boys" to her and the women "the girls." One Washington veteran recalled that Florence invited newspaperwomen to cruise down the Potomac with her on the presidential yacht and then startled the group by slapping one of them on the back and exclaiming, "Well here we are, all girls together." She even invited women reporters to interview her and then, wearing a rose-colored negligee, she spoke with them in her bedroom. Although Ohioan Jane Dixon of the *New York Telegram* was a personal favorite, Florence never showed her preferences and reporters responded by treating her well. Although some of them found her haughty, much of what they wrote was not unflattering. Her claim that she gave them important, newsworthy information is difficult to substantiate because she said she asked them not to name her as a source, and none of them did.

The intentional management of the press extended to virtually every area of Florence's life. Rather than divulge just how precarious her health was, she attributed frequent and sometimes lengthy absences to food poisoning, thus giving the public a picture of a much healthier First Lady than was actually fact. A life-threatening attack of nephritis which she suffered in August 1922, was not re-

Frances Folsom Cleveland

Caroline Scott Harrison

Ida Saxton McKinley

Edith Carow Roosevelt

Helen Herron Taft

Ellen Axson Wilson

Edith Bolling Galt Wilson

Florence Kling De Wolfe Harding

Grace Goodhue Coolidge

Lou Henry Hoover

Eleanor Roosevelt

ported for several weeks and then not in detail. Her two grandchildren did not visit her in the White House so that photographers had no opportunity to catch her in grandmotherly poses that might focus attention on her age. Mindful of the anti-German sentiment that lingered in America after World War I, Florence tailored her ancestors accordingly. Although a prominent historian has concluded that Florence was descended from German Mennonites, she carefully credited her "French grandmother" with teaching her excellent posture and good taste in clothes.

In spite of her expertise in public relations, Florence showed little skill at managing the White House, nor did she seem to care. The 1920s did not place the same importance on domestic skills as had been the case at the turn of the century, and none of the First Ladies of the 1920s spent much time honing her domestic image. Florence had managed only modest-sized houses in Marion and Washington, and she lacked the preparation for taking on an establishment as large and complex as the executive mansion. On first meeting with its staff, she seemed unsure of herself, saying first that she would find a new housekeeper and then that she would retain the old one. Ex-president William Howard Taft, who stopped by the Harding White House to offer advice, judged her completely unprepared for that side of the job. She did make one innovation in the staff, adding a Secret Service agent to the usual retinue of housekeepers, maids, and stewards, and then assigning him sundry tasks that had little or nothing to do with her safety. The surveillance that Eleanor Roosevelt so disliked began in the Harding administration when Florence decided she could use extra help to chauffeur her clairvoyant or keep watch on Warren.

Florence tempered her feminism so that it either fit accepted standards or remained very private. When a woman solicited Florence's views on careers for women, the First Lady replied that one career was about all any couple could manage. "If the career is the husband's," Florence wrote in 1922, "the wife can merge her own with it, if it is to be the wife's as it undoubtedly will be in an increasing proportion of cases, then the husband may, with no sacrifice of self respect or of recognition by the community permit himself to be the less prominent and distinguished member of the combination."

In line with her view that the White House belonged to everybody, Florence worked hard to make it (and herself) available to visitors. One of the maids recalled how Florence would run down the steps to greet tourists, and on New Year's Day she stood to shake hands with thousands of guests even though she needed two days in bed to store up strength for the ordeal and two days to recuperate. Her prediction to Evalyn McLean that being First Lady meant "nothing but work, work, work" proved accurate, and she insisted on expending considerable energy on the job, even when she was seriously ill.

In the end, the calculated secrecy that Florence used in dealing with the press worked against her. Neither she nor her husband (who had a long history of high blood pressure and symptoms of heart disease) had supplied accurate health information, and the public had little preparation for their deaths. On the fatal Western trip in the summer of 1923, Warren's doctor had issued a bulletin citing food poisoning resulting from eating bad crabs, when in fact none had been consumed. When the president died on August 2, many people questioned the cause and some even suggested foul play with Florence as the culprit.

The extent of scandal in President Harding's administration had not yet become public at the time of his death, and Warren's last recorded activity was listening to Florence read from the *Saturday Evening Post* a glowing account of his presidency. The train carrying the president's body across the country for burial passed the largest crowds seen since Abraham Lincoln's death, with a million and a half people gathering in Chicago alone to pay their respects.

Florence made the cross-country trip with her husband's corpse, attended memorial services in the capital, and then traveled to Ohio for the burial. It was during the stop at the White House that she

made her famous nocturnal visit to the president's bier. Evalyn
McLean, who had stayed with her friend, reported that Florence had
gone down in the middle of the night to the coffin in the East Room
and had stood for a long time talking to it. She sounded more like a
mother addressing a dead child when she finished: "They can't hurt
you now."

Florence stayed for a while at the Willard Hotel in Washington
before returning to Marion. She had neither forgotten nor discounted the fortune-teller's prediction about her own death and she
recognized the signs of further deterioration in her health. Her
trusted homeopath died in the summer of 1924, and the following
September, when Evalyn McLean came through Ohio in her private
railroad car, Florence announced that this would be their last visit.
Weeks later, fifteen months after Warren's death, she was dead.

The sum of Florence Kling Harding's influence on her husband's
political career remains difficult to assess, partly because she destroyed much of the physical evidence that could have helped define
it. Of the 350,000 documents that survive of the Harding administration, few relate to her political views or activities, although hundreds of thank-you notes addressed to her suggest that she was not
idle. She contributed to the enigma of her role by juxtaposing
strong and blatant claims of her own power alongside demure self-
effacement. Although she smiled obligingly when her husband's
friends called her "Duchess" in a not altogether complimentary
tone, she seems to have held strong opinions and expressed them
freely. Some historians who have evaluated the evidence have concluded that Florence's influence on her husband has been exaggerated, but most of her contemporaries insisted it was real, and many
of them offered specific instances to support that point of view.

Harry Daugherty, the campaign manager who later served in the
Harding cabinet, reported being summoned to the White House
one evening to referee an argument between the Hardings on the
wording of a presidential address. In the end, Florence got her way.

Secretary of State Hughes called Florence "her husband's most faithful counselor."

Nicholas Murray Butler, a guest at the White House during a discussion about accepting a mansion as a residence for the vice-president, reported that it was Florence Harding who applied the veto. Senator John Henderson's widow had offered to donate her house on Sixteenth Street for the use of the vice-president, but Florence Harding would not hear of accepting the gift. "Not a bit of it," she fumed, according to Butler. "I am going to have that bill defeated. Do you think that I am going to have those Coolidges living in a house like that? A hotel apartment is plenty good enough for them." Whatever the reasons, Congress turned down the gift and the vice-president remained without a permanent official residence for forty more years.

To the widespread view that politicians' wives should form a social backdrop, Florence Kling Harding, as she always signed herself, offered a notable exception. Early in her White House tenure, she had reportedly inquired of a senator whom he judged the most successful First Lady in history. When he replied, "Dolley Madison or Frances Cleveland," Florence Harding retorted, in what might be considered a slogan of her mature years: "Watch me!" She only partly concealed her partnership in her husband's political decisions and yet she received little of the criticism leveled at her predecessor, Edith Wilson. Few of the Hardings' friends would contest the view that she imposed a strong discipline on herself and that she showed exceptional determination throughout her life.

GRACE GOODHUE COOLIDGE

G RACE GOODHUE COOLIDGE, who followed Florence Harding into the White House in 1923, would have virtually no influence on any of her husband's political decisions. Not long after her marriage, she had prepared to go hear her husband speak but he had stopped her with a laconic "Better not," and that separation between politics and family continued for the rest of their time together. While he progressed from state representative to mayor of Northampton, then state senator, lieutenant governor, and governor of Massachusetts, Grace and her two sons remained in half of a house they rented in Northampton. After his work took him to Boston, Calvin commuted home on weekends. Grace later wrote that she knew nothing at all about politics—she considered that subject outside her "province." If she had shown any interest, she said, she would have been quickly put in her place.

Grace's description of herself should not obscure the fact that, unlike any of her predecessors, she attended a coeducational university and prepared for a career of her own. Although Lucy Hayes is often credited with being the first president's wife to have graduated from college, hers was a women's academy that did not offer the same curriculum that would have been offered to men students.

Grace Coolidge earned a bachelor's degree at the University of Vermont and then went on for additional training so that she could teach the deaf. Many nineteenth-century presidents' wives had taught school, but only temporarily, in order to earn some money and perhaps put some distance between themselves and their parents. Their letters convey little sense of education as a career or lifelong interest. Although Grace Coolidge worked only three years between her college graduation in 1902 and her marriage in 1905, she would maintain a permanent interest in training the deaf.

Grace's husband showed little regard for any of her accomplishments. Calvin had made clear his contempt for his wife's general education when, early in their marriage, he quizzed her on Martin Luther and her answers did not satisfy him. He gave no indication that he ever consulted her on any important question; in fact, she had to learn of his decision not to run for president in 1928 from friends because he had not bothered to tell her. By her own admission, Grace's monthly meetings with wives of cabinet members did not go beyond social schedules and the "insoluble problems" that have confronted cabinet wives since the country's founding.

It would be wrong, however, to conclude that Grace played no part in Calvin's success. He had announced that "the business of America is business," and he proceeded to act as though government were an arm of business. In his appointments and in his actions on tax and tariff matters, he paid careful attention to the needs of the business community. Having a wife who did not divulge her opinions on any important matter fitted in with his image of the president as corporate head.

But Grace was hardly inconspicuous, and Calvin profited from her visibility. For a politician who found it very difficult to show interest in the people around him, having a wife who charmed everyone she met was a decided advantage. Grace was frequently photographed hugging children or playing with her pet raccoon or her dog, Rob Roy. Florence Harriman, who was acquainted with several presidents, pronounced Grace's "vivacity and savoir faire" the biggest success of the administration. Grace characterized her role as Calvin's "safety valve." A 1926 *New Yorker* profile described her as his "psychological frame" and after offering the supreme accolade—a comparison with Dolley Madison—concluded, "Few

White House chatelaines have been so genuinely popular in Washington." *Good Housekeeping* included Grace on its list of most admired women, the only one without a profession of her own, and the *Pictorial Review* praised her for complementing her husband's personality and giving him "the light touch."

Visitors to the White House who had a chance to see Grace Coolidge in action reinforced this view with their own stories. When their son John brought his fiancée to dinner, she was noticeably nervous, and although the daughter of a governor and accustomed to meeting important people, she could not quite manage her plate of fish. A large piece plopped on her lap. The president broke the ensuing silence with his New England twang: "Miss Connecticut has spilled on her lovely gown," and it remained for a thoughtful First Lady to provide the talcum powder.

At official receptions, the president curtly nodded to people and quickly passed from one obligatory handshake to the next while Grace's exceptional memory for names and her genuine concern for guests' comfort made them feel at ease. People meeting her for the first time reported they liked her immediately. A tourist who managed to get an invitation to one of the twice-weekly receptions confessed that she felt awkward and feared she would do something wrong, but the president's wife assured her that would only make her more interesting.

The sharp contrast between charming Grace Coolidge and taciturn Calvin mystified many of their closest friends. The only child of a Vermont engineer and his wife, Grace showed such irrepressible humor and outgoing personality all the way through the local schools and the state university that nobody, least of all her mother, could see what attracted her to the rather eccentric lawyer whom she married. Not long after their wedding, the Coolidges attended his tenth reunion of the Amherst Class of '95, and another young wife remarked to her husband that she could not see "how that sulky, red-haired little man ever won that pretty, charming woman." Dwight Morrow, whose wife had made the comment, offered his own opinion that they would all hear one day from the sulky little man, but his wife replied that it would be because of Grace. Like many First Ladies, Grace apparently recognized somewhat sooner than others the potential for success in the man she married.

Many stories emphasize the impish sense of humor that Grace and Calvin Coolidge shared, and that trait may explain their attraction to each other more than any other. That they perceived incongruity and humor in diverse ways increased the magnetism. She had been watering flowers at Clarke Institute for the deaf, where she taught, when she happened to look up one morning and see a man shaving himself near the window. What drew Grace's attention was the felt hat he had planted firmly on his head when his only other garments were his underwear. Grace laughed so loudly that he noticed her and very soon he arranged a meeting to explain to the slim, dark-haired teacher that he anchored the hat on his dampened hair in order to help control an unruly lock of hair.

Regarding his wife's cooking, Calvin Coolidge was merciless. He delighted in dropping one of her freshly baked biscuits on the floor and stomping his foot loudly at the same time to emphasize its lack of delicacy, and he suggested that her pie crust recipe should go to the road commissioner as a substitute for the paving material currently used. Grace, who had no illusions about her ability as a cook, took this as well as his other ego-deflaters in the same imperturbable way. Sometimes she came back with some of her own, frequently zeroing in on his reputation as a man of few words.

On one of their weekend cruises on the Potomac, Calvin had sat silently through an entire meal without so much as acknowledging the two women seated beside him. The next morning, one of the women entered the dining room as Calvin was asking Grace where the two guests were and heard Grace explain that they were resting because they had been "exhausted by your conversation last evening." Calvin's refusal to say very much led to many stories, including one about two men discussing the Coolidges. The first man pointed out that Grace had taught the deaf to speak, and the second responded, "So why didn't she teach Cal?"

Grace Coolidge appeared to accept with equanimity this quirk in her husband as well as his frugality, which she had encountered very early in her marriage. When they returned from a one-week honeymoon in Montreal, cut short so Calvin could campaign for election to the local school board, they moved into a hotel suite in Northampton, Massachusetts. A few months later, they rented the quarters which they continued to occupy until Calvin won national office. When the local hotel went out of business, the Coolidges purchased the supplies so that for years their linens and silverware carried the marking "Norwood Hotel." Grace would tell a joke about how Calvin, soon after their marriage, had presented her with socks to be darned. Since there were fifty-two pairs of them, she decided that he must have been saving them for some time, and she inquired if that was the reason he had married her. "No," he had answered, "but I find it mighty handy."

On only one subject did Calvin forget his frugality. In purchasing clothing for Grace, he could be very extravagant. Nothing was too good for her. When he saw a particularly striking dress or hat, he brought it home for her to try and she cooperated by wearing his selections even when her friends pronounced the colors too flamboyant or the styles inappropriate. While he was still a struggling lawyer, saving postage costs by sending his secretary out on foot to deliver bills, he paid $19.98 for a rose picture hat for Grace and no one recalled his regretting the expenditure. In the White House, he pouted if she wore the same gown twice, causing her secretary to conclude that she had never seen a man who took more interest in his wife's clothes than did Calvin Coolidge.

Grace's natural dignity and determination to remain just what she was earned her the praise and the satisfaction that no clothing extravagance could have matched. She arrived in Washington, conspicuous as the wife of the vice-president, but with little experience outside small towns. Rather than try to compete with other, more sophisticated women, she relaxed in what she was, and later confessed that she could not remember a single embarrassing moment. She recalled that at her first big party, she had stood in a "simple gown by a village dressmaker" and received guests alongside the hostess "resplendent in a gorgeous creation of brocaded white satin by Worth." Yet she remembered it as "all very gay" and "a wonderful time."

Grace Coolidge's casualness appeared refreshing to Washingtonians accustomed to formality and pretentiousness in First Ladies. As wife of the vice-president, Grace presided capably over meetings of Senate wives but she rarely missed a chance to play the comic. On one occasion when someone stood up to thank her for providing ham and potatoes, she banged a fork on the table and reminded the group, "Don't forget I brought a cake too."

Although Calvin Coolidge permitted his wife to give no interviews while she was in the White House, her exuberance generated so many stories that the public felt an acquaintance with her as with few other First Ladies. On shopping trips to the local department stores, she was often recognized. When a salesclerk remarked on her resemblance to the First Lady and suggested that she must often be mistaken for her, Grace murmured, "Sometimes I am," and continued her shopping.

Her husband laid down strict rules for Grace's White House tenure, and she followed them in the manner of an obedient child. Once when she had decided that the White House stables provided an excellent opportunity, she secretly outfitted herself and went out with a riding instructor. The next day Washington papers carried prominent headlines: "Mrs. Coolidge Learns to Ride." At breakfast the president read the item and then turned to his wife: "I think," he said, "you will find that you will get along at this job fully as well if you do not try anything new."

That dictum continued to limit her activities for the rest of her husband's term. When she appeared one day in a stylish culotte outfit, Calvin suggested that none of the Coolidges had ever worn anything like that and she returned it. He bragged that no photographer had ever caught him with a cigar in his mouth, although he chewed one frequently, and she carefully confined her smoking to private places. On one of the rare occasions when Grace found herself out dancing and having a good time at a party, someone volunteered, "I wish your husband could have been here." Grace replied quickly, "If he were, I wouldn't be."

In explaining her White House years, Grace Coolidge projected the same detachment that later characterized Eleanor Roosevelt's statements. Grace wrote, "This was I and yet not I—this was the wife of the President of the United States and she took precedence over me; my personal likes and dislikes must be subordinated to the consideration of those things which were required of her." Not until her husband's presidential term had ended would she express herself more fully.

The most extensive remodeling of the White House since the turn of the century was done during the Coolidge administration but Grace had little choice in undertaking her part in it. The Office of Public Parks and Buildings had informed the Coolidges in 1923 that the mansion had deteriorated badly and needed extensive renovation, but work did not begin until early 1927. The president's family moved to a house on Dupont Circle and then took an extended summer vacation in South Dakota. When Grace returned to Washington, she obtained Congress's permission to accept period pieces to furnish the White House, but Americans were not in a generous mood and few gifts arrived. Her own offering was a coverlet which she had crocheted, one small square per month, for the Lincoln bedroom.

The Coolidge sons, John (born 1906) and Calvin, Jr. (born 1908) absorbed some of Grace's view that politicians' families should remain in the background. When Calvin, Jr. received a letter addressed to "First Boy of the Land," he responded, "You are mistaken in calling me the First Boy of the Land since I have done nothing. It is my father who is President. Rather the First Boy of the

Land would be some boy who had distinguished himself through his own actions."

This particular anecdote was recalled by Grace Coolidge after Calvin, Jr.'s death. In the summer of 1924 when his father was about to be nominated to run for a term of his own, Calvin, Jr. got a blister on his toe. He left it unattended, developed blood poisoning, and died within days. Whatever ideas the Coolidges had about preserving privacy in the White House, this tragedy thrust them even more into the national spotlight, and hundreds of thousands of messages poured into Washington. The president's wife wore black and tempered her usual gaiety, but she resumed a full schedule within weeks.

A woman with Grace's spirit might have brought a new dimension to the job of president's wife but she chose to accede to the wishes of her husband and limit her activities to those her predecessors had made traditional—working with the Girl Scouts and giving receptions. When prevailed upon to give a speech, she injected a note of humor by using sign language, which she had learned in her work with the deaf, a language that no one else in the room understood. She remained the most uncontrolling of individuals, never seeming to mind how many guests showed up unannounced for lunch or when she would learn what Calvin expected of her next. When White House staff inquired about her travel plans, she frequently replied that they should inform her as soon as they learned the answer from the president.

If observers perceived her as mysterious, they were mistaken— she simply waited until she left the White House to "come back to myself." After Calvin's term in Washington ended in 1929, she published her poetry, and after his death in 1933, she gave interviews. In a series of articles entitled "The Real Calvin Coolidge," Grace revealed a great deal about herself. During the nearly twenty-five years that she survived her husband, she matured beyond the childlike woman who had been First Lady and began to speak out on issues such as early intervention in World War II. She sold the house she had shared with Calvin (and the furniture in it), toured Europe, and then went to live with a friend in Northampton. When the WAVES came to train at Smith College, she offered them the use of her house. Her work to win better education for the deaf continued until her death in July 1957.

During their marriage, Calvin's choice of a political career almost certainly limited his wife's actions. What she might have done in other circumstances, without the constraints imposed by marriage to the president, remains unknowable, but she herself related an anecdote which lends interest to the question. A painter came to the White House to do her portrait, in which he rendered her uncharacteristically solemn. When Grace's son asked why, the painter replied, "Because I once saw in your mother's face a look of resignation."

LOU HENRY HOOVER

Lou HENRY HOOVER, who replaced Grace Coolidge in the White House in 1929, differed in style and interests from her predecessor but was just as complex. Rather than reflecting the comic-serious dichotomy of Grace Coolidge, Lou Hoover helped make way for an activist and modern First Lady while remaining very much a retiring gentlewoman of the nineteenth century. In so doing, Lou showed many of the same contradictions that marked her husband's administration.

Although the Hoovers moved into the White House in March 1929, confident and optimistic about their chances for success, the president lost his halo with the stock market crash in October 1929. Before his term ended, the Bureau of Labor Statistics would report that one in four Americans was jobless, lending credence to the judgment that this was the most devastating depression in the country's history. The president reluctantly reexamined his own views about the role of government and took contradictory positions on the matter—first saying that it was not government's responsibility to intercede, then later establishing the Federal Farm Board and Reconstruction Finance Corporation with billions of dollars to assist farmers, banks, and businesses.

When asked about her own interests and accomplishments, Lou's pronouncements were just as puzzling and inconsistent: "My chief hobbies are my husband and my children," she explained in 1921, failing to note that she had given speeches on two continents in behalf of a long list of causes and that her translation into English of a Latin mining text had won an important professional award.

The remarkably parallel lives of Lou Henry and Herbert Hoover began the same year (1874) in small Iowa towns less than one hundred miles apart but did not intersect until twenty years later when they met in California. Lou's youthful interests had run closer to those of boys than of most girls. With only one sister, eight years younger than she, and a sickly mother, Lou's energy drew her to her father, who introduced her to the pleasures of camping, horseback riding, and hiking. When time came for college, she chose first a normal school that boasted "the best gymnasium west of the Mississippi" and then switched to a teachers' college from which she earned a certificate in 1894. Neither of those schools nor a clerking job in her father's bank satisfied Lou, and not until she had a chance encounter with geology did she find her direction. A public lecture by a Stanford professor led her to enroll in the university as the first woman to major in geology.

Herbert Hoover's route to the same department in the same university had been more direct, and during Lou's freshman term, he was already a senior. By the time she graduated, he was already earning $40,000 a year as an engineer in Australia.

The same Stanford degree in geology, when earned by a woman, got fewer job offers, and Lou taught school for a few months before Herbert wired his proposal from Australia. He wanted to accept an invitation to head China's mine program if she would go along as his wife, so his proposal had two parts: marry him and live in China. Almost from their first meeting, the Hoover partnership had a particularly international and ecumenical quality. In order to catch a ship for China the next day, they rushed their marriage ceremony, and because they could locate neither a Quaker minister (Herbert's religion) nor an Episcopalian (Lou's faith), they settled for a civil ceremony performed by a family friend who happened to be a Catholic priest. With little time to pack for their honeymoon, they filled their suitcases with books on Chinese history and culture, so that they had plenty to read on the long trip to Tientsin.

Within months of arriving in China, the Hoovers found themselves in the middle of an attack, supported by the Empress Dowager Tz'u-hsi, to rid the country of all foreigners. In late 1899, a secret society, the "Boxers," began to launch violent attacks on the parts of the international community that had an influence on the local economy and culture, such as railroad construction, missionary work, and mining. The Hoovers quickly decided that expeditions into the country's interior were too perilous for Lou, although she had originally intended to go, and by June 1900, Herbert called in all his workers.

To protect themselves, Tientsin's foreigners barricaded themselves in their homes along the edge of the city behind a wall fashioned out of bags of sugar and grain. Then they watched their numbers multiply as Chinese nationals, who had aligned with outsiders by converting to Christianity or taking jobs with international companies, asked for refuge. Supplies became scarce as days stretched into weeks. A herd of dairy cattle furnished milk and meat, but the closest water source lay outside the barricade and residents had to sneak out at night with buckets. With only two physicians to tend the wounded, Lou Hoover volunteered to help, even though that required dodging bullets to ride her bicycle to the makeshift hospital.

Because their own house at the edge of the settlement seemed particularly vulnerable, the Hoovers moved to a friend's residence at the center of the compound but then returned just before their area came under attack. An American journalist who had taken refuge in the Hoovers' house told how Lou had run to the door at the first shelling to see where it had hit. A big hole in the backyard told her the answer. Expecting other shellings to follow, she sat down in the living room and dealt herself a game of solitaire. Even though a Japanese soldier in front of her house was blown to bits and the post of the stairway behind her splintered, she continued turning over the cards.

Although she lived in Tientsin for less than two years, Lou developed a lifelong interest in China, particularly in porcelains of the Ming and K'ang Hsi periods. She added Mandarin to the other languages she spoke fluently—an achievement her husband never matched—and after they left China she kept his very limited Chinese vocabulary usable by relying on Mandarin whenever she needed to communicate privately with him in the presence of others.

With their usefulness in China ended, the Hoovers moved to London, the world's mining capital during what Herbert called "the golden age of mining." Herbert became a partner in Bewick, Moreing and Company and until 1908, when the partnership ended, their "Red Roof" house served as home base for their family and as a gathering place for London's foreign community. Herbert had undergone no social metamorphosis since college. Conversational awkwardness still marked him in all discussions but those of mining —one woman described him as "the rudest man in London"—but his wife's charm compensated and drew guests to their table.

Lou's balancing of household management and travel in the first decade of her marriage invites comparison with Louisa Adams a century earlier. When two sons were born to the Hoovers in 1903 and 1907, Lou took them on the road almost immediately: Herbert, Jr. left London to go to Australia when he was five weeks old and his brother, Allan, began his first trip to Burma at the same young age. The Hoovers, after circling the globe more than once with their sons, insisted that infants traveled more easily than adults. After 1908, the family moved less, but Herbert still ran mining consulting offices around the world from San Francisco to Petrograd. In one year (1910) his wife and sons joined him in the British Isles, France, Russia, Burma, Korea, and Japan.

While her children were still toddlers, Lou Hoover undertook her one enduring intellectual achievement—the translation into English of a sixteenth-century text on metals. *Agricola's De Re Metallica* offered a significant challenge because its German author, George Bauer, had coined some of the terms when he published the work in Latin in 1556. Finding English equivalents required extensive knowledge of both science and language—an unlikely combination in one person, as reviewers pointed out when the Hoovers finally finished the task after five years. When the work was privately printed in 1912, with both Hoovers sharing equal billing in its translation, it won the Mining and Metallurgical Society's gold award and considerable attention from the scholarly community.

War broke out in Europe in the summer of 1914 while the Hoovers were in London preparing to return to California. Herbert delayed his trip to assist stranded Americans find sailings home and then to oversee food distribution to Belgium and northern France. While her husband earned a reputation as an efficient food administrator in Europe, Lou Hoover traveled with less fanfare back and forth between England and the United States. In London she worked with the American Women's Committee to set up canteens, maintain a war hospital, and operate a fleet of Red Cross ambulances. She even helped start a knitting factory to assist unemployed women. In the United States, she gave speeches to attract money for her European activities, raising $100,000 in the San Francisco Bay area alone. At the invitation of the Stanford faculty, she spoke to them about unrestricted German submarine warfare.

When the United States entered the war in the spring of 1917, Herbert returned to Washington to serve as food administrator, and Lou complemented his role by publicizing strategies for food conservation. She invited reporters into her home to show how she achieved "wheatless and meatless days" and cut sugar consumption below the suggested limits. The same woman who would later cringe and refuse when reporters sought interviews with her in the White House allowed the *Ladies Home Journal* to publish "Dining with the Hoovers" in March 1918, and include information on what she fed her family. Besides acting the part of public model housewife, Lou helped start a club, a cafeteria, and a residence, all for young women who had come to Washington to work during the war.

After 1921 when her husband entered President Harding's Cabinet as secretary of commerce, Lou Hoover continued her public, activist role. The time seemed right to finish what Elizabeth Monroe and Louisa Adams had begun a century earlier, and Lou resolved to stop the mindless "leaving of cards" that had been traditional for cabinet wives since the beginning of the republic. According to Herbert, she rebelled at wasting several afternoons a week and she got the cabinet spouses to agree to an announcement that the afternoon calls would stop.

Nothing about Lou Hoover in the early 1920s suggests she would ever retreat from active leadership, especially of women and young people. In 1924, in the wake of revelations about the Teapot Dome scandal of the Harding administration, she called a special conference to emphasize women's responsibility to speak out on the dangers of dishonesty in government. Lou persuaded the National Amateur Athletic Association, on whose board she served as the only woman, to form an advisory council of athletic directors to encourage physical education for women "in every institution" in the country. When invited to speak to a convention of teenagers, she used the opportunity to exhort the girls to plan to combine marriage with a career, and she volunteered her own opinion that anyone who fell back on children as an excuse for not working outside the home was "lazy."

After her husband became president, Lou Hoover sized up the White House as though it were just another of the many residences where she would make a "backdrop for Bertie" and pronounced it "as bleak as a New England barn." She quickly rearranged virtually every piece of furniture in it and added some of her own things from California. Within three months, nothing movable remained where the Coolidges had left it, causing one house employee to quip that Lou would next reverse the positions of the elevator and the spiral staircase. Of more permanent importance, Lou organized a systematic cataloging of the mansion's furnishings and assigned her friend and secretary, Dare Stark, to write a book about the White House. Although Stark did not complete that project, she did publish articles calling attention to the dearth of reliable information about the house and its furnishings.

Unlike other presidents' wives who felt motivated by their new visibility to make themselves over, Lou Hoover seemed to retreat even from the accomplishments she had. Learning a new language, high on the agendas of many First Ladies, held little urgency—she already spoke five—but when questioned about her ability, she equivocated. Other White House chatelaines had embarked on ambitious buying trips to outfit themselves beyond criticism, but Lou, whose bank account would have allowed for any extravagance, paid little attention to clothes. Rather than attempting to slice a couple of years off her age, she seemed to take pleasure, one maid decided, in looking like the grandmother she was.

The White House staff found the new First Lady a contradictory mix of international customs and small-town America. At Christmas, when she arranged for the family to trek through a darkened house, the girls and women ringing handbells and the men and boys carrying candles, the staff dismissed it as "ghostly" and "another of

Mrs. Hoover's ideas." Although she had a reputation for liking to talk (servants called it "broadcasting"), she relied on hand signals during official parties to communicate with employees. Each dropped handkerchief or raised finger carried a specific command: move the guests more quickly through the reception line, or more slowly; replenish the punch. What Lou had concocted as an efficient innovation—or perhaps a variation on the dressage exercises she learned as a rider—appeared to the staff as dehumanizing and complicated. They had trouble "reading" her, they complained, and sometimes waited carefully for a particular signal and then missed it because of the subtlety with which it was delivered.

Unlike the Coolidges, who were unaccustomed to having servants and tended to treat them as equals, the Hoovers had supervised a large household staff since their days in China. More than one disgruntled White House employee complained in print about the Hoovers' uncaring treatment. The housekeeper, Ava Long, described how "company, company, company" often arrived on such short notice that she had to contrive out of leftovers enough servings for dozens of people. On one occasion she had shopped for six, only to learn at twelve-thirty that forty guests would arrive for lunch at one. She instructed the cook to grind up all the icebox's contents and serve the result as a croquette with mushroom sauce. When one guest requested the recipe, Long dubbed it, with a touch of sarcasm, "White House Surprise Supreme." The Hoovers liked company so much, the housekeeper reported, that they dined alone only once a year, evidently oblivious to the work they imposed on their employees. Eventually Long quit the job, and her colleague, the head usher, singled out the Hoovers as among the least likable of his bosses when he published *Forty-two Years at the White House.*

Other observers praised Lou Hoover's interest in people as her greatest asset. She was indefatigable, they said, in her willingness to welcome groups to the White House, and in her busiest year (1932), she gave forty teas and received eighty organizations. Camp Rapidan, the Hoover retreat in the Shenandoah Mountains, became an extension of the capital when Lou Hoover invited representatives of the Girl Scouts to accompany her there or used the camp as a setting to speak by radio to the country's youth. Much of her generosity, including funds for a school for poor children near Camp Rapidan, was supported by her own pocketbook.

A very deep prejudice against publicizing her personal life kept secret from most Americans the more appealing side of Lou Hoover. She shared with her husband a deep resentment, he later wrote, "of the intrusion of the press and public into our family life." Even he did not know, until after his wife died in 1944 and he was settling her estate, how many people benefited from her largesse. Some of those whom she had supported regularly for years wrote when their checks stopped, wanting to know what had happened. A desire to protect the privacy of people she had helped contributed to the decision to keep her papers closed until forty years after her death.

What makes Lou Hoover's attitude toward publicity more intriguing is her willingness to take a public role as First Lady. Recognizing the value of radio, which had begun to carry inauguration ceremonies in 1925, she arranged to speak to a nationwide audience. She even set up a lab on the second floor of the White House to "test" her performances and improve her radio talks. A speech professor who later analyzed recordings of the talks, judged Lou's voice "tinny," but admitted that the equipment was poorly adjusted for women's voices since so few of them had the opportunity to use it.

Unimaginative in phrasing, Lou's radio speeches to young people had a definitely feminist slant. On a Saturday evening in June 1929, when she spoke from Camp Rapidan to a group of 4-H club members, the National Broadcasting Company carried the message coast to coast. After praising the joys of camping, Lou urged her listeners to help make their homes more attractive places, a responsibility, she said, as much of boys as of girls. She urged her listeners to consider what home meant and then chided the boys to help with the dishes and the cleaning: "Boys, remember you are just as great factors in the home making of the family as are the girls."

In other ways, Lou Hoover exerted a surprisingly modern and liberated influence on her husband's administration. She invited noticeably pregnant women (who had traditionally been excluded) to join her in reception lines, and she encouraged women to pursue individual careers. When her husband issued Executive Order 5984 in December 1932, it amended the Civil Service Rule VII to require nominations "without regard to sex," unless the duties to be performed could be satisfactorily performed by only men or women. Myra Gutin, a careful student of the Hoover record, believes that Lou influenced her husband's decisions in this and other matters. In his single term, President Hoover named seven women to positions requiring Senate approval, bringing the total up to twenty, double what it had been in 1920.

On matters delicate to the Washington political community, Lou Hoover preferred to increase her work load rather than offend anyone. When a protocol feud erupted between Dolly Gann, prominent sister of the vice-president, and Alice Roosevelt Longworth, longtime leader in capital society, Lou gave two parties so that neither would be assigned precedence over the other. Such a solution caused one *New York Times* reporter to announce "a particularly Quaker victory."

When the time came to entertain wives of congressmen, Lou Hoover had to decide what to do regarding the wife of Chicago congressman Oscar DePriest, the first Negro to serve in the legislature since Reconstruction. No black had been a guest at the White House since Theodore Roosevelt dined with Booker T. Washington in 1901, and Lou Hoover understood that an invitation to Jessie DePriest could bring unpleasant repercussions. She sounded out a few of the other wives, found twelve who would not embarrass the congressman's wife, and then gave a separate tea for them.

When word of the invitation got out, several Southern publications objected that Lou Hoover had "defiled" the White House, and the *Mobile Alabama Press* charged that Lou had offered the nation "an arrogant insult." Social mixing of the two races would not do, newspapers charged, especially in the nation's most famous home.

Lou Hoover's decision to follow through with the DePriest tea, in
spite of criticism, reinforced her reputation as extremely egalitarian.
She drove herself around Washington and invited a wide variety of
people to dinner, causing one reporter to note in *Woman's Home
Companion,* "She does not keep the rules, but mixes the great and the
near-great with the obscure and the near obscure."

A woman willing to brave so much controversy might have been
expected to open up to the press, but she was far less open with
reporters in the White House than she had been in her early days in
Washington. The Hoover White House provided such a dry spell for
thirsty reporters that one of them, Bess Furman of the Washington
AP, contrived to enter the family quarters by passing herself off as a
Girl Scout Christmas caroler. Dressed in the traditional uniform,
hair tucked under her cap, Furman went in "as one of the taller
girls" and moved undetected within arm's reach of people who
encountered her everyday as a reporter. During the carols that she
could not sing, Furman kept her face down, furtively taking in details so she could write an account of how a president's family
celebrated Christmas. In a burst of bravado, Furman sent a copy of
the article to the First Lady, who marked it "nice story," without
ever discovering who supplied the details.

Lou Hoover's reticence in the White House extended to policy
matters as well as publicity, thus underlining the traditional side of
her view of a wife's role. If she differed with Herbert on any significant matter, she kept the difference to herself. She tailored her own
suggestions for economic recovery to fit her husband's remedies,
and her public pronouncements on how to end the Great Depression reinforced her husband's reputation for relying on voluntarism. In March 1931, when the country edged toward the trough of
unemployment, she went on radio to thank American women for
their donations of food and clothing. The First Lady urged women
to volunteer in one of three ways: by identifying people in need and

determining how they could be helped, by working in hospitals and visiting-nurse programs, and by setting up recreation opportunities for unemployed young people. Even after Herbert lost the 1932 election (and Lou heard that one indignant mother had changed her young son's name from Herbert Hoover Jones to Franklin Roosevelt Jones), she took to the airwaves to encourage women to volunteer. If everybody helped, she said, there would be plenty of food and clothing for all.

More than most of her predecessors, Lou Hoover had exceptional ability and training for leadership, and she foreshadowed Eleanor Roosevelt in her formidable energy and active participation in her husband's presidency. Alice Roosevelt Longworth (who was never particularly charitable to her famous cousin) credited Lou with being the first president's wife "to take a public part on her own." But Lou's natural reticence unfortunately isolated her. Lou preferred a safe course, protecting her husband by inviting guests to the White House for his pleasure rather than for his growth, and diverting conversation from difficult topics. While other presidents' wives sought to watch out for their husbands' health, Lou gave the impression of standing guard against challenges to Herbert's thinking—challenges that might have moved him in other directions than those he took.

Not long before her death in 1944, a letter that Lou Hoover wrote to her sons and husband contains a revealing message about herself. This woman who started out camping and fishing like a boy, and then proceeded to earn a geology degree equal to her husband's, ended up describing her life as entirely peripheral to him and their sons: "I have been lucky," she wrote, "to have my trail move alongside that of such exceptional men and boys."

Together, the three First Ladies of the 1920s reflect that decade well since they present contradictions and inconsistencies rather than one clear line of development. But they also form a bridge to the period that followed, and it is difficult to imagine Eleanor Roosevelt initiating the changes she did without the foundations laid by her immediate predecessors—in experimenting with the press, speaking out on important issues, and extending women's rights and opportunites.

Breaking Precedents and Reaffirming Old Ones
1933–1961

EVEN BEFORE THE 1932 presidential election, the new First Lady made clear that she meant to break some precedents if her husband won. Just how much she was responding to the special urgency of the Great Depression remains unclear. Perhaps she would have been just as active and innovative a First Lady if her husband had presided over a prosperous nation. But most Americans in 1933 were neither prosperous nor optimistic. The previous summer, Midwestern farmers, disgusted by the low prices they were receiving, dumped their milk. Then thousands of jobless veterans marched to Washington and set up camps of shacks and tents, dubbed Hoovervilles. By the time Franklin Roosevelt took his oath of office in March 1933, many of the country's banks had closed and business halted.

ELEANOR ROOSEVELT ROOSEVELT

Surely the desperation and difficult times Americans confronted in the early 1930s called out for new approaches, and Eleanor Roosevelt (1933–1945) complied on several fronts. She had hinted during the presidential campaign in 1932 that she and Franklin sometimes disagreed, but the real shocker was her announcement that she meant to keep—even if she became First Lady—the job she had held while Franklin had served as New York's governor. During his four years in the Albany state house, Eleanor had traveled down to New York City to teach three days a week at her school on East Sixty-fifth Street, and she saw no reason why his transfer to Washington should alter her schedule or stop her from doing what she "enjoyed more than anything I have ever done."

Such independence came late to Eleanor Roosevelt, after a childhood notable for its loneliness and lack of strong female models, and a marriage dominated for many years by her mother-in-law. The only daughter of an exceptionally beautiful woman, Eleanor had suffered greatly as a child when she heard herself described as an unattractive "Granny." Nor did her confidence grow after her mother's death when she and her younger brother, Hall, came under the control of a stern and distant grandmother. Only the erratic attentions of her *bon vivant* father saved that period from becoming, for Eleanor, an uninterrupted bad memory. Much later in her life, after she had married and had children of her own, she singled out the times spent with her father as the best of her life.

When his excessive drinking and playboy lifestyle led to an early
death, those pleasant interludes abruptly ended and strict Grandmother Hall took an ever larger role in Eleanor's life until, at age
fifteen, she was enrolled in a boarding school in England. There she
met a strong, thinking, caring, Parisian, Marie Souvestre, who had a
powerful impact on her young student. "She gave me an intellectual
curiosity and a standard of living which have never left me," Eleanor
wrote years later. On trips across Europe Souvestre exposed her
young student to the pleasures of good food and comfort but also to
the responsibility of caring how other people lived.

Three years with Mademoiselle Souvestre could hardly cancel out
the fifteen years that went before, and Eleanor returned to New York
to do the expected: make her debut and marry at the first opportunity. Although she later admitted that at the time of her marriage,
she had little idea of what loving or being a wife and mother meant,
she quietly accepted the mold that had been cast for women of her
class and time.

Urbane and handsome Franklin Delano Roosevelt could not have
seen beauty or sophistication or confidence in his bride in 1905, but
like many of the men who later became president, he made an
advantageous marriage. In this respect he illustrates a remarkable
pattern evident in presidents' lives. Most of the men who later
achieved the country's highest office married up into socially or
economically superior strata of American society, while the women
married into more adventure, travel, or risk than they had found in
their parents' home. Franklin's choice of his distant cousin was
hardly social climbing, but the marriage helped him in two ways. As
Joseph Lash, the Roosevelts' biographer noted, young Franklin's
"dissemblings contrasted with Eleanor's scrupulousness." Lash
concluded that she appealed to Franklin because he recognized the
need to temper his frivolous, easygoing approach to life. Another
motive may have been working, at least subconsciously. Eleanor's
uncle, Theodore Roosevelt, then resided at the White House, and a
politically ambitious young man—even one who intended to align

with the Democrats—could do worse than marry the favorite niece of an immensely popular Republican president.

For her part, Eleanor recognized the difficulty of fitting into Franklin's world. His mother, Sara, with whom the couple lived, imperiously controlled the household; and Franklin's friends, with their cigarette smoking and quick wit, made Eleanor so painfully aware of her rigid views and conversational inadequacies that she often begged to stay behind when he went out partying.

Six pregnancies between 1906 and 1916 left Eleanor little time to gain confidence or acquire control over her life. Even the nurses she hired for her children intimidated her and made her feel inadequate. She tried to improve her French and German but found such study unrewarding, and when she ventured down to the Lower East Side to teach in a settlement house, her mother-in-law advised her to stop because of her fear that Eleanor might bring home diseases.

If Eleanor had shared her husband's interest in politics, she might have found a way to break out of her mold earlier but on that subject she lacked both knowledge and curiosity. The intricacies of government remained a mystery to her, and she later admitted that at the time of her marriage she could not have explained the difference between state and national legislatures. At the 1912 Democratic convention in Baltimore, she found the confusion and noise so objectionable that she left early and joined her children at the family's summer retreat on Campobello Island in New Brunswick, Canada. When Franklin's jubilant telegram arrived later to announce Woodrow Wilson's nomination, she failed to comprehend the reason for his excitement. Her husband's support of woman's suffrage about the same time shocked Eleanor, and she realized that she had never given the matter serious thought, although it had been the central objective of the feminist movement for more than half a century.

About 1917, the shy and insecure Eleanor Roosevelt began a metamorphosis so enormous in its consequences that historians have debated its causes. By then in her thirties, she had already

managed a partial escape from her domineering mother-in-law
when Franklin's appointment as assistant secretary of the Navy took
them to Washington in 1913. Sara Roosevelt still came down to
rearrange the furniture, but as soon as she left, Eleanor could put it
back. And put it back she did. More important, Eleanor had the
examples of other Washington wives who were breaking away from
old traditions and accomplishing something on their own.

In part, they were drawn out by the necessities of war. In Washington, as in other American cities, the entry of the country into World
War I created shortages of male workers so that women ran street-
cars, delivered mail, and took other jobs that under peacetime conditions they would not have gotten. Eleanor Roosevelt joined with
wives of other government officials to open canteens for servicemen
stationed in the capital and to visit wounded and sick men. This was
the kind of activism and involvement that she had so admired in
Mademoiselle Souvestre, and Eleanor could hardly conceal her enthusiasm: "I loved it," she wrote later, "I simply ate it up." Her
cousin, Alice Roosevelt Longworth, singled out the war years as the
time when Eleanor went "public."

About the same time that Eleanor found reasons outside her
home to draw her out, she found others inside to push her in the
same direction. She had opened by mistake a letter to Franklin and
found irrefutable evidence that he was having an affair with Eleanor's former social secretary, Lucy Mercer. He refused Eleanor's
offer to divorce him, and the marriage continued until his death. But
the union became a formal one, the distance between the two partners rather formally defined and rigidly observed. She frequently
referred to him in the manner of a trusted employee discussing a
superior, waiting for "my regular time to see him." When he announced he would run for governor, she learned of his decision by
radio, along with other New York voters.

In writing about her life, Eleanor acknowledged that she began to
change some of her attitudes before 1920, but she avoided marital
problems in detailing the reasons. Her Grandmother Hall had died

in 1918, Eleanor explained, causing her to wonder whether that woman's life and those of her children might not have been happier had she developed her own interests rather than attempting to live vicariously through others. Grandmother Hall had shown artistic talent in her youth but had died without developing her ability to paint, and Eleanor resolved not to miss such opportunities for herself.

Most of the credit for Eleanor's increased self-confidence went, by her own account, not to negative examples but to positive ones. Politically shrewd, risk-taking ancestors may have motivated her—relatives sometimes noted that she resembled her Uncle Theodore, her father's brother, more than any of his own children did. Eleanor herself pointed out that her Uncle Theodore often included his two sisters in discussions during his governorship and presidency. The older sister, whom Eleanor called "Auntie Bye," lived in Washington, and Eleanor recalled that she could not think of one serious subject that came up during his presidency that Uncle Theodore did not discuss with his sister. "He may have made his own decisions," Eleanor concluded, "but talking with her seemed to clarify things for him."

The League of Women Voters also exposed her to the excitement of political participation, and the Women's Trade Union League reawakened her interest in helping others. She owed a large debt, she often said, to settlement house leaders such as Mary Simkhovitch and to League workers such as Elizabeth Read and Esther Lape. By helping her understand politics and social movements, they built her confidence in herself. Eleanor failed to note what her friends saw so clearly—that the public activities gave new meaning to her life and close friendships that substituted for the lack of warmth in her marriage.

To one tutor Eleanor Roosevelt gave particular credit. Louis Howe, the wizened newspaperman who took her husband as his protegé, recognized during Franklin's 1920 run for vice-president that Eleanor had the potential to campaign and speak out on issues, but not until Franklin's bout with polio in 1921 and subsequent paralysis did the necessity of developing her skills become clear. If Franklin meant to pursue politics, he needed an exceptionally active and supportive spouse. Louis Howe urged Eleanor to take speaking lessons to increase her self-confidence and lower her high pitch. When she balked at facing crowds, he cajoled her into trying until eventually she could speak comfortably and effectively to large groups.

Eleanor's energy and confidence grew rapidly in the 1920s, inspired by the support of other women, cheered on by Howe, and persuaded by the necessity of her husband's career. The exuberance of her colleagues who felt they could accomplish whatever they set out to do also affected her. She formed two business partnerships with other women: one to operate a school in New York City and the other to manufacture furniture at Hyde Park. As though bursting with long-stored energy, she became involved in New York State politics and served on the Platform Committee at the 1926 state Democratic convention. Buoyed by her new success, Eleanor began publishing magazine articles, some of them advising other wives how to run their households and care for their children. The shy bride who had retreated from managing her own family had matured into a confident teacher of others.

In August 1930, *Good Housekeeping* singled out the prolific wife of New York's governor as the "ideal modern wife." In an interview with the author, M. K. Wisehart, Eleanor outlined what she thought being a wife meant. It still combined the three roles of mother, homemaker, and husband's partner as it always had, but she explained that the relative importance of each had shifted. While women had formerly put most emphasis on motherhood, they now stressed being full partners to their husbands. "Everything else depends upon the success of wife and husband in their personal relation," Eleanor was quoted as saying. "Partnership. Companionship. It is a major requirement for modern marriage." Eleanor also urged wives to develop interests of their own so they would not smother their children with excessive attention or depend too heavily on their husbands' careers for their own sense of achievement.

Her own definition of marriage evidently guided Eleanor in the White House, which she had entered reluctantly. "I never wanted to be a President's wife and I don't want it now," she told her good friend Lorena Hickok in 1932. "You don't believe that. Very likely no one would except some woman who has had the job." But now that she had the job, Eleanor showed that she meant to use it—on the side of causes she believed in—rather than let it use her.

All though the 1930s, Eleanor's letters reveal uncertainty as to how to combine her own private concerns with the demands of her public role as wife of the president. When Hickok attempted to distinguish between Eleanor the "person," whom she preferred, and Eleanor the separate public "personage," Eleanor wrote back, "I think the personage is an accident and I only like the part of life in which I am a person." It was a dichotomy not easily dismissed, however, and Joseph Lash reported that it became an "old discussion" among her friends as to whether she gained prominence as a "result of being the President's wife" or because of her personal skill in using the "opportunities afforded her as First Lady." Lash's own conclusion was that the person and personage eventually merged into one, but that Eleanor insisted on dividing them. In describing a trip she took in 1933, she explained that she had driven up "in the capacity of ER, and only on arriving became FDR's wife."

Many decisions called for working out the competing claims of the two roles. Eleanor arranged for a leave of absence from her teaching, but she stubbornly continued her other professional activities, including lecturing and writing. When the question of doing radio broadcasts came up, Eleanor wavered, first refusing and then reversing herself. To counter criticism that the president's wife had no right to a profitable career of her own, she donated much of her income to organizations such as the Women's Trade Union League and the Red Cross. After seven years as First Lady she explained to reporters that she had earned a "great deal," but that she had "not one cent more of principal or of investment" than in 1932. "I have the feeling that every penny I have made should be in circulation," she said.

The earning of money, not the spending of it, appealed to Eleanor because it was money that resulted from her own efforts. She liked the feeling of having funds apart from the trust income she had inherited from her family and the allotment she got from her husband. Her paycheck was hers to do with as she wanted, or as she said, to do "just things that give me fun." Often that meant gifts for her family and friends but rarely an extravagance for herself. Clothes held no interest at all and a friend observed that Eleanor frequently wore dresses in the $10 range.

Having felt the satisfaction of making her own money, Eleanor acted on more than one level to combat prejudice against married women working. She encouraged Ettie Rheiner Garner, who had worked as her husband's secretary for many years and did not want to stop when he became vice-president in 1933, to continue. On a public level, the First Lady teamed up with Molly Dewson, then prominent in the Women's Division of the Democratic National Party, to denounce the Economy Act of 1933, which permitted firing women in civil service if their husbands also had government employment. Her news conferences, which she had begun immediately upon becoming First Lady, served as forums for Eleanor to speak out on wives' right to work if they wanted to (although she carefully noted that each woman should make up her own mind about whether to work outside the home or not). When individual states sought to enact laws that would have permitted firing working wives, Eleanor used her conferences with women reporters to fight back.

Multiple biographies of Eleanor Roosevelt make clear that her concerns extended beyond women's rights and well-being, but she broke precedent in putting the power of First Ladyship to work on the side of women—both married and single. When the Civilian Conservation Corps offered jobless young men the chance to get out of cities and earn money, Eleanor teamed up with the labor secretary, Frances Perkins, to gain equivalent opportunities for young women. The Federal Emergency Relief Administration responded by setting up camps for women, and although the number enrolled totaled only about eight thousand, compared to two and a half million men in the CCC, this victory marked another small strike against the double standard.

In her attempt to influence New Deal legislation, Eleanor worked through every channel she could find. Before moving into the White House, she had helped her friend Molly Dewson obtain leadership of the Women's Division of the Democratic National Committee, a post from which Dewson could effect the appointment of other women to party jobs in the various states and in federal agencies. One of Dewson's early victories was the naming of Frances Perkins as secretary of labor in 1933, the first woman to serve in a president's cabinet. Dewson also orchestrated a remarkable increase in women campaign workers, from 73,000 in 1936 to 109,000 by 1940. It was this kind of pyramiding that made Eleanor Roosevelt such an effective proponent—she carefully laid the groundwork for change and made way for women at the lower echelons in government and politics so that they could prepare for the bigger jobs. Her efforts achieved remarkable results. In slightly more than twelve years, the number of women holding jobs requiring Senate confirmation doubled, and countless lesser jobs were filled through her influence.

Always sensitive to charges that she held inordinate power, Eleanor frequently issued disclaimers. "I never tried to influence Franklin on anything he ever did," she announced at one press conference, "and I certainly have never known him to try to influence me." When the *New York Times* credited the president's wife with achieving the appointment of a particular woman to attend an international conference, Eleanor wrote to Secretary of the Interior Harold Ickes, who had made the selection, that she had been merely passing along the president's thoughts when she informed Ickes of the woman's qualifications. "There is such a concerted effort being made," Eleanor wrote, "to make it appear that I dictate to FDR that I don't want people who should know the truth to have any misunderstanding about it. I wouldn't dream of doing more than passing along requests or suggestions that come to me." When one man publicly credited Eleanor with obtaining a job for him in Washington, she reprimanded him, pointing out that he had put her "in a very embarrassing position by having made it appear that I had used my influence."

At the very same time she was issuing these disclaimers, Eleanor peppered her letters to friends with references to her attempts to influence both legislation and appointments, and she discussed powerful Washington figures as colleagues rather than superiors. After meeting with Postmaster General James Farley and his aides to "start them off on patronage for women," she judged both Harry Hopkins, head of federal relief efforts, and Secretary of Interior Ickes "good to work with"; and when Hopkins came through with improvements in school lunches, she upgraded her estimate of him to "swell." Eleanor admitted that she used the occasion of a dinner for senators to "throw bombshells about federal controls and setting minimum standards."

Her own children offered rather different descriptions of Eleanor's influence with Franklin. James Roosevelt, who acted as his father's secretary, assigned her a significant role, even "if he didn't always sympathize with her causes" and called her part of the "kitchen cabinet." His sister Anna, who lived at the White House for several years, described her parents' lives as very separate and Franklin as so intolerant of Eleanor's primness and shrillness that he sometimes barred her from his study when he entertained his friends. Anna thought her mother often miscalculated people's moods and tried to bring up serious matters when everyone wished to relax and be frivolous. Whenever Eleanor joined Franklin for a predinner cocktail, Anna recalled, she usually planned to use the occasion to make an appeal.

Although much of her influence remained private, Eleanor Roosevelt became increasingly outspoken on controversial subjects. Just before the 1932 election, Alice Rogers Hagen had written in the *New York Times* of an "unwritten law that the First Lady gives no interviews and makes no public utterances," but within hours of taking the job, Eleanor broke the law. Two days before Franklin got around to talking to the press, she took reporters on a tour of the White House, and then announced that she would meet with them regularly to answer their questions. Just three years had elapsed since Bess Furman had had to disguise herself as a caroling Girl Scout in order to enter the White House and gather material on how the Hoovers spent Christmas, but Eleanor invited Furman to sit down with her colleagues and talk about whatever came to their minds. Such luck seemed too good to believe and one of the journalists pronounced Eleanor "God's gift."

During her slightly more than twelve years as First Lady, Eleanor Roosevelt held 348 press conferences, the last on April 12, 1945, just hours before Franklin's death. Except for the summer months when she left the capital, the meeting was part of her weekly schedule. Questions ranged from trivial inquiries about the habits of visiting royalty to Eleanor's views on substantive matters. Very quickly it became apparent that she did not intend to obey her own rule that forbade political topics but she would continue to limit attendance at the press conferences to women only. When she scooped the president in January 1934 by announcing that wine would once again be served in the White House, thus signaling an end to prohibition, news services who employed no women reporters decided to enlarge their staffs to ensure that they had a representative present. United Press (UP) hired its first woman, Ruby Black.

Eleanor Roosevelt's magazine articles, which in the beginning had stuck to innocuous topics such as family camping trips and baby care, gradually took on such matters as the president's plan to enlarge the Supreme Court, the correct level of preparedness for war, and a war referendum amendment. Beginning in 1936, she also wrote a newspaper column, "My Day," in which she offered her own

pithy judgments of people and policies. In 1939 she used the syndicated column to publicize her resignation from the Daughters of the
American Revolution because of the organization's refusal to permit Marian Anderson to sing in Constitution Hall, thus causing *Time*
to describe her as "increasingly vocal these days."

Such a visible and unconventional First Lady raised many eyebrows and she became almost immediately the subject of carica-
tures. In June 1933, the *New Yorker* carried a cartoon showing a
group of miners deep under the ground, one turning to the next
and announcing, "Gosh, here's Mrs. Roosevelt." By 1940, the criticism appeared on campaign buttons, "And we don't want Eleanor
either." But the First Lady took it all as part of the job. On entering
the White House, she had told Lorena Hickok, "I shall very likely be
criticized, but I cannot help it," and there is little evidence that she
changed her mind. One reporter, who preserved shorthand notes of
many of Eleanor's news conferences, observed that she responded
cordially to all questions, even those clearly hostile to her, except
when she "took on an edge to her voice when asked an unwelcome
question about one of her children."

Eleanor could pass off much of her activity as helping Franklin,
and he shrewdly saw the advantages of having a visible, politically
involved wife who was known to disagree with him. When asked if
her liberal views might not taint him for the more conservative
voters, he could answer, "Well, that's my wife, and I can't be expected to do anything about her." Yet at the same time, he gained
support from those who saw Eleanor as their own champion. She
simply served as "his eyes and ears," it was sometimes said, when
she inspected mines, toured slums, interviewed families of the urban poor, and then relayed her impressions to him.

That a woman raised in one of New York's oldest families, when
considerable attention went to learning to curtsy to one's elders,
would turn up her collar and cuffs and go down in the mines to see
conditions for herself or off to the Pacific to inspect military opera-
tions for her husband, surprised many people and marked a new

level of performance by a president's wife. Eleanor's letters show that by the time she occupied the White House, she had become bored by the kind of activities that still concerned her wealthy relatives. After visiting a cousin in Rhode Island in 1933, she wrote "Newport is so smug," and after seeing her mother-in-law off on a European trip, Eleanor noted how far she had moved from the older woman's world. Her mother-in-law would be visiting the King and Queen of England and staying at the U.S. Embassy: "Lord I would hate it & how she will love it," Eleanor wrote.

Eleanor preferred to spend her time working for her own friends and projects. When the Congressional committee headed by Martin Dies summoned several Youth Congress members to testify in 1939 about possible connections to communism, she went to witness their treatment. Later, she described in her *Autobiography* how she had silently intervened: "At one point, when the questioning seemed to me to be particularly harsh, I asked to go over and sit at the press table. I took a pencil and a piece of paper, and the tone of the questions changed immediately. Just what the questioner thought I was going to do I do not know, but my action had the effect I desired."

Eleanor's multitude of activities in the 1930s led reporters to describe the Roosevelts as a team. Arthur Krock suggested that she might try to succeed her husband in 1940, and in 1941 Raymond Clapper, a syndicated journalist, selected Eleanor as one of the ten most powerful people in Washington, along with John L. Lewis and General George C. Marshall. "She has had," Clapper wrote, "almost the importance of a cabinet minister without portfolio. She deserves credit for many humanitarian projects of the administration, including the National Youth Administration, nursery schools, slum clearance and others. Count Mrs. Roosevelt not only the most influential woman of our time but also a most active force in public affairs."

Such popularity required many adjustments, and Eleanor's childhood had not prepared her for being on a first-name basis with the rest of the world. She tried to adapt. When her husband asked her to go to the Pacific in World War II, she was taken aback in Guadalcanal to hear a young serviceman say loudly, "There's Eleanor," but she decided to accept it as a compliment and respond with a wave and a smile.

The confidence she gained in her mature years led Eleanor Roosevelt to adventures she would not have attempted in her youth and encouraged her to break out of the old limits imposed on women of her time. She flew in a plane piloted by the famous Amelia Earhart, who, for that occasion, wore a long evening dress while she sat at the controls. Eleanor told reporters that she would "love to cross the Atlantic by plane" well before she had the opportunity, and when the time came for her to go to Europe and to the Pacific, she flew. In 1933, *Good Housekeeping* dubbed her "our flying First Lady," and in 1939, she titled one of her own articles "Flying Is Fun." At a time when most Americans still thought flying too dangerous to try, Eleanor Roosevelt delighted in leading the way. She was photographed alongside planes and interviewed inside, doing more for the aviation industry, it was sometimes said, than anyone since Charles Lindbergh.

Eleanor also used her influence in the cause of achieving civil rights for black Americans. Her years as First Lady coincided with events that emphasized very old, strong traditions of racism in American culture: the continued migration of blacks out of the South and into Northern and Western cities, and the renewed reliance on lynching, which had long served in the South to help maintain white dominance. She reacted by involving herself in the campaign for equal rights as no other president's wife had ever done. In this respect she led, rather than followed, her husband, and she earned the permanent admiration of many Americans. She worked for the appointment of blacks to high office, appealed directly to officials to remove disabilities faced by black workers on their jobs, and served as go-between when civil rights advocates sought the ear of the president. Only the threat of harming Franklin's chances prohibited her from doing more, and she once confessed, "I frequently was more careful than I might otherwise have been."

Whatever Eleanor's direct influence in these and other appointments, she could not have acted on so many fronts had not her incredible energy level permitted her to pack into one day more than most people could do in a week. In a typical day, she breakfasted with guests, read several newspapers, attended a conference, returned to the White House to hold her own press conference, made a radio broadcast, and dictated her own column—all before lunch. In the afternoon she saw callers, attended a five-cent dinner to learn how people on WPA wages managed, met with her husband, and then worked on her mail until three in the morning. Eleanor managed all this activity with a tiny staff. Only her personal secretary, Malvina Thompson, was a regular, full-time employee, assisted by various White House staffers who worked on temporary assignments. Eleanor admitted she had the benefit of a very healthy body and insisted that she never permitted herself to feel hurried. If anything kept her awake once she had gone to bed, she never admitted it.

Eleanor Roosevelt set a new standard against which all later First Ladies would be measured. Much of what she did simply extended the activities of her predecessors. Identified as the humane side of the presidency, its conscience and link with the underdog, she continued a long tradition associated with First Ladies since Martha Washington. Eleanor's unique contribution lay in braving criticism by opening up to the press and using her influence as a force separate from the president's, especially in extending opportunities for women and others lacking equal chances. In the process she helped destroy some old, strong prejudices against combining substantive political action with "ladylike" behavior.

When Franklin died suddenly on April 12, 1945, just eighty-two days into his fourth presidential term, Eleanor, then sixty-one years old, had to work out whether she still existed as a private "person" apart from the "personage" who was Franklin's wife. She had always objected to the "fishbowl" aspect of living in the White House, and she prepared to take up residence in a rented apartment on Washington Square in New York City. Reporters who met her train as she arrived in Pennsylvania Station got from her a terse "The story is over," but of course it was not.

Until her death on November 7, 1962, Eleanor Roosevelt continued an active public life, representing her country at the United Nations, where she surprised both her American colleagues and her Russian counterparts by showing firmness in the drafting of the Universal Declaration of Human Rights. In December 1948, when the Declaration passed the General Assembly and the other delegates rose to applaud Eleanor Roosevelt, one of her old political adversaries, Michigan Senator Arthur Vandenberg, conceded publicly what many people were thinking privately: "I want to say that I take back everything I ever said about her and believe me, it's been plenty." Her final appointment came in 1961 when President John Kennedy named her to head the Commission on the Status of Women.

In the seventeen years that she survived her husband, Eleanor Roosevelt achieved recognition as "First Lady of the World"—a status that would have been impossible to attain without the springboard of the White House. Living there longer than any of her predecessors, she had experimented with the role of president's wife and changed it, opening up what had been hidden and breaking down barriers that had stood firm for a century and a half.

ELIZABETH "BESS" WALLACE TRUMAN

E LIZABETH VIRGINIA ("BESS") WALLACE TRUMAN (1945–1953) moved into the White House with little known about her background and interests, despite the fact that Harry had served in Congress and lived with his family in Washington since 1935. In more than twelve years of the Roosevelt administration, journalists had concentrated so heavily on Eleanor that they had paid little attention to those waiting in the wings. Other Senate wives could offer little insight into Bess, and even the Democratic Party lacked accurate biographical information on the wife of the new president and erroneously reported that she had once taught school.

Margaret Truman called her mother the "least understood" member of the family. Bess's deep desire for privacy evolved out of her view that publicity was undignified and unbecoming a lady, a bias that guaranteed her a different relationship with the American public than her predecessor had cultivated. Neither Eleanor Roosevelt nor any other First Lady exceeded Bess in her commitment to help her husband but she wavered on just what that meant. At first she had agreed to have Eleanor introduce her to reporters; but then, on the train back to Washington after the Hyde Park funeral of Franklin Roosevelt, she had sounded out Frances Perkins on the subject. "I'm not used to this awful public life," Bess explained, and Perkins consoled her, assuring her that Eleanor was unique in thriving on the exchange with reporters. When Bess learned that no other president's wife had held regular press conferences, she promptly canceled hers and never scheduled another one.

Ceremonial appearances could not so easily be avoided, much as Bess would have liked to limit them. Her hands perspired profusely at White House receptions even when things went smoothly, and when some mishap occurred, Bess detested being at the center of attention. One of her least pleasant public appearances, permanently recorded on film, occurred only weeks after Harry's inauguration. Scheduled to christen two hospital planes, she approached the first one and swung the champagne bottle in a way she hoped would befit a lady but also break the bottle. Neither that strike nor the eight others that followed had any effect and finally an exasperated Bess turned to a military aide for help. His four swings failed as well because no one had scored the bottle first.

Margaret Truman, who accompanied her mother that day, found the spectacle amusing, but Bess was nonplussed as she moved on to the second plane. This time the bottle had been prepared too well and her first strike showered her with champagne. The navy lieutenant in charge of the ceremony suggested that reporters describe it as though it had gone perfectly, but they preferred the real version and gleefully relayed all the details. Harry Truman tried to make a joke of it all by teasing his wife about losing the tennis champion's arm of her youth, but she refused to be placated and retorted that she would have liked to have cracked the bottle on his head.

Actually, servants and neighbors, visiting royalty and newsmen, all agreed that the Trumans were the closest family they ever saw in the White House. With their daughter, a senior in college when Harry became president, they were dubbed by their staff the Three Musketeers. All of them laughed a lot, but particularly Bess, who, one maid observed, acted as though she had invented laughter.

Neither Bess nor Harry concealed the fact that their partnership extended to his work. Her family connections in politics had helped launch his career. In 1944, when a reporter asked what role she would have in Harry's campaign for vice-president, Bess replied that she would make no speeches but would help him write his "because we've done that so long, it's a habit." When it was revealed that she had been on his Senate payroll, Harry defended hiring her: "She's a clerk in my office and does much of my clerical work. I need her there and that's the reason I've got her there. I never make a report or deliver a speech without her editing it."

The foundation for strong mutual respect between Bess and Harry was established when they were very young. His family had left their Missouri farm when he was six and moved into Independence so that he and his brother could get a "town" education. The Trumans owned hundreds of acres, but like many farmers, they had borrowed heavily in order to buy. They always owed money, Harry once said, to somebody. First in Sunday school and then in the Independence elementary school, the bespectacled Harry was permanently smitten by a blond, blue-eyed classmate (whose family rarely owed money to anyone). Almost sixty years later he wrote her from the White House, "You are still on the pedestal where I placed you that day in Sunday School in 1890."

Bess Wallace's maternal grandfather, George Gates, had moved to Independence from Vermont in the 1850s and had established a profitable milling business that produced the nationally famous "Queen of the Pantry" flour. For his wife and three daughters, he built a seventeen-room Victorian mansion that was still impressive when it became the summer White House almost a century later. One reporter described it as a residence that, no matter where it was, "would command respect."

When one of Gates's daughters, Madge, the "queenliest woman" Independence ever produced, married David Wallace, the son of the town's first mayor, it seemed a perfect match. But neighbors later concluded that Madge's egotism made her a less than sensitive wife. One story that made the rounds of Independence had it that when Madge had her dress splattered by a cantering horse, she had immediately registered her surprise. "Doesn't he know who I am?" she asked, leaving it unclear whether she referred to the rider or the horse.

Whatever his reasons, David Wallace put a gun to his head and took his life when he was forty-three, leaving Madge with four children. Bess, the oldest, was just eighteen, and according to Margaret Truman, this tragedy, more than any other single event, produced Bess's unusually great insistence on privacy. Mrs. Wallace moved her family back into her father's house on North Delaware Street but she never quite recovered from the shock. Bess, the dutiful daughter, did not go away to college, but remained in Independence and commuted to Barstow Finishing School in nearby Kansas City. Thus, she could begin a long correspondence with Harry Truman, who was working his parents' farm ten miles out of town.

Harry, the most faithful of writers, constantly chided Bess about owing him a letter and reported his own activities with a combination of self-doubt and braggadocio. He insisted that if she married him he would try to provide the same level of luxury she had in the Gates mansion or, failing that, he would supply equivalent prestige. "How does it feel being engaged to a clodhopper who has ambitions to be Governor of Montana and Chief Executive of U.S.," Harry wrote in 1913, but continued, "He'll do well if he gets to be a retired farmer." He would add, "You'll never be sorry if you take me for better or for worse because I'll always try to make it better."

Although Bess admitted that she found Harry to be an enigma, she appreciated his devotion. He repeatedly offered to buy tickets for whatever show she would consider seeing with him. Aware of her tennis prowess, he constructed a playing court at the Truman farm to tempt her to come visit him on Sundays.

Whatever Harry could offer her, he never seemed to think it enough, and while he tried first one scheme and then another, he compiled the longest courtship record of any president. He later complained that he never understood why she made him wait fifteen years to marry her. Bess's mother, the hard-to-please Madge Wallace, judged a farmer like Harry unworthy of her only daughter, but

Harry was partly to blame, too, because he wanted to make good first. When the farm did not produce as he had hoped, he turned to mining and then to drilling for oil. In 1917 he enlisted in the Army and opened a canteen.

Fighting in France evidently tempered Harry's expectations about what he should be able to offer his bride or changed Bess's ideas about how long she wanted to wait. They had announced their engagement before he sailed, and when the war ended, he could not conceal his eagerness. She rejected his suggestion that she meet him in New York so that they could marry there, and their wedding took place in Bess's hometown church with the appropriate number of attendants on June 28, 1919. Madge Wallace continued to doubt that the bridegroom would ever amount to much. He had shown up for the wedding in a figured wool suit, she noted disapprovingly, when linen would have been more appropriate.

Harry's mother-in-law was not the only one surprised by the marriage. The bride and groom, both in their mid-thirties, differed so much from each other that even their daughter Margaret, born when her parents were almost forty, marveled at the contrast. Bess, an athletic young woman who developed into a controlled and very private person, made Harry look particularly bookish and impetuous. As a child, he stuck to his books because he feared breaking his spectacles, and he never did learn to mask his sharp temper. While he became widely read in American history, she liked a good murder mystery. He delighted in winning small stakes at poker, but she preferred bridge. Theirs was, apparently, one of those unions of sharply different partners who chose to team up in maturity after both had developed very separate identities.

Harry did not immediately set out to win political office. After he failed at running a men's store, opened in partnership with an army buddy, he accepted the invitation of another army friend, James Pendergast, nephew of Jackson County's political boss, and tried for a judgeship. When Harry Truman assumed that office in January 1923, he began a government career that lasted, with the exception of two years, for three decades. Bess reluctantly faced the prospect of being a political wife.

Unlike Eleanor Roosevelt, who seemed intent on carving out her own niche in Washington, Bess merged her identity with Harry's. In 1945, when questioned about her past, Bess replied, "I have been in politics for more than 25 years." But it was a subtle participation with her public and private lives kept very separate. Her public role consisted of keeping quiet and making sure her hat was on straight; her private life was her own business, although it was understood in Washington that she did not lack opinions.

This apparent contradiction led to considerable confusion. Although *Good Housekeeping* named Bess Truman one of Washington's ten most powerful women in 1949, the public knew little about her because she refused to tell much. After nine months in the White House, she went Christmas shopping alone and unnoticed. When the *New York Times* published a feature article on her in June 1946, the headline read, "The Independent Lady from Independence," and three years later readers of *Collier's* learned that Bess was "still a riddle."

Bess Truman remained very much an enigmatic, introspective woman. Unlike Eleanor Roosevelt, Bess thought travel by plane was too fast to be dignified (she took the train) and refused even to try public speaking. She kept carefully in her husband's shadow, and on a 1948 trip to Cuba, Bess would not even attempt to speak Spanish, a language she had studied, because she feared an error might be reported in the newspapers.

In defining just what a First Lady should do, Harry and Bess Truman apparently agreed that Bess's activities were mostly her own business. Except for an occasional appeal that people buy savings bonds or contribute to the March of Dimes and the Girl Scouts, she rarely issued public statements; her announcement in 1949 that she hoped Congress would repair the old White House rather than taking the cheaper option of constructing an entirely new mansion was an exception.

All information for the press about the First Lady came from her two secretaries: Reathel Odum, who had formerly worked for Harry, and Edith Helm, whose White House experience went back to the Wilson years. Reporters soon learned to expect from Odum and Helm only the barest facts, none of them very informative about the Trumans. After much badgering, Bess finally consented to respond to reporters' written questions but even then she used "No comment" for nearly one-third of their queries. She revealed that she thought the two most important characteristics for a First Lady were good health and a strong sense of humor but, she added, a course in public speaking would also be helpful. Perhaps her most telling response came to the question of whether she had wanted her husband to be president. "Definitely did not," she wrote, underlining "definitely."

In the absence of other information, reporters wrote about her comings and goings, her housekeeping, which was "excellent," and her "mind of her own about menus." Her refusal to speak out on matters of public concern gave readers the impression she knew less than she did.

Much of the information reported was simply wrong. One national news magazine informed readers that Bess Truman "neither drinks nor smokes." Another ran a photograph of her refusing a glass of wine, with the caption: "No prohibitionist, Mrs. Truman just doesn't like the taste of the stuff." When Bess and daughter Margaret chose orange juice over cocktails at a New York dinner, they made the *New York Times* and received an approving letter from a Binghamton (New York) Methodist church. Bess politely thanked her supporters but failed to enlighten them about her drinking preferences.

White House employees made clear in their published memoirs that the Trumans liked a cocktail before dinner. In fact, they had definite preferences in how their drinks were mixed, something the staff had to learn. According to J. B. West, who worked many years in the White House, Bess rang for the butler her first night there and ordered old-fashioneds for herself and the president. Since the butler had once worked as a barman, he took considerable pride in his mixing abilities, and he confidently added fruit slices and bitters to the drinks before serving them. Bess made no comment about the fruit slices but pronounced her drink too sweet. The next evening an identical order received even greater attention from the butler but the same reaction from the First Lady. Finally on the third night an exasperated butler poured straight bourbon into the glasses. This time Bess smiled. "That," she said, "is the way we like our old-fashioneds."

Such stories became known only after the Trumans had left the White House—not because Bess altered her ways to fit popular tastes but because she refused to talk. In fact, what endeared her to many people was her insistence on remaining unchanged by her prominence. She invited the entire membership of her hometown bridge club to stay at the White House and see Washington from the top. Each time she returned to Missouri she made clear that she wanted no fuss from her neighbors and that she expected to be treated like everyone else. In spite of heavy commitments as the president's wife, she kept her mother with her until Madge Wallace died in December 1952. Bess's brothers had volunteered to help but she insisted that it was a daughter's duty.

Beyond the household management and the ceremonial appearances, Bess Truman spent much of her time answering about one hundred letters a day. It was a far less demanding schedule than Eleanor Roosevelt had kept, but one congressman thought she ought to be compensated. Calling her job the "only case of involuntary servitude in the USA," Representative James G. Fulton (Republican, Pennsylvania) proposed giving the president's wife an annual salary of $10,000. The country provided for widows of presidents, Fulton said, but did little "for wives who are in there working on their job every day." The proposal was quickly dropped as not being authorized by law, and Bess continued working as presidents' wives had before her—for nothing.

Much of Bess's value lay in her tempering influence on her husband. When his salty language and fiery temper got him into trouble, she reprimanded him. Her frequent "You didn't have to say that" became a joke with the White House staff. Liz Carpenter, later press secretary to Lady Bird Johnson, remembered seeing Bess take her husband by the collar and back him into a hotel room when she thought it unwise for him to go out.

Harry repaid his wife with frequent vows of devotion and swift attacks on her critics. Harry's most noted outburst of indignation— the fiery letter he sent to Paul Hume, music critic of the *Washington Post* who had disparaged Margaret Truman's singing ability—appeared in print because the president wrote it and mailed it himself rather than checking it out with Bess or the usual White House channels that were equipped to save him from his own excesses.

A lifetime of correspondence between Harry Truman and his wife reveals how much he valued her judgment and how often he conferred with her on important matters. Not all the letters survived, as their daughter pointed out. After he had become president, Harry found Bess burning some papers and inquired what they were. "They're your letters to me," she said, and he responded, "Well, why are you burning them? Think of history." "I have," she replied, and kept on burning. Enough were saved, however, to make more than one book, and in 1983, hundreds of Harry's letters, written to his wife over half a century, were published in *Dear Bess.*

The correspondence shows a continued sharing of thoughts with so much background information missing that the writer must have assumed no need to repeat it. In September 1941, for example, Harry wrote from his hotel in Kansas City that he had spent hours with various Democratic Party leaders who were all asking what he was going to do for the Party. "What should I do?" he asked his wife.

Harry Truman continued to defend his confidence in Bess's opinions long after he had left office. In a 1963 interview with the Washington reporter Marianne Means, he explained that he had

talked over with his wife the use of the atomic bomb, the Marshall
Plan and post-war rebuilding, and the Korean military action: "I
discussed all of them with her. Why not? Her judgment was always
good." The Trumans' daughter later underlined her mother's impact on the administration by crediting her with obtaining increased
funding for the National Institutes of Health and with arranging for
theater groups to tour the world under the auspices of the State
Department.

In one of her more revealing statements, reported in *McCall's* in
1949, Bess chose the Monroe administration as the period in American history that she found "interesting." She did not explain
whether it was the lack of party rivalry that drew her to the early
nineteenth century or the reputed skill with which Elizabeth Monroe
shunned the public's curiosity about her. Perhaps Bess felt a special
sympathy for Elizabeth Monroe, who followed the popular Dolley
Madison into the White House and had to redefine the limits of
being a president's wife. Like Elizabeth Monroe, Bess Truman realized how different her own training and inclinations were from
those of her predecessor, and she insisted on working with what she
had and letting those who followed do the same. After leaving the
White House in 1953, she and Harry retired to Missouri, where they
lived quietly in the old Gates house built by Bess's grandfather.
Following Harry's death in 1972, Bess rarely left Independence, and
she died there in 1982 at age ninety-seven.

MAMIE DOUD EISENHOWER

D URING Mamie Doud Eisenhower's years in the White House (1953–1961) her name became a trademark for a certain style or taste. The First Lady's favorite color became known as "Mamie pink," and she surrounded herself with it, from the pink furniture in her bedroom down to pastel cloth covers on her lipstick holders. In the 1950s femininity meant opinionless dependence, and although Mamie Eisenhower did not invent that model for women, she represented it well, making clear by her every public utterance that she thought a wife's role entirely secondary and supportive. Her thirty-six years of marriage had been a series of moves, averaging almost one per year, as she trailed her army husband from one assignment to another.

Even a magazine named *Independent Woman* accepted this concept of the perfect wife and put Mamie on its January 1953 cover. The new First Lady had adapted to each change in her husband's career, Lenore Hailparn wrote, quickly rearranging successive new homes for his comfort. Mamie even carried swatches of her favorite colors to save time in the redecorating. To the reporters who inquired in 1952 how she felt about her life, she replied she was "thankful for the privilege of tagging along by Ike's side."

Born in Boone, Iowa, to a successful businessman and his wife, Mamie Geneva Doud resembled in many ways her Swedish mother, Elivera Carlson Doud, who at age sixteen had married a man considerably her senior. Before she was twenty-two, Elivera had borne him four daughters and in many ways acted as a fifth. When the family moved to Denver for the benefit of the health of one of the girls, Elivera made their house on Lafayette Street a gathering place for the neighborhood. The red carpet that lined the front porch steps served as seating for whoever came by and distinguished the rather ordinary structure from others on the street. A staff of four performed all domestic chores while the woman of the house ran around Denver in her Rausch and Lang electric auto, an extravagance that reportedly cost her husband $4,800 in 1910.

On one of the Doud family's winter trips to San Antonio, Mamie met young Second Lieutenant Eisenhower, who came from a family of seven boys and had received none of the pampering that Mamie and her sisters had. Ike had supported one brother through college, then gotten himself an appointment to West Point so that he could attend free. His pacifist mother had overlooked the implications of his going to a military academy, he said, because of her determination to see all her sons through college. Mamie's parents, who paid no attention to cost, put far less importance on schooling for their daughters, and Mamie stopped after one year of finishing school. In 1916 Dwight Eisenhower and Mamie Doud were married, on the day he was promoted to first lieutenant in the Army.

Although Mamie suffered generally poor health as an adult, one illness figured in the central tragedy of her life. In the winter of 1920–1921, her firstborn son, then three years old, became sick and was hospitalized. Mamie, suffering at the time from a respiratory infection, was not permitted to go near him. Weeks later, when he died, her grief was multiplied because of her sense of helplessness. Ike called his first son's death "the greatest disappointment and disaster in my life." For Mamie, the loss was at least as traumatic. Even after the birth of a second son, John, in 1923, she did not appear completely recovered from the tragic loss suffered earlier.

By the time Ike was assigned to the Philippines for a four-year stint (1935–1939), Mamie was already spending much of her time in bed. A weak heart and respiratory problems caused doctors to forbid her to fly and then when they permitted her to go up in planes, they suggested she not exceed five thousand feet.

During World War II, when General Eisenhower was catapulted to fame as Supreme Allied Commander in Europe, Mamie ("Mrs. Ike") was singled out by reporters for both her breezy manner and her example of the patient wife. "Eisenhower's Wife Finds Wait Tough, the armed forces' newspaper, *Stars and Stripes,* reported in an article later carried in the *New York Times.* Part of the public's interest in her personal life caused her great discomfort—especially the reports that her husband was romantically involved with his Irish driver, Kay Summersby. While Mamie waited in Washington, she could not fail to hear speculation about the two, who were frequently photographed together. Summersby, a willowy ex-model who was young enough to be Mamie's daughter, had first been assigned to drive Ike around England. Later she followed him to Africa, and after the death of her fiancé in 1943, speculation increased about the relationship between her and her boss.

Evidence of just what happened between Summersby and Dwight Eisenhower is not easily assembled. Years later, Summersby wrote her own account of their liaison. John Eisenhower published his father's wartime letters to Mamie to bolster claims of Ike's devotion to his wife.

Whether or not the relationship threatened the Eisenhower's marriage, reports of it circulated freely and continued to be part of Washington gossip even after Ike became president. Mamie kept up a cheerful front, and she was quoted in *Look* magazine as saying that there could have been nothing improper between her husband and Summersby because "I know Ike."

Between 1945 and 1952, when Dwight Eisenhower served first as chief of staff, then as president of Columbia University, and finally in Paris as commander of NATO forces, Mamie perfected her skill at entertaining large groups of important people. She paid close attention to centerpieces, menu selections, and seating arrangements, giving reporters every reason to believe that being a good hostess

would continue to be her focus in the White House. In contrast to
Eleanor Roosevelt and Bess Truman, who both disliked that part of
the job, Mamie insisted she enjoyed it, and at her first press conference she read a projected schedule for herself, listing what one
reporter described as "tea by inexorable tea."

The Eisenhower White House years (1953–1961) presented its
occupants as a typical family with Mamie as familiar and folksy as the
woman next door. She insisted that reporters call her Mamie "because it's so much friendlier," her close associates revealed that she
greeted them with "girls" or "kiddo," regardless of their ages and
that she signed her letters, "Bless you, Mamie E." Mamie announced that she often bought clothes off the rack, and that once,
after having spotted a $17.95 dress in a store window during a
campaign, she had mailed off an order for it. Instead of expensive
jewelry, she wore costume pieces and had a costume jeweler design
a set of pearls and rhinestones for the inaugural ball.

In spite of her protests that she spent no more than most women
on clothes, Mamie Eisenhower made the Dress Institute's roster of
Best Dressed Women, a list enlarged in 1952 beyond the usual ten
to accommodate two from the world of politics: Mamie and Oveta
Culp Hobby, later named secretary of health, education and welfare. Both women had started out slowly in the polling, the Institute
announced, but had ended up tying for eleventh place. The ward-
robes of presidents' wives had been a recurring topic of conversation since the earliest days of the republic, and Mamie's popularity
promised that her taste in clothes would affect cash registers.

In a decade that put more stress on women's youthfulness than on
their intelligence, Mamie became a national heroine. Reporters frequently noted that she looked younger than her years, and she
herself admitted that she hated "old lady clothes." Pink strapless
evening dresses that she chose for White House parties differed
little from those selected by high school seniors for their proms.
Because she felt "too young to be a grandmother," she urged her
grandchildren to call her "Mimi," and to maintain a figure in line

with that image of herself, she made frequent trips to an Arizona spa.

Mamie cheerfully admitted that she had no ear for languages, and although she had lived all over the world, in Panama, the Philippines, and France, she spoke little Spanish or French. Later, in March 1959, when St. Joseph College in Emmitsburg, Maryland, conferred an honorary degree on her, Mamie had such a case of "mike fright" that she called on Ike to relay her thanks.

As for her responsibilities as First Lady, when one group after another descended on the executive mansion for a personal greeting from the president's wife, Mamie always tried to satisfy as many requests as possible. When she could not manage to receive 1,600 members of the Federation of Women's Clubs who wanted to come by for tea on short notice, she went down to their convention center to soothe hurt feelings. She shook hands with thousands of people averaging more than 700 a day in 1953, and managed, her admirers said, to make each greeting individual and different. Rather than complaining, she gave the impression, *Time* reported, of being a "happy household manager."

What her husband called her "unaffected manner" made Mamie's choices for the White House a reflection of popular taste rather than a showcase of high culture. She liked to call on band leader Fred Waring or on male quartets to entertain her guests, one of whom reported that Mamie's favorite number was "Bless This House." Her publicized preference for gladioli and for taking her dinners off TV trays rendered her a familiar, friendly figure. She made the White House "livable and comfortable," her husband said, and therefore "meaningful for the people who came in."

Behind the scenes, the staff gave a different picture—one that reflected Mamie's "spit and polish" army background. She checked for cleanliness by running a white glove over windowsills as she passed through rooms, one of the staff reported, and she insisted that vacuum cleaners be run frequently to erase evidence that anyone had walked on the plush carpets. J. B. West, assistant chief usher, argued that Mamie was simply establishing her command, having developed in her years as an army officer's wife a "spine of steel" and a complete understanding of how a large household worked. "She could give orders," West wrote, "staccato crisp, detailed and final, as if it were she who had been a five-star General."

Americans less acquainted with the running of the White House saw only Mamie's "softer" side and they found her thoroughly charming. For a woman who spent much of her energy on how she looked, there could be no headier reward than a bevy of ubiquitous photographers. She obliged them cheerfully. In 1952 Mamie had accompanied Ike on the campaign train and she posed with him even if that meant getting up in the middle of the night to satisfy well-wishers who had waited for hours to catch a glimpse of the famous general. On one occasion she had gone out on the platform in her bathrobe; when some photographers, who had missed the shot, asked for a replay she gamely acquiesced even though it meant putting her hair back in curlers.

For occasional rests, Mamie sometimes went off to her mother's house in Denver or to the Gettysburg farm that the Eisenhowers had bought, the only home they used for any length of time during their entire marriage. To speculation that these trips were really drying-out spells for alcoholism, Mamie never gave a reply during the White House years, but in 1973, she admitted in an interview that she was aware the stories had circulated. They had begun, she said, because of the effect of a condition, carotid sinus, which put excessive pressure on her inner ear and upset her sense of balance. So severe was the disequilibrium that she was frequently covered with bruises because she collided with objects, but since her condition had no cure, she had learned to live with it.

Mamie's first term in the White House showed no decline in her health and in some ways she seemed better, but her physical condition again became an issue in the 1956 campaign. The Republican national chairman Butler referred indirectly to Mamie when he ventured that the incumbent would probably not run for reelection because of a "personal situation in the Eisenhower household." The reference was not quite indirect enough, and the president and his supporters denounced Butler for bringing up Mamie's health. James Reston, the widely read columnist, objected, "To drag a President's wife into the political bear pit is a dubious maneuver. It has been tried before but never with notable success." Mamie's mother had fueled the speculation by declaring that her daughter could not stand another four years in the White House.

By the time of renomination in the summer of 1956, the country's attention focused more on the president's health than on that of his wife. In September 1955, while visiting Mamie's family in Denver, the president had suffered a coronary thrombosis, and the first reports from Denver indicated that the entire family united to urge him not to try for another term. John Eisenhower later reported it had been Mamie, aware of the consequences for Ike if he was forced into inactivity, who encouraged him to run again. The final decision was the president's, of course, and he announced at a news conference, in response to a reporter's question about family influence, that he had made up his own mind and the family had gone along in good military fashion.

In 1961, after eight years in the White House, Mamie Eisenhower left the job of First Lady much as she had found it, except for one small change. The *Congressional Directory* of March 1953 acknowledged for the first time the distaff side of the Executive Office when it listed Mary McCaffree as "Acting Secretary to the President's wife." Mamie's name did not appear, but the foundation was laid for a much expanded staff under her successors.

Before she died in 1979, Mamie witnessed a considerable change in the job of First Lady. From their Gettysburg farm, where the Eisenhowers retired, she observed a young glamorous Jacqueline Kennedy put her stamp on the White House and then an issues-oriented Lady Bird Johnson continue in the activist tradition of Eleanor Roosevelt. By the time she met Rosalynn Carter in 1977, public expectations for the First Lady had permanently altered, and

Mamie marveled at the difference the few intervening years had made: "I stayed busy all the time and loved being in the White House," she told the new First Lady, "but I was never expected to do all the things you have to do."

The Turbulent Sixties

IN FEBRUARY 1960, when the field of likely nominees for that year's presidential election had narrowed to five, *Newsweek* compared the men's wives and predicted that one of them would preside over the White House in the next four years. As it turned out, two of them did; and before the decade ended, three of the five had served as First Lady. With very different personalities and priorities, each carved out an individual response to a turbulent period in American history—one of exhilaration, then questioning and delusion as attention turned from space exploration and the Peace Corps to John Kennedy's assassination and then to Vietnam. In less than a decade, the style of First Ladies changed too, so that campaigning for their husbands became almost a requirement. Acting as White House hostess dropped as a priority; spear-heading substantive reforms rose. In short, the president's wife moved out of the society columns and onto the front page.

Of the five singled out by *Newsweek* before the major parties convened to choose their candidates, only Evelyn Symington fell from national prominence. Muriel Humphrey, the most traditional of the five and the one who described herself as a "mother of an ordinary family," never lived in the White House, but she saw her husband become vice-president in 1965, and after his death she served briefly as a United States senator from Minnesota. The remaining three women on *Newsweek*'s list, Pat Nixon, Lady Bird Johnson, and

Jacqueline Kennedy, all had the opportunity to preside over the White House.

JACQUELINE BOUVIER KENNEDY

T HE FEW YEARS that Jacqueline Bouvier Kennedy spent in the White House (1961–1963) were ones in which the First Lady's glamour, sophistication, and love of the arts were clearly evident. But Jackie took little pleasure in the political game, with the long hours of handshaking and small talk that went with the winning of primaries. Soon after her husband's nomination for president in 1960, her pregnancy was announced and Jackie retired to the family home in Hyannisport, Massachusetts, for the rest of the presidential race. Yet even if she did not mingle with the crowds and chose to remain aloof from much of her husband's campaigning, Jackie Kennedy had the uncanny knack of intriguing a nation.

Born on Long Island in 1929 to a stockbroker and his society-conscious wife, Jacqueline Bouvier attended the fashionable Chapin School in New York and then the prestigious Miss Porter's in Connecticut. After her parents divorced and her mother remarried Hugh Auchincloss, who was considerably wealthier and more successful than Jack Bouvier, Jackie and her younger sister Lee divided their time between Merrywood, the Auchincloss estate outside Washington, and Hammersmith Farm in Newport, Rhode Island. When the time came for college, she took two years at Vassar and a year in Paris before being graduated from George Washington University. Her stepfather arranged through a family friend for her to go to work for a Washington newspaper and soon she had her own byline for a column, "Inquiring Photographer."

Although many other women in the 1950s compiled similar records of international travel, multilingual competence, and careers of their own, none of the others topped off their accomplishments with marriage to a senator who seven years later won the presidency. Jackie's youth (she was only thirty-one when she became First Lady), her wit, and her flair for fashion all put her in sharp contrast to her immediate predecessors. She would have aroused curiosity even if she had restricted herself to being White House hostess, but she resolved to do more.

Just weeks after John Kennedy's victory over Richard Nixon in 1960, Jackie gave birth to a son, and within days, she was announcing through her social secretary, Letitia Baldrige, "sweeping changes," so the White House would become "a showcase of American art history." Following this precedent-breaking, pre-inaugural announcement, Jackie assembled a large staff; Baldrige reported that she eventually had forty people at work in the "First Lady's Secretariat."

Astute observers did not fail to note how the wife of the president-elect tailored her public statements to complement his upbeat, energetic approach to the office. While John Kennedy incorporated phrases about a "new frontier," his wife talked of "new beginnings" and the "best" of everything. The *New Yorker,* in an amusing article entitled "Mrs. Kennedy's Cabinet," underlined the parallels when it compared the Kennedys' appointments. Both John and Jackie had included Republicans (Letitia Baldrige and Douglas Dillon), the *New Yorker* pointed out, and both had rewarded early boosters (in her case, the hairdresser Kenneth). Their most important selections, however, had come slowly, with both Kennedys announcing on the same day the designer of her inaugural wardrobe (Oleg Cassini) and his secretary of state (Dean Rusk). Both Cassini and Rusk had been, the *New Yorker* explained, "rather dark horses."

As soon as her husband was sworn in, the new First Lady moved to leave her imprint on his administration. Within a week of the inauguration, she had begun her campaign to upgrade the taste of the nation. On January 25, she met with an old friend, the artist William Walton, and experts from the Commission of Fine Arts and the National Gallery to discuss plans for restoring to the White House its original furnishings. That same afternoon she took tea with George Balanchine, the Russian choreographer who headed the New York City Ballet. By the end of her first week as First Lady, she had made clear that although she had listed her priorities in the same order as had Bess Truman and Mamie Eisenhower, placing husband and children first, she meant to handle the duties in a different manner.

For a start, Jackie became the first president's wife to employ her own press secretary. However, Pamela Turnure, the twenty-three-year-old woman who got the job, functioned less as a press secretary than as link between the First Lady and the president's staff. The president's press secretary, Pierre Salinger, estimated that he handled 95 percent of all the information about the First Lady, deciding what information went out to the public and when, and handling memos from Jackie exhorting diligence in shielding her children from publicity.

The popularity of the young First Lady escalated the demand for information about her, and reporters admitted that they engaged in "shameless" tactics to get their stories. Helen Thomas, who was assigned to the White House, recalled that she and her colleagues were insatiable for news about Jackie Kennedy. They queried her hairdresser, her caterer, and her pianist. They even sought information from the White House diaper supplier and watched carefully how much alcohol the First Lady consumed at receptions.

Interest in the new First Lady quickly spread around the world and photographs of her (and of other women bearing a striking resemblance to her) appeared in commercial announcements. A Scottish tweed company used her photo, implying she endorsed its product, until requested to stop. Less than three months into the

Kennedy administration, the "Jackie look" was being debated in Polish magazines, and one of them, *Swiat,* predicted she would dictate the "tone and style for the whole civilized world."

When the First Lady accompanied the president to Europe, she multiplied her exposure and her admirers. Combining youthful beauty, fashionable clothes, and faultless French, she so engaged the crowds that she quickly became an international star. Vienna and London brought similar ovations, and at the end of 1961, Jackie Kennedy was voted "Woman of the Year" by the editors of more than a hundred international periodicals. The Public Opinion Research Institute in Argentina selected her and Pope John XXIII as the two outstanding models for the world.

As First Lady, Jackie Kennedy took as her own project one that had traditionally been the province of presidential wives. Each White House family had enjoyed considerable freedom to choose what to bring into the mansion and what to discard. Over the years many valuable pieces had simply disappeared—sold at auction or carted off as junk. Presidents did not usually involve themselves in the decisions (James Monroe and Chester Arthur were the notable exceptions), and wives could choose to reflect their own personal preferences or treat the mansion as a museum of the country's treasures. Following structural renovations in the 1920s, Grace Coolidge had prevailed on Congress to pass legislation permitting the president to accept appropriate antiques, but so few were forthcoming that the law had little effect. Lou Hoover had attempted to stimulate interest in the White House by asking a secretary friend to write a book on the subject, but depression times were hardly conducive to attracting donations of the Federal or Early Empire styles.

The early 1960s found Americans in a more giving mood, especially when a popular First Lady and new tax laws encouraged them in their generosity. Jackie prevailed on wealthy individuals to contribute, assembled a professional staff to oversee the collection, and engaged scholars to give guidance and advice. The sale of White House guidebooks, which began July 4, 1962, would help finance the project. To ensure that her efforts could not be canceled by a successor with different tastes, Jackie secured passage of legislation defining the furnishings of the White House as "inalienable property."

The First Lady's efforts to restore the White House (she did not like the term redecorate) received considerable publicity, including a one-hour special on national television in early 1962 during which millions of viewers watched her move through the mansion and describe the provenance and significance of the furnishings and artworks. Jack Gould, television reviewer for the *New York Times,* pronounced her an extremely able historian, art critic and narrator.

Jacqueline Kennedy insisted that the White House serve as showcase for "the best in the arts, not necessarily what was popular at the time." According to one aide, she acted as "White House impresario" and invited the country's top opera singers, ballet dancers, and instrumentalists to perform at presidential parties. But she remained selective about public appearances for herself. Citing obligations to her two young children, she frequently refused to attend the luncheons and teas that typically fill a First Lady's calendar. Sometimes she sent her husband or her secretary or enlisted the vice-president's wife, but she adamantly preserved most of her time for herself.

Jackie Kennedy insisted on being her own person—breaking all kinds of precedents for First Ladies by going off on her own on extended vacations. Previous presidents' wives had limited themselves to dutiful family trips (such as Bess Truman's summers with her mother and daughter in Independence) or to serious, fact-finding missions (such as Eleanor Roosevelt's car trips to both the East and West Coasts), but none gained the attention of Jackie's luxury-packed international forays. She often vacationed away from Washington without her husband, yachting one time in the Mediterranean with Aristotle Onassis and friends, another time riding elephants in India with her sister, still another summer introducing her daughter Caroline to the sights of Italy.

Just returned from a vacation in Greece, Jackie consented to make one of her rare political trips with her husband in November 1963. Partly to mend Democratic fences in preparation for the 1964 election, the president and vice-president went together to Dallas, where, with the assassination of the president, the Kennedy administration ended. Thus it happened that Lyndon Johnson, unlike other vice-presidents in similar circumstances, was there to be sworn into office on the afternoon of November 22, 1963, just ninety-nine minutes after John Kennedy died.

The quickly improvised ceremony aboard Air Force One was delayed until Jackie Kennedy arrived; photographs of the inauguration show her standing, in a pink suit stained with her husband's blood, alongside the grim-faced Johnsons. This marked an unprecedented appearance of an ex–First Lady, as though her presence might help confer legitimacy on the transition even though the details of the assassination—who killed John Kennedy and why—remained unclear. No woman widowed as First Lady had ever been present for the inauguration of her husband's successor—even Eleanor Roosevelt did not attend Harry Truman's inauguration in 1945 although she was still in the White House at the time.

In planning for John Kennedy's funeral, Jackie assumed a far more prominent, publicized role than had any of her predecessors in similar circumstances. Presidential widows had attended their husband's funerals since 1881, and both Florence Harding and Eleanor Roosevelt had made important decisions about the services, but none of them provided quite the drama Jackie Kennedy did.

Six years earlier when her father died, she had decisively handled plans for his funeral. She oversaw the flower arrangements, located a particularly appealing photograph, and insisted that the obituary be hand-delivered to the *New York Times*. Now turning that same determination and confident taste to her husband's funeral, she chose the smaller St. Matthew's Cathedral, within walking distance of the White House, rather than the huge Shrine of the Immaculate Conception.

Only thirty-four at the time of her husband's death, Jacqueline Kennedy lived to raise her two children and continue an active interest in the arts, especially ballet, and in architecture, especially the preservation of landmarks. Her 1968 marriage to Greek tycoon Aristotle Onassis made headlines (the only other presidential widow to remarry had been Frances Cleveland in 1913) and her employment as a book editor made history (none of her predecessors had taken a full-time job after leaving the White House).

In early 1994 Jacqueline Kennedy Onassis was diagnosed as having non-Hodgkin's lymphoma, and in the next few months she was hospitalized several times. On May 19 she died at her New York City apartment on Fifth Avenue "in her own way," her son announced, surrounded by family, friends, and the things she loved.

John Kennedy, Jr., later added in his funeral address that he and his sister had searched for the themes that had shaped their mother's life and had settled on three: love of words, emphasis on family, and desire for adventure. She was buried at Arlington National Cemetery beside the graves of her first husband and the two children who had predeceased them.

In April 1996 Sotheby's in New York conducted a sale of her personal possessions. It yielded more than $34 million, several times what the same items would have brought had they not belonged to one of the most enigmatic and celebrated of all First Ladies.

CLAUDIA ALTA "LADY BIRD" TAYLOR JOHNSON

CLAUDIA ALTA ("LADY BIRD") TAYLOR JOHNSON had lived in Washington for many years prior to her stay in the White House (1963–

(1963–1969), having arrived in the capital as a bride in 1934. Except for the years 1935–1937, she had spent at least part of every year in Washington while Lyndon progressed from being secretary to a congressman to congressman himself (1937–1949) and then U.S. senator (1949–1961) and majority leader (1955–1961). Despite that long acquaintance with the capital, she apparently never expected to live in the White House, and in November 1963, she described herself as feeling as though she were "suddenly on stage for a part I never rehearsed."

The nickname "Lady Bird" had been conferred on Claudia Taylor many years earlier, soon after she was born in a small town in east Texas in 1912. A nursemaid had pronounced the baby "pretty as a ladybird," and the name had stuck. Later, when she met and married Lyndon Baines Johnson, he seized on the coincidence of their initials and proceeded to extend it to every possession or offspring—daughters, dogs, and ranches. Lady Bird confessed she had come to live with her name (friends and family called her "Bird") although she had suffered some embarrassment when, traveling through Europe with her husband, she heard the nobility-conscious ask, "Lady Who?"

When Lady Bird Taylor was five, her mother died. Her sickly, unmarried Aunt Effie assumed responsibility for much of Lady Bird's upbringing, and although she initiated her niece into the pleasures of literature and nature, she left other areas untouched. "She never taught me how to dress or dance," Lady Bird later remembered, and her aunt's weakness and frailty presented a model of what to avoid, rather than what to attempt. Although Aunt Effie had genuinely poor health, Lady Bird suspected "that some of it must have been psychosomatic," and she saw how inhibiting it was to be so weak and full of illnesses. Instead of following her aunt's example, she set her sights on being more like her father, whom she described as "one of the most physically strong people I have ever known."

Bright and quick, Lady Bird finished high school at fifteen but arranged to rank third in her class, one-half percentage point behind second place, because she feared giving the graduation speech required of the top two students. Still too young to enter college, she enrolled for an additional year at St. Mary's Episcopal School in Dallas, a choice that was hers rather than her father's. He had not been impressed with the school but accepted her wishes, showing a faith in a fifteen-year-old's judgment, she later said, that she hoped she extended to her own daughters.

Later, when she enrolled in the University of Texas, Lady Bird had more than the average student. She drove her own car, enjoyed an unlimited expense account at Neiman-Marcus, and had a checkbook that required only that she fill in the numbers. Yet hers was neither a glamorous nor luxurious life. She wore her aunt's cast-off coats and never emerged as a belle at parties, showing early evidence of both the shyness and careful spending habits that she retained through adulthood.

This carefulness extended beyond money to other areas of young Lady Bird's life. Having completed requirements for her liberal arts degree at the University of Texas, she remained another year to earn a journalism degree as well, and just to make sure that she had prepared for all contingencies, she perfected her typing and stenographic skills. She had hoped to become a newspaper reporter but carefully enrolled in courses that would qualify her for a teaching certificate, not because she ever wanted to teach but because she hoped to go to some faraway place "like Alaska or Hawaii."

A woman as careful as that might be expected to proceed very cautiously in choosing a husband, but after years of plotting to get herself out of small-town Texas, Lady Bird Taylor made the most important decision of her life in uncharacteristic haste. Following a two-month courtship, carried on mostly by mail and telephone between her home and Washington, where Lyndon Johnson worked, she married the tall, overpowering Texan who, she later admitted, resembled her father in many ways.

Twenty-six-year-old Lyndon, then employed as Congressman

Kleberg's secretary, had been visiting his home state when a friend introduced him to Lady Bird and he immediately engaged in a courtship that she herself described as "whirlwind." He arranged a date with her at the earliest possible moment, which happened to be breakfast the next day, and then regaled her with every detail of his life story: how he had come from a poor family, worked his way through Southwest State Teachers College, taught briefly, and then taken a job in Washington. He even told her how much life insurance he carried. Lady Bird admitted she was impressed. "I knew I had met something remarkable," she later said, "but I didn't know quite what."

Two months after that first encounter, Lyndon returned from Washington to marry her, and even though she remained unconvinced, he loaded her in his car, told her "now or never," and started off toward San Antonio. Her Aunt Effie had counseled caution, but Lady Bird's father was pleased with Lyndon and told his daughter, "This time you brought home a man." In spite of the fact that her aunt "was scared to death" for Lady Bird, the marriage took place on November 17, 1934.

After a short honeymoon, the Johnsons settled in Washington and Lady Bird, at twenty-two, began what she later described as her education in politics. She had not previously shown any interest in the subject but Lyndon proved a persuasive teacher. He brought home a list of counties and told his bride to learn the names of them so that when she traveled with him she would be prepared.

At home, Lady Bird learned that a political wife had other responsibilities as well. Their small Washington apartment became "open house" for Lyndon's political friends—and those he hoped to bring into that category. For a woman who had never cooked a meal, she learned fast, not only to prepare food for her husband but also for whatever number he brought with him unannounced. She did this all on a minuscule budget. When Lyndon's salary totaled only $265 a month, he took $100 for his car, insurance, and other personal expenses, leaving her $165 to pay for everything else, including an $18.75 savings bond every month.

When a Texas congressman died in 1937, leaving his seat vacant, Lyndon decided to try for it. Lady Bird borrowed against her inheritance, still under her father's control, to pay for the race. Although Robert Caro, one of Lyndon's biographers, later concluded that the campaign cost many times the $10,000 that Lady Bird put up for it, she took much of the credit for financing it, and she admitted that she carried with her the relevant bank withdrawal slip until it became too faded to decipher. Lyndon's campaign manager later recalled how Lady Bird had attempted to use her financial support as leverage to influence how that first political race was run: "She came and told me that she was helping pay for this campaign and she wanted her husband to be a gentleman." She did not think it proper for him to speak out against other candidates.

In the end it was more than Lyndon's victory in 1937 that drew Lady Bird to politics. She found her husband more vibrant and exciting during that first difficult race for Congress than ever before or after, and she loved being part of it all, if only from a back seat. Lady Bird lacked both the confidence and the inclination to campaign openly. Such participation would have been highly unorthodox in Texas at that time as candidates' wives still stayed in the background in the 1930s and 1940s. The state had elected a woman governor in 1924 but she had been a stand-in for her husband, who had been impeached, convicted, and removed from the same office.

Lady Bird Johnson might never have moved beyond such a definition of her role had not World War II intervened. Lyndon Johnson had represented Texas's 10th Congressional District a little more than four years when Japan attacked Pearl Harbor in December 1941. Within hours, he asked to be assigned to active duty, at an officer's pay that was one-third what a congressman earned. Lady Bird took charge of his office and managed it without compensation until he was called back, along with other congressmen, a few months later. She frequently singled out this period as a turning

Bess Wallace Truman

Mamie Doud Eisenhower

Jacqueline Bouvier Kennedy

Lady Bird Taylor Johnson

Pat Ryan Nixon

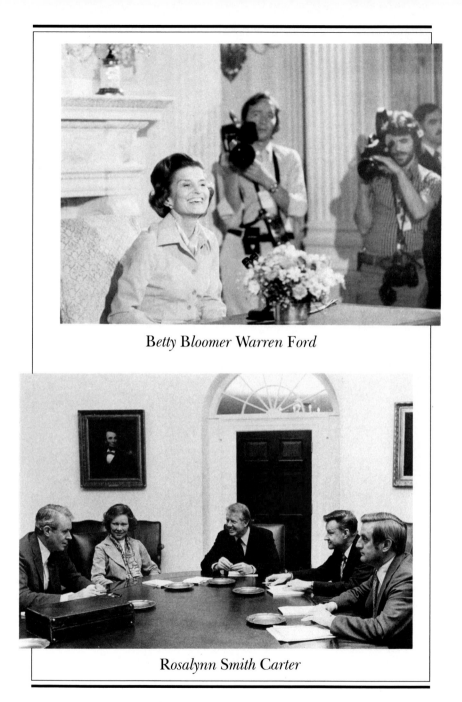

Betty Bloomer Warren Ford

Rosalynn Smith Carter

Nancy Davis Reagan

Barbara Pierce Bush

Hillary Rodham Clinton

Laura Welch Bush

point in her life, because it helped her understand her husband better, but more importantly, it gave her confidence that she could do things on her own. She attended to the needs of Lyndon's constituents (a word written with a capital *C*, she sometimes said) as though they were her own, providing detailed answers to their inquiries and escorting those who came to the capital to see the tourist sites.

Rather than setting out on her own, Lady Bird played the supportive wife—a designation that in this case involved financial support. Her own modest inheritance would never have financed Lyndon to the top of the political ladder, and elective office itself paid little. The Johnsons then set out to make the money that would support them during his career in government. When an almost bankrupt Austin radio station went up for sale in late 1942, Lady Bird took more of her inheritance, borrowed an additional $10,000 from the bank, and bought the station.

As television gained popularity and technical sophistication, the revenues of Lady Bird's Texas Broadcasting Corporation skyrocketed and the market reached beyond Austin. When asked about her phenomenal success, Lady Bird attributed it to timing and a good staff, saying her family had entered the field just as the industry underwent great expansion and they had profited from the work of an exceptionally astute group of employees. She suggested that her own role in management of the stations had been exaggerated, and evidence suggests that Lyndon maintained a close, protective eye on what happened to the corporation, even after he became Senate majority leader.

It would be wrong, however, to conclude that Lady Bird functioned merely as a figurehead for the business interests of her husband, whose political aspirations made too close identification with the company unwise. She continued to review weekly packets of information on the corporation all her Washington years (until the presidential period when the holdings were placed in trust), and after Lyndon's death, she resumed an active role in the corporation.

The family ranch was turned over to the National Park Service before Lyndon's death because he apparently decided that his wife would not want to manage it, but the considerably more valuable broadcasting corporation remained under family control. After 1977, when her business manager died, Lady Bird increased her role, and when an interviewer asked how it felt to be "back as a business woman," Lady Bird answered that it had happened in a way that she had not anticipated, but that she was "enjoying it." Her daughter Luci remarked in 1984 that she had never appreciated her mother's business acumen until she sat with her on corporation boards and understood how hard she had worked "to build up a family business for us all."

While marriage to Lyndon may have pushed Lady Bird to meet new challenges, such as buying a radio station, it had its trying side as well. He frequently berated his wife in front of others, criticizing her clothes or her makeup. Lyndon's list of "Don'ts" included full skirts and T-strap shoes because he thought they made her look fat. Lady Bird dieted and exercised because her husband made no secret of his preference for svelte women, and she wore the reds and yellows he liked and struggled with high heels even though she admitted she "hated" them. Rather than complaining, Lady Bird insisted—in the manner of a diligent student defending the excesses of an overzealous teacher—that his likes were her likes: "What pleases Lyndon pleases me."

The petite woman who had, one friend said, the "touch of velvet and the stamina of steel," found few critics except those who disdained her unfailing loyalty to her husband. Even Lady Bird once admitted that her view of her role might be too traditional for some tastes: "I really wanted to serve my husband and serve the country," she asserted.

This was no easy assignment Lady Bird set for herself, and reporters marveled at how she managed. News correspondent Nan Dickerson remembered that Lyndon once called Lady Bird from an Austin airport saying that he was bringing home nine reporters for the weekend. When they arrived an hour later, everything was prepared for their comfort.

More than household management was involved in Lady Bird Johnson's political education. After Lyndon accepted second spot on the Democratic ticket in 1960, she took speech lessons and then traveled 35,000 miles in two months to speak to voters. Before 1960, Lady Bird's work for Lyndon had been within the traditional woman's sphere—telephoning, stuffing envelopes, and shaking hands at tea parties—but her new role, as wife of the vice-president, imposed other demands. Because Jackie Kennedy frequently refused to appear on ceremonial or political occasions, Lady Bird substituted. Sometimes this meant preparing in only a few hours to speak to large audiences; and when Lady Bird filled in for Jackie on national television, one reporter deemed her "Washington's Number 1 pinch-hitter."

In November 1963, when Lyndon became president, Lady Bird's opportunities for action increased, and she proceeded to alter the public's expectations of what a First Lady might do. As an ex-journalism student and loyal wife, she understood the value of maintaining good relations with the press. More importantly, Lady Bird had lived in Washington long enough to know that privacy for a presidential family was a naive fantasy—she accepted curiosity about her as part of her job. Lady Bird appointed as her press secretary Liz Carpenter, who had worked in Washington since the days of Eleanor Roosevelt. With Carpenter's help, Lady Bird set out to win over the press. She had come to the conclusion, she later said, "that if you're available and talked over something with folks and explained why you couldn't do this or believe in that, or whatever, you would fare better in the end than if you either ran away or just evaded."

Much of what Lady Bird accomplished is detailed in her book, *A White House Diary*, which resulted from the tapes she made during her husband's presidency. It was the most complete record of a First Lady's tenure since Eleanor Roosevelt turned out her daily col-

umns. Comparisons between the two women came quickly, with
many observers noting that both grew along with their husbands'
political successes to personalities of their own. Unlike Eleanor
Roosevelt, Lady Bird did not thrive on the controversies inherent in
politics, and she disapproved of First Ladies who involved themselves in issues that might divide the country. Lady Bird kept her
views on civil rights and Vietnam to herself, and she never sought an
individual constituency for herself or pursued a political or diplomatic career in her own right. After her husband's death, she withdrew from public life and compaigned only when her son-in-law,
Charles Robb, who would become Virginia's governor, sought help.
It had all been fun, she said, and she had learned a lot but "politics
was Lyndon's life," and thirty-eight years were "enough." She preferred spending her time on wildflower preservation.

    While Lyndon lived, his ambitions always came first with Lady
Bird, and she put all her energies into helping him. He could have
won the 1964 election without carrying states below the Mason-
Dixon line, but his wife volunteered to campaign there because she
did not want to lose those states "by default." Many Southerners
had vigorously opposed President Johnson's stand on civil rights
and any move from him to change their minds seemed doomed to
failure, but his wife's campaigning was something else. On a train
dubbed the "Lady Bird Special," she wound her way out of Washington into the Carolinas and over to New Orleans, giving forty-
seven speeches along the way. Assisted by daughter Lynda for the
first two days and then by Luci, she enticed local politicos to join her
(although many of them would have balked at being photographed
with the president). Because they could pass off an appearance at
Lady Bird's side as simple chivalry, one after another recalcitrant
Democrat climbed aboard. Some of the holdouts sent their wives.

    Lady Bird did not meet individuals to bargain on specific matters
—her husband's staff had come along to perform that task—but in
her deep Texan accent she pleaded with crowds of Southerners to
understand that her husband was one of them. When hecklers tried

to outshout her, she waited a moment and then said, "Now you've had your say. Will you give me mine?" "There will always be somebody in the audience," she later pointed out, "who will say, 'that's fair.' " For a woman who had always hated giving speeches, she did remarkably well. When the trip ended, just about everybody agreed that she had helped win votes for Lyndon—the disagreement came over how many. Making the president's wife appear all the more courageous, her Republican counterpart in that election took only a traditional handshaking role.

After Lyndon Johnson achieved his own clear victory in 1964 and held the presidency in his own right, Lady Bird resolved to do more for the success of the administration. Choosing an area in which she held a deep and lifelong interest and one in which her staff believed Lyndon would not interfere, Lady Bird Johnson launched her "beautification" project. The early 1960s offered a propitious time for encouraging Americans to care more for their environment. Rachel Carson's book, describing a "silent spring" when birds could not sing and trees could not green because of the effects of harmful chemicals, was published in 1962, the year before Lyndon became president.

Focusing attention on the environment, contests sponsored by the Committee for a More Beautiful Capital rewarded neighborhood participation, and the First Lady lauded historic preservation that linked people with their past. Her beautification efforts did not stop in Washington—she went national—and in thousands of miles of traveling around the country, she planted trees, shot rapids, and urged people to care more about the world they would pass on to their children. Headstart, an education program for preschool children that Congress initiated in February 1965, stayed on her agenda and she became its honorary chairman, but for most Americans she was permanently associated with environmental concerns.

Lady Bird's highway beautification program was promoted on many fronts. Federally sponsored conferences on the subject began in early 1965, and regional meetings were scheduled to involve governors and city officials. The administration prepared drafts of several bills on the subject, and Lady Bird went to work lobbying. She telephoned congressmen and urged her friends to do the same. Guest lists for White House dinners and receptions reflected an interest in enlisting votes, and when Lady Bird spoke to members of the Associated Press, she encouraged editorials on the subject. Reporters who followed her suggestion received a personal thank-you. Liz Carpenter, Lady Bird's chief of staff, recalled that the First Lady had gone to Capitol Hill to call on members of Congress. The program needed every vote it could get, she said, "for the billboard lobby was active and well-healed."

The president pressured the congressional committee to report the measure out and then he urged the House to act during a night session. Notwithstanding some grumbling about the measure being a present for Lady Bird, the Highway Beautification Act became law in October 1965. Neither the president nor the First Lady felt that the law went as far as they would have liked, but it marked a beginning.

Lady Bird's association with the Highway Beautification Act was not unprecedented—and the reaction was predictable. Cartoons featured her as they had once pointed to Eleanor Roosevelt's activities—one picture showing a maze of highways running through a forest, with the caption, "Impeach Lady Bird." Criticism remained lighthearted, however, and she wrote in her diary, "Imagine me keeping company with Chief Justice Warren!," whose impeachment had been sought by some right wing groups.

The busy First Lady made more than seven hundred various appearances and over a hundred and fifty speeches while her husband was president. Lady Bird underlined her prominence by appointing a larger and better-trained staff than any previously seen in the East Wing of the White House. The press section of six full-time employees, under the direction of Liz Carpenter, represented quite a change from the preceding administration. A team of four handled details of the social secretary's office, and another four answered correspondence. Two staff members dealt only with beautification issues, and even this entourage did not complete the team since others came from the president's wing to work on temporary assignments.

Lady Bird was a remarkably well-organized businesswoman and ran her side of the White House in the manner of a chairman of a large corporation. Leaving details of flower arrangements and menus to assistants, she was tutored on the issues by the best advisers available, including McGeorge Bundy and members of the Council of Economic Advisers.

The successfull combination of energy, organization, and experience won Lady Bird many admirers. Within two years of moving into the White House, observers pointed out that she had altered the job. "What Lady Bird Johnson has done," Meg Greenfield wrote in the *Reporter,* "is to integrate the traditionally frivolous and routine aspects of the East Wing life into the overall purposes of the administration and to enlist the peculiar assets of First Ladyhood itself in the administration's behalf. They are assets no one fully understood until Mrs. Johnson moved into the White House—or at least no one fully understood their potential political clout."

The Texan First Lady once said that any woman in that job should look out for the president's well-being but she should also ask herself what makes her "heart sing. What do you know about? What do you care about? What can you do to make this a better administration?" By the time she left Washington in early 1969, Lady Bird Johnson had made clear her own answers to these questions.

THELMA CATHERINE "PAT"
RYAN NIXON

IN JANUARY, 1969, when Pat Nixon moved into the White House following her husband's election, she had to reconcile her own ideas about the job of First Lady with the new models popularized by her immediate predecessors. Pat's entire Washington apprenticeship had been served under First Ladies Bess Truman and Mamie Eisenhower, neither of whom moved beyond ceremonial appearances and social leadership. But styles had changed by 1969, and many Americans expected a First Lady who was actively involved in issues and causes.

To complement her husband's agenda for social welfare measures, Pat planned to concentrate on adult education and job training, but her efforts received little public notice. Through the Education Office, Pat announced the formation of a "Right to Read" program, and when that project produced little, she spoke of becoming "more active in the environment field" and, the following year, of improving "the quality of life."

To ignite the country's enthusiasm, any one of these projects needed a crowd pleaser—someone who spoke easily to large groups. Although Pat Nixon could be very charming when talking with people in small groups, she stiffened in front of large audiences and television cameras, causing some observers to characterize her as cold and unfeeling.

Pat Nixon's youth, truncated like that of several First Ladies by the death of a parent, may explain some of the restraint in her personal style. For most Americans, she was quintessential Irish, because of her name, Pat Ryan, and her birth just hours before the dawn of St. Patrick's Day in 1912. Few people realized that her mother Kate had immigrated from Germany and was a miner's widow with two young children when she met and married William Ryan. Later she bore him two sons and a daughter, Pat. Like many of the Europeans who immigrated to the United States around the turn of the century, Kate Halberstadt Bender Ryan never lived to see her adopted country deliver on its promises. But before she died of cancer in her early forties, she had convinced her second husband to give up the dangers of mining for a more healthful, but never prosperous, small farm outside Los Angeles.

Even with the housekeeping chores that Pat assumed after her mother's death, she continued to excel in school. She caught up in grade level with her two older brothers and, at the same time, took part in many extracurricular activities. When she won election to vice-president of her class and secretary of the entire student body, she impressed those she worked with as masking a "strong personality" behind a "very quiet" exterior.

Pat's father died of tuberculosis about the time she graduated from high school. Orphaned and with little money, she earned her way by sweeping floors and working as a teller in a local bank. When the chance came to drive an elderly couple to New York, she took it, although in 1932 superhighways had not yet smoothed the hills or straightened the curves across the continent. The couple's old Packard performed imperfectly and Pat later told an interviewer that at age twenty she was "driver, nurse, mechanic and scared."

For two year Pat Ryan worked in New York as an X-ray technician, and by the time she returned to Los Angeles, she had saved enough money to enroll at the University of Southern California. Before she was graduated in 1937 she had prepared herself for several careers, having earned a merchandising degree and two traditional backups —a teacher's certificate and secretarial skills. She had even found work as a movie extra, but full-time jobs were scarce in the Depression years, and in the end she accepted an offer to teach commercial subjects at Whittier High School.

Little about Pat Ryan up to that time suggested the reserved figure whom Americans would later remember in the White House. In fact, her students at Whittier had found her so lively and likable that they selected her to advise the Pep Committee, organized to arouse school enthusiasm. Robert C. Pierpoint, who later covered the White House as a correspondent for CBS, was a member of the Pep Committee, and he remembered Miss Ryan of his Whittier student days as "approachable, friendly and outgoing. She was happy, enthusiastic, sprightly. Her disposition was sunny, not intermittently but all the time," Pierpont recalled, and the students "liked her enormously."

Since Whittier encouraged its teachers to take part in community activities, the new commercial subjects instructor went down to try out for a production of the local drama club. A young lawyer, Richard Nixon, back in his hometown after graduating from Duke, auditioned the same night and his attraction to the new teacher was so immediate and immense that he proposed marriage that same evening. "I thought he was nuts or something," Pat later recalled. He was ten months younger than she and not yet established in his profession but he pursued her with the same diligence he turned to just about everything he did. Two years later, when she was twenty-eight years old, she accepted.

The arsenal of skills that Richard Nixon's wife had carefully accumulated now went to help support his career. While he served in the Navy during World War II, she worked in a San Francisco bank, and when he got the chance to run for Congress in 1945, her savings helped finance the campaign. She contributed her considerable secretarial skills to winning that election and then to running the congressman's office, all without a paycheck of her own.

Whenever Pat Nixon was questioned about her use of time, she emphasized her domesticity. Until 1952, when her husband ran for vice-president, she did her own housework, and she once confided to reporters that whenever she had a free evening, she took down her husband's suits and pressed them. Rather than talking about what she read or her views on national issues, she shared her thoughts on sewing dresses for her daughters and stitching up draperies on her home machine. Her husband emphasized the same helpmate quality in Pat when in his famous "Checkers" speech, he referred to her as a "wonderful stenographer."

Pat Nixon retreated farther and farther from the vivacity of her youth as her husband moved up in politics. She performed as energetically as anyone on the campaign trail, but she showed more stoic determination than real pleasure and her disillusionment with politics grew. Although she encouraged Richard to make the speech that could clear his name of improper handling of campaign funds, she resented the humiliation of having to bare the family's finances for the entire nation. As her husband put it in his *Memoirs,* she "lost zeal in 1952 for politics." By the mid-1950s she so strongly wanted her husband out of office that she obtained a written promise from him not to run again, but after signing the pledge, he broke it four times: in 1960, 1962, 1968, and 1972.

Nevertheless, Pat Nixon dutifully accompanied her husband on every trip where her presence was requested. When Dwight Eisenhower sent his vice-president on all kinds of international missions and advised him to "take Pat," she went. In Caracas, where the Nixons were spat on, had their cars stoned and windows broken, they feared for their lives. Other trips proved less dangerous, but very tiring, requiring that the Nixons leave their two young daughters Julie and Tricia, for weeks at a time. Pat later estimated that she spent only a fraction of her time at home.

In spite of her many public appearances, Richard Nixon gave no evidence that he considered Pat's opinions when framing his own. In his books, Richard refers to his wife's looks or to her courage and patience but not to her ideas. Several of his key White House staff treated Pat's projects very condescendingly, and researchers who later sought information on her years in the White House were likely to receive the curtest of refusals from Richard Nixon's office. In her book *Pat Nixon* (1986), Julie Nixon Eisenhower, who insists her parents were closer than people thought, offered only one instance of her mother's attempting to influence policy. According to Julie, Pat encouraged her husband to appoint a woman to the Supreme Court.

Pat Nixon turned her most productive efforts to restoration of the White House, where she was allowed more freedom. Helen McCain Smith, an aide to Pat Nixon throughout the White House years, noted that Pat's contributions lay in two areas: she made the mansion more accessible (by arranging special tours for disabled and blind persons, preparing a booklet on the gardens, adding exterior lighting, and changing the guards' uniforms to less imposing blazers); and she restored authentic antiques to the state rooms. Many of Jackie Kennedy's acquisitions had been copies, Smith noted, but Pat Nixon managed to bring in, without congressional appropriation of any kind, chairs that had once belonged to the Monroes, Duncan Phyfe pieces, and other authentic American furniture. She also restored the Map Room and arranged for the transfer, either by gift or on loan, of several important paintings of presidents and First Ladies. Pat, always a modest woman, played down this particular aspect of her tenure, and when television cameras came to tour the White House, Tricia provided the commentary.

During Richard Nixon's second year in office, the number of visitors to the White House broke all records. Pat chatted endlessly and tirelessly with hundreds of people. She also paid careful attention to the mail she received and insisted on an individual reply to each letter. Pat refused to use a facsimile of her signature, even in the face of staff arguments that no one could tell the difference. For four or five hours a day, she looked over responses that had been prepared, sending back for revisions those she deemed in need of improvement. She followed up on some of the requests herself, helping an immigrant woman, for example, with her citizenship problem. Right up to her husband's resignation, when the White House seemed in disarray and confusion, Pat Nixon persevered in answering the mountain of mail she was receiving.

Much of Pat's work as First Lady went unnoticed because of her sincere desire for privacy. "I know a lot," she said when offered a large sum of money to do a syndicated column, "but you have to keep it to yourself when you're in this position." On another occasion, when asked about the extreme poverty in which she grew up, she told Jessamyn West, a writer and her husband's cousin, "I don't like to think back. . . . It is behind me."

Pat's dissatisfaction with her image conveyed by the press is reflected in her having named three different press secretaries in five and a half years. Constance Stuart replaced Gerry Vander Heuvel in October 1969, and then in 1972, Helen McCain Smith was named. For a while, Smith seemed to be presenting a "new" Pat who traveled alone to Africa to represent her husband at the inauguration of the Liberian president. Later, on the pages of the *Ladies Home Journal*, Pat modeled pants suits, although she had not previously worn them in public.

Her daughter Julie pointed out that Pat was the most widely traveled First Lady (eighty-three nations), crisscrossing the United States many times. These could be grueling trips, as the *New York Times* noted in covering one Western visit. Pat was "pelted by rain, sleet, snow and hail, then sat serenely through sheets of rain in an outdoor amphitheater" before proceeding on to another city where she dedicated a new industrial arts building and addressed a crowd of 5,000 young people, most of whom were not old enough to vote. "I do or I die," Pat Nixon was frequently quoted as saying, "I never cancel out."

Her White House residence ended in 1974, after Richard Nixon resigned from office as a result of the Watergate scandal, following the break-in at the National Democratic Party headquarters in the summer of 1972.

In his final speech as president, and ever since, Richard Nixon refused to accept blame for acting improperly. For him, the culprits were news reporters who had treated him unfairly. He hinted that he might have fared better had he destroyed the tapes he made of meetings held in the Oval Office, but his lawyers had convinced him, he said, not to destroy evidence.

Pat Nixon, whose counsel the president apparently rejected or never sought, had reasoned otherwise, and reportedly told her friend, Helene Drown, that the tapes should have been burned or destroyed "because they were like a private diary, not public property." The First Lady's press secretary gave corroborating evidence that Pat had urged her husband to destroy the tapes before they had become the subject of litigation, but he did not listen.

In August 1974, when the television crews gathered at the White House to record Richard Nixon's last words as president, Pat stood behind him, apparently struggling to hold back tears. In a speech so rambling that it frightened some listeners, he spoke warmly and at length about his mother whom he called "a real saint," but did not mention his wife. As the Nixons walked with Gerald and Betty Ford to the helicopter that would take the Nixons on the first leg of their trip to retirement at San Clemente, Betty remarked on the red carpet that had been rolled out for them. Pat Nixon replied that after seeing a lot of red carpets, "you'll get so you hate them."

In her earlier announcements expressing interest in volunteerism, literacy, and the environment, Pat Nixon showed that she envisioned a role for herself that went beyond White House hostess. But she never quite managed to change the country's perception of her as a helpmate in the shadows. The failure, resulting from her own uneasiness about a public role and from a lack of consideration in the president's wing, meant that she did not enlarge the job of First Lady. In the years following her husband's resignation, illness and her own preferences prevented public appearances so that she was left to be remembered, as she frequently said she hoped to be, as the "wife of the president."

New Dimensions
to the Role of
First Lady
1974–1997

O VER THE YEARS the job of First Lady gradually moved beyond the exclusively private and ceremonial. As though to accelerate the trend begun in the 1960s toward strong, more activist First Ladies, some particularly determined, energetic women lived in the White House in the 1970s and 1980s. What had once been a daring exception, much commented on in the press, became commonplace. Elizabeth ("Betty") Bloomer Warren Ford, in the job less than a full term (August 1974 to January 1977), spoke with candor about subjects that had formerly been taboo, and her support of women's rights made headlines. Rosalynn Smith Carter (1977–1981) continued Betty Ford's example of using First Ladyhood as a platform for women's issues; and she added a new component by going off on international missions, which the White House billed as "substantive," and then testifying in front of a congressional committee on a mental health program. Nancy Davis Reagan began her Washington tenure in 1981 by insisting that she had little to say about presidential decisions. But by July 1985, when Ronald Reagan underwent surgery for cancer, she displaced the vice-president from the front pages of the country's newspapers and announced herself at a White House reception as "the President's stand-in." Unlike Edith

Wilson, who had faced charges of "petticoat government" and "rule by regency," these three First Ladies encountered only the mildest criticism. By 1993, the credentials of First Lady Hillary Clinton looked very much like those of the President.

ELIZABETH "BETTY" BLOOMER
WARREN FORD

B ETTY FORD appeared particularly eager to make her own mark, and she apparently had her husband's support. President Ford publicly acknowledged that he valued her opinions and admitted that in one of his most criticized moves, the pardon of Richard Nixon, she had wielded considerable clout. Gerald Ford told an aide that he and Betty had talked over the Nixon pardon and had decided to take action because the uncertainty about what would happen to Nixon was "tearing the country to pieces." On another occasion, Gerald Ford volunteered to an interviewer that Betty "obviously has a great deal of influence."

That special partnership had begun twenty-six years before it reached the White House when, in 1948, Gerald Ford and Betty Bloomer Warren were married. Born in Chicago in 1918, Betty had married William Warren, a man from her hometown of Grand Rapids. When that marriage ended in divorce five years later, she was working as a fashion coordinator for a local department store.

Gerald Ford, a thirty-five-year-old bachelor making his first run for Congress, had not included a Washington career in his original marriage proposal to Betty. Betty Ford later admitted that she had lacked preparation to "be a political wife." From the moment he arrived late for their marriage ceremony due to a campaign appearance, she began learning the long, sometimes painful lesson that Gerald Ford's family frequently came second to his work.

During his time in Congress, she dutifully joined the appropriate wives' clubs, taught Sunday school, and saw to most of the details of raising the three boys and one girl born to them in the first seven years of their marriage. As her husband's ambitions grew to include Speaker of the House, so too did his absences from home, but these were not the campaign trips that aspiring presidential candidates make with spouse in tow. Gerald Ford appeared in his Republican colleagues' home districts to bolster their election chances—and in such contests, his wife played no part.

While Gerald Ford accepted as many as two hundred speaking invitations in one year, Betty became so accustomed to chauffeuring their sons to the emergency room of the local hospital after minor injuries that she laughingly suggested that the family car could make the trip on its own.

In addition to the strains resulting from her husband's absences, Betty Ford suffered from a pinched nerve and arthritis. Finally, in 1970, she sought professional help, and as a result of several months of counseling, she resolved to keep more time for herself and to persuade her husband to leave Washington after his congressional term ended in 1976. Those plans abruptly changed in late 1973 when Vice-president Spiro Agnew resigned and Gerald Ford was named to that job. Instead of preparing to end her Washington residence as the unknown spouse of a Michigan congressman, Betty Ford moved into the center of national attention.

Maintaining her equilibrium was not easy when within a year Richard Nixon resigned the presidency in 1974 and Gerald Ford moved up to that office. The entire Ford family, none of whom had ever campaigned in a constituency larger than half a million people, became the focus of more scrutiny than they had ever imagined possible. Magazines profiled the four Ford children, and Betty Ford, the woman *Good Housekeeping* said "nobody knows," quickly became someone whom everybody sought to meet.

Having arrived in Washington when Bess Truman was First Lady, Betty Ford had come to admire (as many other Washington wives had) the way Bess combined being in the spotlight with staying "so humble." Bess's example guided her, she wrote. Perhaps Betty Ford felt particular sympathy for another Midwesterner, who like herself had moved without much warning or preparation into the White House. Certainly the two women shared little in their attitudes toward privacy or in their views about whether presidential wives should take sides on controversial matters. While Bess Truman refused to speak up on any matter more divisive than that of restoring the White House, Betty Ford appeared willing to talk more freely.

The country's disillusionment with government influenced the new First Lady. The United States' recent military involvement in Vietnam and the rumors of doctored casualty reports and other concealments, Spiro Agnew's "nolo contendere" response to charges that he had accepted bribes, and Richard Nixon's alleged complicity in the Watergate crimes committed during his 1972 campaign—all added to a consensus that honesty had value but that in government it was rare. Betty Ford explained that she felt a need to be open. "I tried to be honest," she later wrote in her autobiography. "I tried not to dodge subjects. I felt the people had a right to know where I stood."

In discussions with reporters, she spoke with disarming frankness about her children, her own health problems, and how she felt about being a political wife. When she hired a press secretary, she gave her two assignments, one of which was to provide "honest answers." This was no new guise contrived to impress the public. Betty Ford had always had a reputation for candor, and she had already shocked reporters when, as wife of the vice-president, she gave as explanation for her drowsiness: "I take a Valium every day." Her announcements received much attention from the press; and in

short order, Betty Ford made honesty something chic—and reticence, passé. Helen Thomas, veteran UPI reporter, echoed her
colleagues when she pronounced Betty Ford a "real friend" of the
press, and Rosalynn Carter, who succeeded Betty, credited her with
"making it easier to talk."

This new approach became immediately evident when Betty Ford
scheduled her first press conference less than a month after her
husband's swearing in as president. One hundred and fifty reporters
heard a slightly nervous Betty Ford announce that she intended to
work for substantive changes, especially in the campaign for ratification of the Equal Rights Amendment. This was quite a different
exchange than the one in March 1933, when fewer than three dozen
reporters attended Eleanor Roosevelt's first press conference and
heard her promise to avoid substantive issues and never comment
on pending legislation. In Betty Ford, feminists finally had a First
Lady who worked for them openly, rather than discreetly behind the
scenes.

Her outspokenness continued when a reporter asked how the new
First Lady stood on abortion, and Betty Ford described her position
as "definitely closer" to that of Nelson Rockefeller, who supported
the Supreme Court's decision leaving the matter up to the woman
and her physician, than to that of Senator James Buckley, who
thought the Court had gone too far. Reporters could hardly fail to
notice that Gerald Ford would have answered differently. In Alabama, a few days later, Betty Ford spoke to the fears of many American mothers when she speculated that her children had probably
experimented with marijuana. Later, she raised some eyebrows
when she confessed that when voting she had often been "tempted
to split" her ticket.

In September 1974 a routine physical examination revealed that
Betty Ford had breast cancer, and she entered a Washington hospital for surgery. Less than twenty years before, the Eisenhower White
House had refused to use the word "hysterectomy" in describing
the First Lady's surgery, but the Fords made "mastectomy" a house-

hold word. Other famous women, including Alice Roosevelt Long-worth and former child star Shirley Temple Black, had had similar surgery performed, but they had not received quite the same attention as the First Lady.

The decision to level with the public came naturally to the Fords. Ron Nessen, the president's press secretary, later explained that while Betty was still on the operating table, the staff produced doctors for briefings. While Nessen seemed to concentrate on the political rewards of being open and candid, Betty Ford emphasized the humanitarian value. If she had cancer, then many other women had it, she said, and "If I don't make it public, then their lives will be gone."

Articles on the First Lady's surgery went beyond her individual case to discuss different treatments—comparing the advantages of radical mastectomies over more limited versions and discussing the necessity of follow-up drug or radiation treatment. In the process of satisfying their curiosity about the woman who lived in the White House, many Americans learned a great deal about breast cancer, one of the leading causes of death among women. Physicians reported a tenfold increase in requests for examinations. Some of these mammograms revealed cancers at an early stage and increased the chances for successful treatment and cure. For Betty Ford, this marked a new understanding of the clout held by First Ladies: "Lying in the hospital, thinking of all those women going for cancer checkups because of me, I'd come to recognize more clearly the power of the woman in the White House. Not my power, but the power of the position, a power which could be used to help."

For the rest of her time in the White House, Betty Ford continued to use that power for causes she believed in such as the Equal Rights Amendment. When the time came for votes in states considered likely to approve the amendment, the president's wife got on the telephone and lobbied wavering legislators for their votes. Her press secretary, Sheila Rabb Weidenfeld, reported that Betty used a very gentle approach, but that she could be persuasive. "I realize you're under a lot of pressure from the voters today," she told one woman legislator from a rural district in Missouri, "but I'm just calling to let you know that the President and I are considerably interested. I think the ERA is so important." The president's wife installed a separate telephone line in the White House for her lobbying. When asked about the propriety of intruding in state politics, Betty's press secretary insisted this was a national issue since an amendment to the Constitution was at stake. To those who thought such activism inappropriate, Betty Ford replied that she would "stick to my guns," and she did, even when mail ran three to one against her and pickets marched in front of the White House waving "Stop ERA" signs. She appeared undaunted by letters to the editors of major newspapers charging her with "arm twisting tactics" or by more dramatic objections, such as that of a group of black-clad figures who paraded in front of the White House and then were shown on evening television, chanting in unison, "Betty Ford is trying to press a second-rate manhood on American women."

In addition to her work on women's issues, Betty Ford devoted considerable attention to the arts, especially dance. She had begun dancing when she was eight years old and during two summers she had studied with Martha Graham at Bennington College. After graduating from high school, she had rejected college and Grand Rapids in favor of New York City and more dance. Although she never made Graham's main troupe and had to support herself partly by modeling for the John Powers Agency, she retained a lifelong interest in dance.

Art enthusiasts also welcomed an advocate in the White House. Innumerable photographs of her attending dance programs and meeting with artists gave the public an image of a healthy, active president's wife involved in a noncontroversial area. In fact, her association with dance far outshadowed much of her other work as First Lady.

In 1975, the National Academy of Design named Betty Ford a Fellow, the first president's wife to be so honored since the group singled out Eleanor Roosevelt in 1934. In making the award, the photographer Ansel Adams called Betty "the most refreshing character we've had in public life for sometime" (and he significantly did not limit the field to women).

Not all of Betty Ford's press coverage was so kind. In July 1975, she had taped an interview for the television program "60 Minutes," and her press secretary judged that she had come across as articulate and warm. Public reaction to the interview, when it aired on August 10, was something else. The Fords were vacationing in Vail, Colorado, when telephone calls began coming in from reporters who wanted to follow up on Betty's comments. In the interview, the First Lady had been asked what she would do if her daughter, then eighteen years old, told her she was having "an affair." Betty Ford had replied that she would not be surprised but would try to counsel and advise her. She had stressed the need to keep communication channels open between parents and children no matter what the circumstances, but the newspapers took her words out of context and implied that she expected, even condoned, premarital sex among teenagers. White House mail reflected the difference between the television show and printed accounts. Letters supporting the First Lady came from viewers of "60 Minutes," while her critics had read the newspapers.

The president admitted to a Minneapolis meeting of broadcast and newspaper executives that when he heard the interview he predicted it would cost him 10 million votes but after reading the newspapers he had doubled the damage. Betty's press secretary kept insisting that in the long run the television appearance would work to the president's advantage and she was right. A Harris Poll, taken three months later, showed 60 percent of the respondents approved of Betty Ford's handling of the hypothetical question about her daughter, while only 27 percent disagreed. For the pollsters, the president's wife represented "a solid asset" to her husband.

In many ways a very traditional wife, Betty Ford crossed lines to appeal to feminists and to less independent-minded housewives. Her whole life history spoke to the experience of women who, like herself, had never worked a day outside their own homes after their marriages. But her outspoken support of women's issues gained approval from others who could not imagine adulthood without careers of their own. Her candor in dealing with her own experiences—cancer surgery, psychotherapy, and her children's experimentation with illegal drugs—won the admiration of women who were tired of hearing about "super perfect" families in the White House.

Before she had held the job six months, Betty Ford's hope that she would be remembered "in a very kind way as a constructive wife of the President" was assured. Her unfortunate bout with cancer aroused admiration for her courage, and her popularity cut across social and economic lines. The woman almost unknown to the public three years earlier had made large strides, and she would continue in the post–White House years to make headlines with her Betty Ford Clinic and her admissions of her own dependency on alcohol and prescribed drugs. In 1976, all this lay ahead. She had already shown, however, and the 1976 campaign buttons supporting "Betty's husband for President" bore her out—just how valuable an active presidential wife could be.

ROSALYNN SMITH CARTER

BETTY FORD'S Democratic counterpart in the 1976 election proved a formidable opponent, but unlike Betty (or any of the

preceding four First Ladies), Rosalynn Smith Carter was a newcomer to Washington. Her apprenticeship had been limited to the
Georgia governor's mansion and to a long campaign across the
nation.

However, this did not stop Rosalynn from compiling a remarkable list of accomplishments in just four years, and she did it as the
most traditional of wives. "Jimmy and I were always partners," she
would announce, and then proceed to act in such a way that historians would describe her as "surrogate, confidante, and joint pol-
icymaker."

Rosalynn was fifty years old at the time of Jimmy's inauguration
in January 1977. Her life up to that point had been divided
roughly into thirds, with the initial segment ending at age fourteen
when her father died. Like most of her immediate predecessors,
she experienced the death of a parent before she had reached
adulthood, and for her the loss was traumatic. "He thought I could
do anything," she later recalled; and since she was the oldest of his
four children, she took his deathbed request to "look after Mother
for me" more to heart than did the others. Her mother added to
Rosalynn's sense of responsibility by relying on her almost as another adult. "I was devastated," Rosalynn wrote. "My childhood
really ended at that moment."

Her education, however, was just beginning. A seventh grade
teacher who was "young" and "beautiful" appeared to Rosalynn to
know more than anyone she had ever met. She prodded her students to read the newspaper and listen to the radio, thus stretching
their minds about the country and the world, and encouraging
them "to discover a world of interesting people and faraway
places."

High school graduation came first—with Rosalynn delivering the
valedictory for her class of eleven—and then two years at a nearby
junior college. Her real education began, however, when at eighteen, she married the local boy who had already distinguished himself by being nominated to the U.S. Naval Academy. Jimmy Carter,
ready for his first naval assignment, was her ticket out of Georgia.

He always teased her, she said later, about marrying him to get out of Plains.

For a curious and energetic young wife, having a husband whose assignments took them to Norfolk, Virginia, then Hawaii, and finally Connecticut offered opportunities that she could only have dreamed of in tiny Plains, Georgia. While Jimmy was frequently on duty at sea for days or even weeks at a time, Rosalynn managed a household that eventually included three sons born within five years. When her husband came home, she worked with him through courses in the "Great Books" and in classical music. She learned the hula in Hawaii and memorized Shakespeare in Virginia, but most importantly she developed confidence that she could do things for herself. Jimmy assumed that she could manage well, she wrote in her autobiography, "and he always made me feel he was proud of me. So I was forced to discover that I could do the things that had to be done."

The absence of close friends increased Rosalynn's emotional dependence on her husband. Plains had no other girls her age, she recalled later, and the naval assignments, each lasting only a few years, gave little opportunity to forge strong friendships. Her days were filled with housekeeping. "I was the total wife and mother." she later wrote, washing, ironing, cooking and mopping floors, but she was doing it all on her own, without the supervision of either mother or mother-in-law. The new independence suited her, and she recalled, "I was more content than I had been in years."

The third (but first political) segment of Rosalynn Carter's life began inauspiciously when she reluctantly returned to live in Georgia. In 1953, her father-in-law died, and Jimmy decided that his younger brother Billy, still in high school, needed help running the family businesses. Rosalynn disliked relinquishing the independence that she had gained but in "the only major disagreement" of their marriage, she lost. Or in the short run, it seemed that she had. She returned to Plains with Jimmy and their three sons. Very quickly she realized that the town had not changed but she had. With the confidence she had acquired away from home, she set out to explore the opportunities she had not recognized before. She played golf, took dancing lessons, and went off with friends on a trip to New Orleans. Even she had to admit she was "enjoying this life."

More significantly, she became involved in some of the issues that affected the small town—issues that often had direct and personal implications but on the local level seemed solvable. Jimmy's appointment to the school board put the Carters in the middle of the integration struggle, or as Rosalynn describes their position, off to a minority side of it. "Though we were both raised in the South and had accepted segregation as children," she explained, "Jimmy and I had traveled enough to see a different way of life." Not many of their neighbors agreed with them, however, and so they kept their views to themselves.

The Carters' work in their church and other local organizations led them into politics, but it was Jimmy who took the lead. On his thirty-eighth birthday, he announced his candidacy for the state Senate. Rosalynn had already taken over the bookkeeping at the family's peanut warehouse, and she could evaluate, just by checking the accounts, which sections of the business made money and which lost. While Jimmy spent more time at legislative sessions in the state capital, she had to make more business decisions. Her own public service was very limited—the idea of delivering speeches made her physically ill, and when Jimmy first ran for governor in 1966, she and her sons did nothing more than pass out brochures and smile for photographs in front of a vehicle marked "Carter Family."

Jimmy Carter lost that election, but in his next try in 1970, the entire family resolved to work harder. For Rosalynn, that meant conquering her fear of public speaking. Jimmy encouraged her to stop memorizing her script so she could speak extemporaneously from notecards, and the results surprised even her. She found that people listened attentively and wanted to hear more. That kind of response gave her "a wonderful feeling" and represented "quite a breakthrough."

Successful in that second gubernatorial race, the Carters moved into the spotlight of the state capital. It was a larger transition, she frequently said, than that she later made from Georgia to the White House. Other presidents' wives (including Edith Roosevelt and Eleanor Roosevelt in Albany and Ellen Wilson in Trenton) had pointed to their husbands' governorship years as times of growth, and Rosalynn also reported that she used those years to gain confidence in her social and administrative abilities. Travels around the state exposed her to problems in mental health, education, and care for the aged, and she developed a new appreciation of what government could do to make individuals' lives better. By the time Jimmy prepared to run for president in 1976, she showed almost none of her former reticence about taking a public role for herself. By January 20, 1977, when she strode down Pennsylvania Avenue toward Number 1600, little remained of the tentative teenager who had left Plains, Georgia, thirty years earlier.

Much of the confidence developed during her fourteen months on the road before Jimmy won the 1976 nomination. It was a campaign unequaled among politicians' wives. Victory must have seemed an impossible dream at the beginning when few Americans outside Georgia had heard of Jimmy Carter. Even Jimmy's mother, the indefatigable Lillian Carter, was rumored to have responded to her son's announcement that he was running for president with the question "President of what?" Rosalynn became accustomed to similar replies when she first went out to speak for Jimmy.

The Carters had reasoned that in this difficult, uphill campaign, they could cover more ground if they traveled separately, and when she set out on her first out-of-state appearance to nearby Florida, she was accompanied only by one good friend. Guided by a Florida road map and a slightly outdated list of Democratic Party officials, the two women stopped wherever they spotted a radio transmitter or found somebody willing to gather a few friends together. Rosalynn would make her speech about why Jimmy should be president, answer any questions, and then prepare to speed on to the next town.

Rosalynn later graduated to commercial airlines and then to her own private plane but her schedule never lightened. She described campaigning as "a job, a very demanding job, with pressures and deadlines." From Monday to Friday, she was on the road, and then on the weekend she returned to Plains to rest up, eat "a square meal," confer with her husband, and see the rest of the family, including their daughter, Amy, who was not yet ten years old. "It was not a vocation I would want to pursue for a life," Rosalynn wrote when it was all over, "but it was essential."

Like all successful campaigners, Rosalynn Carter had to decide what to do with victory, and no woman ever entered the White House with a clearer agenda for herself—nor a longer one. She would continue to be active in mental health, because that was what she knew best, and she would work for the ratification of the Equal Rights Amendment, which still needed the approval of three states. She also expected to help the aging and to encourage volunteerism on the local level. To assist her, she appointed a staff of eighteen, headed by her press secretary and East Wing coordinator, Mary Finch Hoyt, a veteran of the Edmund Muskie and George McGovern presidential races. Eventually Rosalynn had a staff of twenty-one, not so large as she would have liked but larger than any East Wing staff in history.

Even before the inauguration in 1977, Rosalynn Carter was busy in her new job. In December 1976, she attended (although not in an official capacity) the inauguration of Mexico's new president, and then she returned to preside over a mental health conference in Philadelphia. After Jimmy took office, she increased momentum and within months had announced a precedent-breaking trip to Central and South America.

While other presidential wives had typically represented their husbands on ceremonial and fact-finding international missions, none had claimed to work out policy. Eleanor Roosevelt's trips

across both the Atlantic and the Pacific during World War II and
Lady Bird Johnson's attendance at the funeral of Greece's King Paul
in 1964 had underlined the surrogate role some First Ladies took,
but neither had claimed to make decisions. Rosalynn Carter's trip to
seven Central and South American countries in the spring of 1977
was treated seriously by the president's office and she underlined
the trip's importance when she revealed that she had prepared by
studying Spanish and by briefings with members of the State Department and the National Security Council. She planned to deliver
in each country a "summary of the administration's foreign policy
approach," and then go on to discuss more specific problems of
local interest.

In Costa Rica she listened to complaints that the United States
was restricting that country's trade, in Ecuador to objections that
her husband should not have vetoed the sale of Israeli jets, and in
Peru to an explanation for that country's arms buildup. When she
returned to Washington, she reported to the Senate Foreign Relations Committee on what she had seen and heard.

The trip brought mixed returns. Heads of state who met with the
American First Lady appeared uncertain as to how they should
react, and while some Latins applauded her enthusiasm for learning
their language, others expressed discomfort about receiving a
United States representative who had been neither elected nor appointed. Reporters in Jamaica questioned whether she had the right
to speak for her husband, and when she got home, the discussion
continued. Meg Greenfield, in a *Newsweek* article entitled, "Mrs.
President," explored the implications of the First Lady's trip and
concluded that if Rosalynn wanted a role in diplomacy, she should
find a way to make herself accountable for her actions. A State
Department official attempted to blunt some of the criticism by
describing Rosalynn's trip as "mainly questioning."

The fact that all her later international travel fell within the older,
more traditional bounds for presidents' wives indicates that the
Carters may have judged the South American venture not entirely

successful, although Rosalynn explained the lack of additional trips by saying that Jimmy was "able to go himself." She continued to signal her significant role in her husband's administration but in other ways—in announcements that she met regularly with him for "working" lunches and that she attended meetings of his closest advisers, including the cabinet.

Most of her energies were concentrated on the projects she had named early in the administration, especially mental health. Because she could not legally serve as actual chair of the President's Council on Mental Health, she took an honorary (but working) title and then accepted invitations to speak on the subject in Canada and in Europe. On February 7, 1979, she went before the Senate Resource Subcommittee to testify in favor of increased federal spending for mental health programs, and there she tangled with Chairman Edward Kennedy over what constituted a satisfactory federal health budget.

As Rosalynn continued to follow her Mental Health Systems Act through the various committees, she made history of two kinds. Not only was she the first presidential wife to testify before a congressional committee since Eleanor Roosevelt appeared in the 1940s, but in this case the chairman of the Senate committee, Senator Edward Kennedy, was a strong contender for her husband's job.

Although the act did not provide for a national health insurance program, it did outline goals to move mental health patients to smaller community facilities, and to increase services to the poor. The act finally passed in September 1980, but the Carter celebration was brief because within weeks Ronald Reagan had won the presidential election. "The funding for our legislation was killed," Rosalynn wrote, "by the philosophy of a new President. It was a bitter loss."

In addition to the average of two meetings per month that she attended on mental health projects, she also met with groups concerned about women's issues and with people working on problems of the elderly. In November 1979, she journeyed to Thailand to inspect refugee camps, and on her return to Washington, she added this as another cause to her agenda.

When President Carter invited Middle Eastern leaders to a meeting at Camp David in September 1978, he involved Rosalynn in a special way, thus demonstrating once more how the elasticity in the American presidency opens the way for including spouses in substantive decisions. Not since Theodore Roosevelt mediated between two foreign powers to end the Russo-Japanese War in 1905 had an American chief executive attempted quite what Jimmy Carter did. In his invitations to both Middle Eastern leaders, Jimmy Carter had pointedly included their wives, telling Rosalynn, "There are going to be a lot of hard feelings and tough fights and the atmosphere will be more congenial if all of you are there."

Rosalynn's role at the Camp David summit extended, however, beyond providing a hospitable setting for the talks and companionship for the wives. Jimmy briefed Rosalynn, she later wrote, because "he wanted me to understand the issues as well as the nuances of certain words and phrases. What we called the West Bank, for example, was Judea and Samaria to Israeli Prime Minister Menachem Begin." Although she lost her chance to sit in on the first meeting of the three leaders because the other two wives were delayed in arriving, she began immediately to keep a record of what she observed and what her husband told her. By the end of the twelve-day meeting, she had almost two hundred pages of notes, which eventually became the basis for one chapter in her autobiography.

Previous presidential wives had played down their influence—Helen Taft insisted her advice stopped when her husband became president; Edith Wilson maintained that she never made any decision; Eleanor Roosevelt patiently reiterated to dubious listeners that she never tried to steer Franklin to any particular course of action. Rosalynn Carter took no credit, of course, for conducting the Camp David talks but she did not minimize her role. It had been her enthusiastic support for the idea that had convinced Jimmy to try for the peace agreement, she wrote, and she went with him through a "see-saw" of emotions during the long negotiations.

Rosalynn played more than one role at the Camp David talks. Partly, she served as the president's cover, returning to the White House to substitute for him at events that had been previously scheduled. Nobody had expected the summit to continue so long, and the president had agreed to meet with leaders of the Italian-American and Hispanic communities and to host a concert for the world-famous cellist, Mstislav Rostropovich. "One of us had to be there," Rosalynn explained, "and it was obviously going to be me," so she helicoptered back to the White House, making every effort to give no premature indications of how the talks were going. Her subsequent description of the summit earned her high marks, and a *New York Times* book reviewer wrote that Rosalynn was a better and franker writer "hands down" than her husband, and that in describing the Camp David summit and other events of the Carter administration, she had written "what may turn out to be the best human account" of that period.

Not all of Rosalynn Carter's press coverage was so kind, and she frequently complained about it. She had selected an experienced press secretary, Mary Finch Hoyt, who had assisted the wives of several presidential candidates, but Hoyt spent much of her time correcting erroneous stories. Reporters seemed unable to agree on what the First Lady was doing—they shifted from emphasizing her weakness to portraying her as having excessive clout. Insisting that she was somewhere in the middle, Rosalynn complained that her image changed from "fuzzy" to "most powerful" after she began attending cabinet meetings in early 1978. She tried to remain philosophical: "I had already learned from more than a decade of political life that I was going to be criticized no matter what I did, so I might as well be criticized for something I wanted to do. (If I had spent all day 'pouring tea,' I would have been criticized for that too.)"

Much as she wished to emphasize her work on substantive issues, the press would not ignore other more personal elements of her life.

She recalled that she had impulsively flown to New York with her assistant Madeline MacBean to buy clothes, but that, hoping to avoid attention, she had not even informed her own press secretary. When she had finished shopping and was preparing to leave a Seventh Avenue building, "flashbulbs blinded me," she wrote, "and it seemed that the whole New York press corps was waiting for me." The press's stories drew attention away from what Rosalynn considered more important topics, but she had little choice in the matter—Americans wanted to know as much as possible about their First Lady.

Although Rosalynn Carter has described as "considerable" the time she spent on ceremonial appearances, she gave the impression of being much more involved in the substantive aspects of her husband's administration than in the hostess part. She never selected a china pattern for the White House collection and did not even spend the full amount of money allotted for refurbishing the family's quarters in the mansion. In her autobiography, *First Lady from Plains,* the chapter entitled "People, Parties and Protocol" is one of the shortest in the book, and researchers who hope to find there descriptions of her clothing, menus, and flower arrangements will be disappointed. Julia Grant's *Memoirs,* which were written (but not published) almost exactly one century before Rosalynn's, contain mostly social details on the White House years, but Rosalynn correctly realized that expectations for First Ladies had changed.

The preceding century had altered (among other things) women's chances for education, employment, and political participation, and Rosalynn Carter followed Betty Ford's example of using her influence to make further changes. She lobbied state legislators to vote for the Equal Rights Amendment and she attended the International Woman's Year meeting in Houston in November 1977. But while Betty spoke of the need for women to "feel liberated whatever their job or family situation," Rosalynn emphasized the justice of equal pay for equal work. Rosalynn also proudly listed her husband's appointments of women to important positions: three cabinet secretaries (out of a total of six in history) and forty-one federal judges. "It was always understood between us," she wrote, "that a woman would be appointed "if a vacancy occurred on the Supreme Court."

Rosalynn's partnership with her husband combined competence with unquestioned loyalty, and her four years in the White House helped extend the job of president's wife beyond what it had ever been. On her own, and with her husband's concurrence, she took a portion of his quest for her own—campaigning full-time and putting her best efforts into making the administration a success.

For her part, Rosalynn was pleased with her demanding role. Once presidents' wives had been confined to "official hostess" and "private helpmeet," she wrote, but the public expectation has changed "and there is a general presumption that the projects of a First Lady will be substantive, highly publicized, and closely scrutinized. I am thankful for the change."

NANCY DAVIS REAGAN

EVOKING Jackie Kennedy's emphasis on elegance and style, Nancy Davis Reagan would bring her own set of priorities to the role of First Lady (1981–1989). Her more formal, glamorous lifestyle contrasted markedly with the unpretentious public image of her predecessor. Especially during the early years of her husband's first term, Nancy Reagan appeared to concentrate her time more on china patterns and luncheons for her wealthy friends than on substantive issues. Washington caterers, whose business in caviar and other imported delicacies increased overnight, and dress designers, whose creations in the four-figure range became *de rigueur* at White House parties, applauded the change. To underscore her efforts to put "the best of everything" in the White House, Nancy invited Letitia Baldrige, social secretary during the Kennedy presidential years, to return to Washington to make sure that things were done correctly. Old discussions about the proper role of a First Lady were revived—whether as a helpmate and homemaker or as a more out-spoken voice to help solve important problems.

For many Americans, Nancy Reagan epitomized an old-fashioned model of womanliness. Nancy had announced on more than one occasion that her "life began when I met my husband" and that seeing to his well-being was her one career. She had gladly let an MGM movie contract expire at the end of seven years in order to dedicate her total energy to her husband and children. Ronald had not pushed her—it was what she had always wanted, she said, and on the questionnaire she completed when she arrived in Hollywood, she had listed as her ambition in life "to have a successful, happy marriage."

Biographers frequently point to the lack of security and perma-nence in Nancy's childhood as the reason for her putting great emphasis on her marriage. Born to an actress, who soon left her daughter with relatives in order to pursue her career, and to an auto salesman who left both of them, Nancy Davis Reagan spent her early years (as Anne Frances Robbins) living in Baltimore with an aunt. When her mother remarried, this time choosing a more settled mate, and took her daughter to live in Chicago, the new husband adopted the girl, providing the name she later used in movies— Nancy Davis. Her stepfather had a son from a previous marriage but Nancy was the only daughter of this successful neurosurgeon and he made the rest of her growing up protected and secure: a debut, four years at Smith, where she majored in drama, and then a try at Hollywood with help from family friends.

Despite criticism that Nancy Reagan went too far in her devotion to her husband, she did play an important part in Ronald Reagan's political ascent. Several of her husband's advisers, even those who had suffered expressions of her displeasure, agreed on her value, and suggested that she deserved as much responsibility for Ronald Reagan's success as he did.

Part of Nancy's value resulted from the unorthodox path her husband took to the top. While most high offices in national politics had typically been gained by working up a ladder of lesser jobs, some of the most visible posts in the 1960s and 1970s began to go to people who had achieved a reputation in one field and then transferred that popularity to government. Astronauts, athletes, and actors turned up as candidates for high office.

Such a horizontal entry into politics at the top (Ronald Reagan took his first political office as governor of California in 1967 when he was almost fifty-six years old) involved considerable money and a support staff that could play a variety of roles. A spouse who could be endlessly amiable and pleasant to prospective contributors was no small asset. Nancy Reagan lunched with wives, and she gamely shared long private plane rides with people she had just met.

Nancy gave every indication of wanting to transfer this supportive wife-style to Washington, and she began by refurbishing the White House. The routine appropriation of $50,000 that Congress allotted each new president was inadequate for her plans, which included a decorator who usually put that much into a single room (art and antiques were additional). To raise the $900,000 she needed, Nancy turned to private donors. Some of the contributions came from old Hollywood friends, but critics were not so sure about the provenance of the rest. President Reagan had ended the remaining price controls on domestic oil and gasoline as soon as he took office, several months before the controls were slated to come off; when names of some who had apparently profited from the move showed up on the list of White House donors, suspicion grew that the largess was not motivated solely by patriotism. Whatever their reasons for giving, the contributors had received tax deductions, and since many of them paid federal levies at the rate of 50 percent, the government was footing half the bill.

Considerably more unsettling to many critics was an announcement that $200,000 would be spent on new china for the White House—an announcement made one day before the administration publicized a plan to decrease nutrition standards for school lunch programs.

Also during Nancy Reagan's first year in Washington, she had to deal with one of the worst experiences of her life—the attempted assassination of her husband in March 1981. For months afterward, Nancy could not even refer to the incident more directly than "that thing that happened," and during a televised interview much later, she broke into tears when describing her reaction. She had announced early in the administration that she would continue with a Foster Grandparents program that she had worked with in California, but the effects of the assassination attempt left her little energy, and public perception of her association with the program was weak at best.

During the second year of the Reagan White House, the president's staff turned its attention to Nancy and set out to temper her elitist image. Her secretary announced that the designer clothes received as gifts would be donated to museums. Nancy Reagan learned to make jokes about herself. To those who referred to her as "Queen Nancy," she quipped that she would never wear a crown because it would mess her hair.

By the middle of the first Reagan administration, it had become clear that Nancy needed to do more, and she began to devote more time to serious problems, particularly drug abuse. Nancy Reagan visited drug care faciles, headed up a series of community-based endeavors billed on television as the "Chemical People," and in April 1985 she invited the wives of other countries' leaders to meet with her in Washington at the First Ladies Conference to discuss drug problems. Nancy Reagan also journeyed to the Vatican to discuss drug abuse with Pope John Paul II, and she arrived in Rome in what one reporter described as an "entourage more appropriate to a visiting head of state."

Nancy Reagan had occasionally explained that drug abuse had always been a top priority for her but that she had been warned away from it by advisers who judged it too "downbeat." Yet whatever the reasons for her changed approach to her role as First Lady, her popularity immediately rose, showing that her involvement in rehabilitation programs was perceived as both genuine and significant.

As the country's economy improved, the president's popularity rose even higher. This show of confidence along with the security of having entered into a second presidential term in January 1985 encouraged Nancy Reagan to take an even more prominent part in the administration. The Reagans had always played down or dismissed accounts that Nancy exerted clout in Ronald's political decisions. However, evidence to the contrary came from high White House sources who publicly described her as "indispensable," "a savvy adviser," and important on political matters and personnel decisions in the executive branch.

What happened in the summer of 1985 added fuel to that speculation. Immediately following President Reagan's surgery for cancer in July, Nancy returned to the White House to receive foreign dignitaries. As soon as it became clear that the president's surgery would require him to work on a reduced schedule, broadcasters speculated on who was "in charge in the White House"—namely the president, his chief of staff (Donald Regan), and the First Lady.

Ronald Reagan lent weight to this interpretation when, in a radio address following his surgery, he spoke about the contributions of First Ladies who, he said, "aren't elected and they don't receive a salary" but "they've all been heroes." He ticked off the most famous: "Abigail Adams helped invent America. Dolley Madison helped protect it. Eleanor Roosevelt was FDR's eyes and ears." Then he added, "Nancy is my everything. When I look back on these days, Nancy, I'll remember your radiance and your strength, your support and for taking part in the business of the nation. I say to myself, but also on behalf of the nation, 'Thank you, partner. Thanks for everything.' "

No wonder the *New York Times* on July 13, 1986, chose to describe Nancy Reagan as having "expanded the role of First Lady into a sort of Associate Presidency." The change was not that the president's wife played a part in important decisions. Spouses had often taken on special responsibilities in times of illness or other crisis, but in the White House that role had often been camouflaged or, as in the case of Edith Wilson, denigrated. But after Betty Ford, who openly disagreed with her husband on a whole list of important national issues, and Rosalynn Carter, who sat in on cabinet meetings and represented Jimmy Carter in substantive talks with leaders in Latin America, Nancy Reagan's initiatives were now taken more as a matter of course.

The fact that perception of the First Lady's influence had become international is suggested by a duo of telephone calls from the Philippines to Washington in February 1986, as the ruling Marcos family decided whether or not to flee. Ferdinand Marcos sought advice by telephone from Senator Paul Laxalt, a close friend of President Reagan's; Imelda Marcos called Nancy.

The idea that wives—who were neither elected nor appointed—participated in their husbands' political careers had clearly become accepted outside the United States by the 1980s. Raisa Gorbachev, the intelligent, chic wife of the Soviet Union's general secretary, received considerable publicity when she accompanied her husband to several international conferences; and cameras from around the world focused on Nancy Reagan and Raisa Gorbachev when the Reagans visited Moscow during the summer of 1988. Reporters speculated that they did not get along. But the novelty was not their friendship—or lack of it—but that even the Soviet Union, once so adverse to discussing the private lives of its leaders, had allowed the wife of a prominent Soviet leader to become a familiar figure to the rest of the world.

Meanwhile, Nancy Reagan's influence would be underscored that year with the publication of *For The Record*, a controversial book by her husband's chief of staff, Donald Regan, who said that Nancy vetoed the scheduling of press conferences and other Presidential appearances despite the objections of staff members. "Mrs. Reagan's concern for her husband's health was understandable, even admirable," Regan wrote, "but it seemed to me excessive, particularly since the President himself did not seem to think that there was any need for him to slow down . . . ." Regan went on to say that Nancy consulted her California astrologist before making some of these scheduling decisions.

In her own defense, the president's wife said, speaking to the American Newspaper Publishers Association, "I'm a woman who loves her husband, and I make no apologies for looking out for his personal and political welfare."

Despite criticism from the press throughout her White House years, Nancy Reagan showed no sign of changing her course. Her inner strength helped her through the stressful times following the assassination attempt on her husband, and through the last months of 1987 when her mother died and then Nancy herself had to undergo surgery for breast cancer. Rather than withdraw in seclusion as nineteenth century First Ladies sometimes did, Nancy Reagan kept her official calendar full. So much was expected of her, she said, that she could not do otherwise.

BARBARA PIERCE BUSH

I N THE presidential campaign of 1988, Barbara Bush was one of a long line of women poised to take over the powerful position of First Lady from Nancy Reagan. During the campaign, the wives of the candidates played an important part, going out on the trail separately from their husbands and speaking in unabashedly partisan tones. Even the spouses of the vice presidential candidates got caught up in the whirl. Marilyn Quayle, wife of Dan Quayle, the Republican choice for vice president, gained considerable attention because she had graduated in the same law school class as her husband.

Attention to the families of the candidates was not new—Americans had wanted to know about their leaders from the earliest days of the republic. But the glare of publicity seemed stronger than ever in the 1988 campaign. This perception may have resulted in part from the length of the campaign—candidates had announced plans to run almost eighteen months before the nominating conventions. Meanwhile, the candidates and their wives had to be prepared to answer frequent questions about their views and personal lives.

Barbara Bush, who was known as a candid, buoyant, down-to-earth individual, confidently replied to many questions directed at her and helped win votes for her husband's campaign. As the wife of the incumbent vice president George Bush, she had already shared the national spotlight for eight years, albeit keeping a low profile.

Barbara Bush had just celebrated her sixty-third birthday when the Republicans nominated her husband as their standard bearer in the summer of 1988 and she had been in political life for more than two decades. Like many previous candidates' wives, she could claim several politically active, civic minded ancestors in her family tree. Her maternal grandfather, James Robinson, had served on Ohio's Supreme Court, and her father's family was distantly related to Franklin Pierce, the fourteenth president of the United States. But politics actually played little part in Barbara Bush's life as she was growing up.

The third of four children born to Marvin Pierce and Pauline Robinson Pierce, Barbara was born on June 8, 1925, and grew up in the affluent New York suburb of Rye. The Pierces had full-time household help, and Barbara's mother devoted her days to gardening and volunteer work, two interests that her daughter later adopted. Marvin Pierce worked for the McCall Corporation in Manhattan, where he started out as an assistant to the publisher and became president in 1946.

Educated at a local public school for six years and then at private Rye Country Day School for the next four years, Barbara spent her junior and senior high school years at a boarding school in Charleston, South Carolina. Ashley Hall, where Barbara's older sister Martha had already enrolled, was a private school that stressed the classics but placed even greater emphasis on the social graces, namely good manners and deportment. During her junior year, when she returned to her family's home for Christmas vacation, Barbara attended several parties, including one where she met the man she would eventually marry.

Although she was only sixteen at the time and he was a year older, Barbara Pierce and George Bush evidently "hit it off" from the start. Barbara Bush later said that she married the first man she ever kissed—"something that when my children hear [about it] they almost throw up." While George Bush finished high school in Connecticut, Barbara completed her junior year in South Carolina, and after he enlisted in the Navy in June 1942, she returned for her final year at Ashley Hall. By the time she graduated in June 1943, Barbara Pierce had been invited to visit the Bush family in Maine, a stay that permanently endeared her to the matriarch of the family, Dorothy Bush. Over the years Barbara would often say that George's mother was a far stronger influence on him than his father ever was. Barbara's athletic prowess and her openness and spontaneity appealed to George's mother—a very down-to-earth woman whose own athleticism made her a nationally ranked tennis player while still in her teens.

During the summer of 1943, George Bush and Barbara Pierce became engaged—a quiet decision that they both remembered as non-momentous, a more-or-less general agreement among themselves and their families rather than one single declaration of intent. George returned to Navy duties and Barbara entered Smith College, which she would attend for little more than a year. Within weeks of beginning her sophomore year, she dropped out to prepare for her wedding, which was scheduled to take place during the Christmas holidays. However, when the bridegroom's return was delayed, the wedding date had to be reset. Finally, on January 6, 1945, Barbara Pierce and George Bush were married.

Until the end of the war in August of 1945, the Bushes lived on various military bases, but by September, George had enrolled at Yale where he and Barbara became part of the young couples crowd. As was very commonplace at the time, young men resumed college educations that had been interrupted by the war and their wives learned to fit night feedings of babies around examination schedules and term papers. Even with the GI bill, budgets were tight, and Barbara Bush earned a little extra money working at the college cooperative until the birth of her first child in 1946. Except for a summer factory job during the war, this would be the only paid employment she ever had.

Much about the Bushes' partnership mirrors that of other couples in which the husband has a busy career, and the Bush family would move from city to city as George Bush went from one job to another, crisscrossing the United States and eventually the world. Meanwhile Barbara Bush's days were taken up with raising their children, three of whom were born within the first seven years of their marriage.

In 1953, the Bushes went through the most trying experience of their lives. Daughter Robin, then three years old, was diagnosed as having leukemia. For seven months George and Barbara Bush devoted all their energies to try to keep their daughter alive—taking extended trips to New York's Sloan Kettering Hospital and consulting with as many specialists as possible. Robin's death was traumatic for both parents, and Barbara's hair began to turn prematurely white. But while George could immerse himself in his career, Barbara found it particularly difficult to resume her normal workload as a mother of two young sons. She often pointed to this period of struggle and grief as one of the lowest periods of her life, but she invariably added that it was her husband's love and support that helped her through the sadness.

Within the next few years Barbara Bush gave birth to three more children—two boys and a girl—and she again found herself doing much of the parenting while her husband concentrated on his work.

When George Bush was elected to Congress in 1966, the first Republican to hold that office from Harris County, Texas, Barbara Bush again played a supportive role. She conquered her fear of public speaking, gamely kept track of the names of political contributors and opponents, and made sure that her own household was running smoothly.

In 1970, after George Bush lost his race for the U.S. Senate, President Richard Nixon appointed him as Permanent U.S. Representative to the United Nations, a job that took the Bush family to New York to live for 22 months. The Bushes later returned to

Washington, D.C., where George chaired the Republican National Committee, and then they traveled to China where he headed the U.S. Liaison Office in Beijing.

Their return to Washington in December 1975 coincided with a period that Barbara Bush later described as one in which she became introspective and took time to consider the course that her life had taken. The secrecy connected with her husband's new job as director of the Central Intelligence Agency meant that much of his work could not be shared. With her children grown or more on their own, Barbara Bush (now fifty years old) faced the question of how to define the remainder of her life.

Like other women of her age and comfortable economic situation, Barbara Bush turned to volunteer work. She would later say that she considered several alternatives before deciding to focus on helping to raise public awareness of the importance of literacy. She may well have been moved by the example of previous First Ladies who appeared to increase their husbands' popularity by taking on a cause of their own. Indeed, her selection of a project coincides with her husband's full-fledged attempt to capture the Republican nomination for President—but she herself had struggled with the reading difficulties of her son Neil, who was dyslexic, and held strong feelings about how low literacy levels were connected to other problems such as drugs and homelessness.

In 1980, when George Bush failed to win the top spot on the Republican ticket and had to settle for second place behind Ronald Reagan, Barbara Bush faced eight years as wife of the Vice President. During that time she remained in the background, volunteering at hundreds of events that advanced the cause of literacy. She contributed the proceeds from a book, purportedly the story of her dog, C. Fred, to literacy groups and she helped organize a public broadcasting project focused on reading. By the time her husband ran for President in 1988, Barbara Bush was well positioned to take on the job of First Lady.

No other woman had gone directly from eight years as the wife of the Vice President to 1600 Pennsylvania Avenue (in Pat Nixon's case, eight years had intervened between the two jobs), and Barbara Bush had used the time wisely. She assembled a large, professional staff, carefully balanced to include several minority women, including Anna Perez, the first African-American to serve as Press Secretary to the First Lady.

Although Barbara Bush played the part of presidential spouse with humility and frequent self-deprecation, she was neither uncertain nor timid. She had a strong sense of who she was and seemed determined not to change. Approaching the position of First Lady with her own indelible style, rather than attempting to model herself after previous First Ladies, Barbara Bush poked fun at her own wrinkles, white hair, matronly figure, and comfortable wardrobe.

During her first year in the White House Mrs. Bush was diagnosed as having Graves disease, a disorder of the thyroid. Although she lost considerable weight, Barbara Bush made no pretense of dieting to achieve the loss. Yet, despite considerable discomfort, the First Lady maintained a full schedule of public appearances and entertaining at the White House.

Although most closely connected with the campaign to improve literacy, Barbara Bush also made public appearances as First Lady on behalf of the fight against AIDS. A widely-circulated photo showing her holding a baby born with AIDS was credited with helping to reduce fear about how easily the disease could be spread. Other appearances were designed to encourage parents to read to their children. When she published *Millie's Book*, the purported autobiography of the White House dog, she turned over the entire post-tax proceeds of the book (which grossed nearly $800,000) to the Barbara Bush Foundation for Family Literacy, an organization she had helped to establish in 1989. Had she not given the money away, Barbara Bush's earnings would have been far larger than her husband's that year, and much higher than any previous First Lady earned while in the White House.

Although it was perceived that Barbara Bush differed with her husband on some issues (including gun control laws and a woman's right to terminate a pregnancy), the First Lady rarely spoke out publicly on these topics, and she generally remained outside controversy. Her interviews and other contacts with the press centered on her family and her hostessing duties—subjects unlikely to engender disagreement. Not since the 1940s and 1950s had a First Lady taken such an approach to the job, and Barbara Bush was frequently compared to Bess Truman who made it a point to keep her own strongly-felt views to herself.

In 1990 this traditional approach to the position of First Lady produced considerable public controversy. The debate peaked after Barbara Bush was invited by Wellesley College officials to speak at graduation exercises. Students objected, saying that her one claim to fame came as a result of the man she married—not because of any achievements on her own. Rather than defend herself against that charge, the First Lady accepted it, responding that she understood the students' point of view and that she respected other women's rights to make their own choices. Then, in an impressive public relations coup, she invited Raisa Gorbachev, who coincidentally would be visiting the United States with her husband at the time of the scheduled Wellesley appearance, to come along to the ceremonies. Thus, students, parents, and others who attended the Wellesley graduation exercises on June 1, 1990, had the unprecedented privilege of listening to two of the most famous women in the world—one, the First Lady of the United States, and the other, in a newly public role for women in her country, the spouse of the Soviet Union's top political leader.

Although White House insiders reported that Barbara Bush could be a fierce protector of her family and a shrewd analyst of political prospects, the public perceived her as a contented, devoted wife and mother who was satisfied to have defined her life around her family. Her taste helped define a new style, and magazines featured advertisements for faux three-strand "First Lady pearls" and for "Nancy Reagan furniture at Barbara Bush prices."

The First Lady's enormous popularity became a featured part of her husband's campaign for re-election in 1992. She had often garnered an "approval level" higher than her husband's, and *Good Housekeeping* readers put her at the top of their list of "Most Admired Women" for four years in a row. At the nominating convention, delegates and millions of television viewers got the chance to hear her speak about her husband's qualifications and her family. The convention had already broken precedent by listing Marilyn Quayle, wife of the Vice President, as a featured speaker. Some observers noted that the Republican convention seemed to applaud women who had devoted their adult lives to homemaking and family nurturing rather than to careers of their own.

When George Bush lost his bid for re-election in 1992, Barbara Bush appeared to find the prospect of leaving Washington not entirely unattractive. She had often said that she hoped her husband would finish up with politics while she still had the vigor to garden. In setting out to locate a new home in Houston, Texas (after having occupied more than two dozen houses during her 48-year marriage), Barbara Bush looked forward to a new stage in her life, a time when her schedule would be simpler and more of her time could be devoted to gardening and grandchildren.

HILLARY RODHAM CLINTON

H ILLARY RODHAM CLINTON entered the White House on January 20, 1993, amid predictions that she would change the job of presidential spouse. For the first time, voters had elected a president born after World War II ended, and his wife (as well as his Vice President and the Vice President's wife) also came from the so-called baby boomer generation. Unlike her predecessors (but like many of her contemporaries), Hillary Rodham Clinton boasted education credentials and professional accomplishments very similar to her husband's. She was not likely, it was thought, to content herself with a domestic or background role; she would participate in personnel and policy decisions at the highest levels.

Much about her younger years underlined a will to succeed. Born on October 26, 1947, in Park Ridge, Illinois, a suburb of Chicago, Hillary Rodham Clinton grew up in a comfortably middle-class home. Daughter of Hugh Rodham, owner of a small fabric store, and Dorothy Rodham, full-time wife and mother, she was the oldest of their three children (and the only girl), and she played the classic role of the firstborn who tries so hard to please. When her parents encouraged her to do everything that her brothers did, she took them seriously. "I was determined," Dorothy Rodham later told *The Washington Post*, "that just because she was a girl didn't mean she should be limited."

Hillary's outlook was also influenced by her religion and by the time in which she came of age. Raised by Methodists who placed strong emphasis on civic duty, she grew up in the 1960s amid much public talk about what young people—whether male or female—could "do for your country." In high school she developed confidence as a public speaker and organizer, but many of her ideas were still evolving. While committed to social progress, she favored a limited role for government, and she entered Wellesley College in 1965 as a Goldwater Republican.

During the next four years her perspective changed. In early 1968 she campaigned for Eugene McCarthy, the antiwar Democratic candidate who helped drive incumbent Lyndon Johnson out of the White House. Besides the Vietnam War, a fledgling feminist movement and new civil rights fight helped shape her views. While majoring in political science, she had ample opportunity to reexamine her thoughts on how change should proceed, and she came to see the positive side of a larger role for government in people's lives.

At Wellesley's commencement in June 1969, when Hillary's classmates selected her to speak for them, she attacked old guard thinking that put too much emphasis on "an acquisitive and competitive corporate life," and she insisted it was not for her generation: "We're searching for more immediate, ecstatic, and penetrating modes of living." *Life* published Hillary's picture alongside photos of several of her contemporaries who had also addressed commencement audiences across the nation.

Yale Law School, where Hillary enrolled in 1969, helped point her toward a career in public service. Encouraged by a Yale alumna, Marian Wright Edelman, Hillary signed on to work the summer of 1970 with a research organization in Washington that Edelman had founded. Assigned to study migrant workers, Hillary became most concerned about the welfare of children as they moved with their parents from one camp to the next. When she returned to Yale in September, she had made up her mind to focus on matters related to children: their health, safety, and legal protection.

This new interest diverted some of her attention from the traditional, required courses and funneled her energy into issues related to family law. She assisted professors writing a Carnegie Council book, *All Our Children: Families under Pressure in the United States*, which examined the work pressures and economic conditions that affect entire families and the improvements that could be shaped to change them.

While at Yale, Hillary Rodham met Bill Clinton, who was one year older but enrolled in the same class. After both graduated in 1973, they temporarily went separate ways: Bill returned to his native Arkansas, and Hillary took a job in Washington with the House Judiciary Committee, investigating President Richard Nixon's culpability in the Watergate break-in and its aftermath. One of three women on a legal team that totaled forty-one, Hillary came to the job with high recommendations and plenty of zeal, and she forged friendships that she took with her to the White House twenty years later. Her first real job proved an exciting one, and Hillary later told Washington reporter Donnie Radcliffe that it had been a "great experience. . . . What a gift! I was twenty-six years old. I felt like I was walking around with my mouth open all the time."

When President Nixon resigned in August 1974, Hillary's job ended, too, and she made her big decision to move to Bill's Arkansas. Although she would have to start from scratch to forge a career for herself on his turf, she had decided to do so. She began teaching at the University of Arkansas Law School in Fayetteville (where Bill also taught), and a year later, on October 11, 1975, they married. When he won his first statewide election to attorney general in 1976, the Clintons moved to the state capital, and she joined the Rose Law Firm in Little Rock, becoming the first woman hired by this prestigious old law firm.

Hillary Rodham (as she was known until 1982, when irate voters convinced her of the wisdom of adding "Clinton") had a remarkably successful career. Work on corporate boards and her legal practice provided a comfortable six-figure income, thus putting her among the top women earners of the time. She was popular with colleagues at work and was twice named to the list of "100 Most Influential

Lawyers in America." Garry Wills singled her out as "one of the more important scholar-activists of the last two decades."

Like many other women of her generation, Hillary combined this success at work with a full family life. Chelsea Victoria Clinton was born on February 27, 1980. After a few months' leave, Hillary returned to her law office full-time, juggling the competing demands of home and job.

All these details remained largely unknown to voters when the 1992 presidential campaign began. Most Americans knew very little about the professional accomplishments of Hillary Rodham Clinton or about her personally. That quickly changed when she went on national television to help her husband reply to a charge made by an Arkansas woman, Gennifer Flowers, who had given an interview to the *Star*, a supermarket tabloid, about "My 12-Year Affair with Bill Clinton." The Clintons chose to make their case to as large an audience as possible, and on January 26, following the Super Bowl game, when 100 million television viewers were expected to be in front of their sets, Bill and Hillary appeared on *60 Minutes*. Not only did Hillary agree to sit beside her husband—she also answered questions and spoke for herself.

Years of facing television cameras and of public speaking paid off for both Clintons, but Hillary was particularly effective. While Bill squirmed a bit and admitted to "bringing pain" to the marriage, but stopped short of confessing any wrongdoing, Hillary challenged voters to consider what the Clintons represented, and if they did not like what they saw, "then heck, don't vote for him." It was generally agreed that she performed remarkably well, avoiding looking like a martyred wife as others in her situation had done.

Hillary's name became a household word. She remained central to her husband's campaign, and when candidate Jerry Brown charged that she had gained professionally from her husband's governorship, she replied that she "could have stayed home and baked cookies" but had chosen not to. The press picked up her comment

and used it out of context to convey the impression that she disparaged women who had no career outside their homes or apart from
their families. In fact, she had gone on to say that she had made her
choices with the hope that she could ease the way for other women to
have more options. But the "cookies" quote dogged her steps and
tagged her in her opponents' eyes as an enemy of traditional family
values.

After Bill Clinton's nomination in July, much more attention focused on his wife's record. The first prospective First Lady to bring
nearly two decades of professional activity to a campaign, she was
bound to have stepped on some toes. As an attorney specializing in
corporate law, she had associated with clients whose past practices
she might not have known about or condoned. As an activist, she
had taken some stands herself, and not all of them found favor with
voters looking at them for the first time. Her detractors pointed to
her work on the Legal Services Corporation, a federally funded
organization established to give legal assistance to poor Americans.
Although the corporation was designed to be nonpartisan, Hillary
had, her critics charged, helped funnel money to openly liberal
causes. Her directorship of a philanthropy, the New World Foundation, coincided with what one writer called support by the foundation for "hard left" causes. Even her work with the Children's Defense Fund, an organization devoted to identifying and protecting
the rights of minors, was examined and described (inaccurately) as
advocating children's right to sue their parents.

In their coverage of Hillary, reporters appeared uncertain what to
consider. Some focused on her hairstyle and clothes, as though she
were simply the candidate's wife, and others looked at her record, as
though she ran in her own name. Conservative journals attacked her
pointedly under headlines such as "The Lady Macbeth of Little
Rock," while more liberal and feminist magazines applauded the
idea that finally a political spouse spoke out and admitted to having
a mind of her own.

After the election in November 1992, speculation centered on a cabinet post for Hillary Clinton, but this idea cooled when it was pointed out that a 1967 law prohibited such employment. President Clinton fed speculation that his wife would play an important advisory role in his administration, albeit an unpaid one, by including her in his initial consultations with congressional leaders and by emphasizing the extent of her participation, noting that "she knew more than we did about some things." Hillary attended interviews with prospective appointees and put forward names drawn from her huge network of professional associates.

As though to temper talk of too much clout in a First Lady, Hillary chose as her first in-depth interview to talk with Marian Burros, a food writer for *The New York Times*. When the *Times* ran the front-page article on February 2, 1993, it included a photo of the new First Lady, glamorously clad in an off-the-shoulder black dress and leaning over a table set for a formal dinner in the State Dining Room. The article delved into Hillary's thoughts on menus, entertaining, and other traditionally domestic and "feminine" topics. Other newspapers picked up on the domestic theme; they carried articles on how she had banned smoking in the executive mansion and encouraged the serving of wholesome foods.

Yet within a few days of moving into the White House, Hillary indicated that she expected to act as more than the hostess. She took an office on the second floor of the West Wing (while her predecessors had been content with the more remote East Wing or even the residence itself), and she appointed able assistants with long experience in Washington. Chief of Staff Margaret Williams, working out of her own West Wing office, boasted Capitol Hill expertise and graduate study in mass communications; she had met Hillary while working as communications director for the Children's Defense Fund.

President Clinton quickly underlined his wife's central role by appointing her to chair the Task Force on Health Care Reform, the group charged with devising a plan to reshape the nation's health care. The assignment carried a huge responsibility, since the President had made health care reform central to his campaign and had promised to alter the medical system to cap costs and to offer health insurance to all Americans, including thirty million not then covered by health insurance. About fifteen cents out of every dollar that Americans spent went toward health care; many people stood to lose (or win) a lot if the system changed. Medical personnel, insurance companies, and others who feared they would be hurt organized to fight back.

When discussions began, physicians sought to participate, but they found they were barred because the Task Force consisted of "government officials" and thus had the right to meet in privacy. The doctors objected that the First Lady did not qualify as a "government official" and since she chaired the Task Force, its meetings must be open to the public. In its initial decision on the matter, a district federal court agreed that the President's wife was neither a "government official" nor, as her attorneys had argued, "the functional equivalent," and the presiding judge called for open meetings. A few weeks later a federal appeals court reversed that decision, citing a "long-standing tradition of public service by First Ladies . . . who have acted (albeit in the background) as advisers and personal representatives of their husbands." Since the Task Force had completed its work and disbanded by this point, the court's ruling had no immediate effect, but it did underline the controversy surrounding an activist First Lady.

Hillary Rodham Clinton made repeated trips to Capitol Hill to woo Congress into supporting the Task Force recommendations, and in the fall of 1993 she broke all precedent by talking with five different congressional committees in the course of one week. The media covered her appearances, and she generally won "rave" reviews from reporters and legislators alike. But Hillary, sensitive to complaints of others who saw such a role in policy as inappropriate for a First Lady, emphasized that she came before committees as "mother, wife, sister, a woman."

Forces opposed to a change in health care weighed in, and in spite of strong support from the President and First Lady, the proposal advanced by the Task Force had little chance of success. Both Clintons eventually conceded that it had been too ambitious in its objectives and its timing. They distanced themselves from it and began to focus on other matters.

Criticism of the First Lady now turned to her past activities. Since Hillary had managed most of the family's finances since her marriage, fingers pointed to her when critics charged that the Clintons had acted improperly in an investment, Whitewater, that went bad in Arkansas a dozen years earlier. When the Treasury Department investigated a related matter, subpoenas went out for Clinton aides —who came from the First Lady's staff as well as the President's. The President's chief counsel, Bernard Nussbaum, an old mentor of Hillary's, resigned.

More suspicions got into print, causing Americans to speculate whether the suicide of Vincent Foster, Jr., deputy White House counsel and Hillary's friend and law colleague, might have been related to some sort of "cover-up" rather than simply the act of a seriously depressed and overworked man, as it had been presented. Accounts of paper shredding at Hillary's old law firm raised other questions. To complicate the First Lady's situation, new evidence emerged that she had traded in futures commodities in 1979 and done it very profitably, converting a tiny $1,000 nest egg into a hefty $100,000 bankroll, and she had accomplished this remarkable feat in a very few months. She also faced questions about how much legal work she had done for an Arkansas bank that had eventually failed, at great cost to taxpayers.

Hillary's situation was complicated by charges that she had acted improperly after moving into 1600 Pennsylvania Avenue. When several members of the White House travel office were fired, some fingers pointed to Mrs. Clinton as the instigator. Rumors also circulated that she had initiated a request for FBI files on hundreds of people, including many prominent Republicans in the preceding administration.

For the first time in history, a President's wife had enough connections to corporate law and to the financial network that she could be interrogated about substantive, ethical matters touching on money and power. When a special prosecutor was appointed to look into the Clintons' involvement in Whitewater and report to Congress, he took sworn testimony from both Clintons.

As the 1996 election approached, Hillary Rodham Clinton moderated her role, seeking to allay criticism that she held too much power. When she traveled to Asia in March, she took along her daughter and made a point of focusing on women's issues. Her book, *It Takes a Village: And Other Lessons Children Teach Us*, drew critical praise and renewed attention to her long-standing interest in families. She muted her voice in the presidential campaign that year and avoided speaking out on controversial issues.

As the details of the 1996 campaign became known, it was charged that she had played a major, behind-the-scenes role in compiling a list of contributors and seeing that many of them were invited to the White House. According to the *Wall Street Journal*, the First Lady's office had helped woo donors: It had cooperated in compiling a database of potential benefactors with instructions on how they might be approached. Her defenders pointed out that anyone concerned with making the White House accessible—as First Ladies have done for two centuries—will surely keep guest lists and that any wife interested in her husband's success will make a special effort to please big donors.

The appearance of donors' names on the White House guest list became even more important after Hillary Rodham Clinton announced her candidacy for public office. Even before she formally entered the race for the U.S. Senate seat from New York, she had to consider how to finance what would surely be a costly campaign in a large state. This was uncharted territory. Never before had a First Lady run for public office. The fact that her husband still presided over the Oval Office and that she had the last word on guest lists for the most coveted invitations in America complicated the matter.

When critics charged that she was using the White House as "Motel 1600," she felt obliged to release the names of all those who had stayed overnight at either the White House or Camp David since she began her Senate race. The 404 names fell into several categories, including friends, supporters, officials and dignitaries, artists and sports figures, family members, and friends of Chelsea Clinton. Only the identities of those in the last group were withheld, in line with the Clintons' policy of keeping their daughter's life private. About one-quarter of the names on the list also appeared on a list of donors to the First Lady's campaign or to Democratic causes, but the Clintons insisted there was no connection.

The Senate run dominated Mrs. Clinton's schedule for the final two years of her husband's second administration. In early 1999 she released a few trial balloons and followed up with "listening tours" of New York State. Since she had never lived in the state and knew that she would face carpetbagger charges, she proceeded cautiously, learning the economic conditions of upstate counties and the various conflicts inherent in the competing ethnic communities of the cities. In polyglot New York City, her Illinois birth certificate and Arkansas voter registration caused little comment, but in the suburbs and farther north, it was a different matter. The state's politics had often split along city–upstate lines, and a Brooklynite could be suspect in Buffalo on many grounds. Accent, urban experience, and sensibilities all marked the urban dweller, and it is safe to say that the typical candidate from New York City knew less about Oswego County, hundreds of miles to the north, than about major issues confronting voters in northern New Jersey or western Connecticut.

The nationalizing of American living had rendered many issues meaningless as state matters, and an intelligent, informed Ohioan often knew as much about other states as about her own. Cheap air fares, round-the-clock news broadcasting, and millions of e-mails crossing state lines daily all helped render state boundaries archaic reminders of the days when most Americans never traveled very far from their birthplaces. Small farmers, unemployed miners, and uninsured children united across the continent, and finding a peculiar state angle for any of their stories, although possible, became more difficult.

As First Lady, Hillary Clinton had resided in Washington, D.C., since January, 1993, but she had little personal experience with the local public transportation system or the homeless and destitute. Had she been asked to name leaders, specify tax rates, and enumerate voters' greatest fears, it is likely she would have done as well by New York State as by Illinois or D.C. The job of First Lady had its own nationalizing effect, and she had, like the President, come to see her constituency in national terms.

In February, 2000, when the First Lady formally announced her candidacy for U.S. Senator from New York, she initiated a new era. For historians who had documented the power base from which any presidential spouse operates, this marked an interesting turn, and they waited to see if she could convert successfully from candidate's wife to candidate, bringing in the funds and backers necessary to win.

Exactly eight months later, on November 7, when Hillary gave her victory speech at the Grand Hyatt hotel in Manhattan, she summed up her campaign as "Sixty-two counties, sixteen months, three debates, two opponents, and six black pantsuits." That understated the enormous effort she had expended, however. She had crisscrossed the state dozens of times, meeting with small groups in tiny towns as she doggedly persisted in hearing voters describe their worst fears and biggest dreams. To prepare for the trivia teasers, she learned the state flower and bird. She gamely studied up on what writers, such as E. B. White, had said about the magnetism of New York. Even the Clinton family summer vacation was planned to maximize her connection with New York. Instead of Jackson Hole, Wyoming, or Martha's Vineyard, Massachusetts, which the Clintons had enjoyed during previous summers, they now looked to the Adirondacks or Long Island beaches.

For her campaign uniform, the First Lady rarely strayed from the black pantsuit, and her haircut preference had finally jelled into a short, brushed-behind-the-ears look that was both becoming for her personally and practical for a professional woman with an exhausting daily schedule. She became such a fixture on the nightly news programs that it sometimes seemed as though she had always been running for office in New York State.

In the three debates with Rick Lazio, her Republican opponent, Hillary improved her standing with many voters. In the first (and most widely watched) debate on September 13, Lazio, wanting to seem authoritative and up to the job, had asked her to sign a statement that she would not spend "soft money" contributions. But his way of asking—he walked over to her podium and waved the paper in her face—angered many voters, especially women, who saw the move as unnecessarily threatening. After the third debate, during which moderator Tim Russert showed a tape of her appearance on a "Today" show when she seemed to blame "a right wing conspiracy" for the whole Monica Lewinsky episode, Hillary won additional votes. To many viewers, Russert's tactic appeared unfair and calculated to embarrass her. Her dignified response, in which she noted that her choice might not have been right for others and their families but it was for her and hers, rang a sympathetic bell.

Her critics—and there were many—still clung to their old objections, that she was untrustworthy and excessively ambitious, and had stayed with her husband to further her own career. Often these arguments came from professional, well-educated, married women much like her, but more frequently they came from men, and the objections (along with money to defeat her) poured in from across the nation.

So that Hillary would qualify as a resident of the state, the Clintons had purchased a Dutch colonial house in Chappaqua, just north of New York City, in late 1999. To meet the down payment on the $1.7 million price, they had at first borrowed from a friend but, in response to criticism, they managed to finance the purchase on their own. This was the first home they had owned in some time, having lived in either the Arkansas governor's mansion or the White House since 1984. Like several other presidential families of the late twentieth century, the Clintons had to make a new home for themselves after Washington. Ike and Mamie Eisenhower had retired to a Gettysburg farm; Barbara and George Bush built a new house in Texas; Californians Pat and Richard Nixon opted for Manhattan and then a New Jersey suburb (after briefly trying their home state); Michigan natives Gerald and Betty Ford bought homes in Palm Springs and Colorado. The only thing unusual about the Clintons' decision was the reason: The move satisfied the wife's career needs.

The Clintons' daughter Chelsea, who had shunned the spotlight during her father's campaigns and two administrations, suddenly became more visible in her mother's campaign. Although she rarely spoke more than the occasional greeting to individuals in the crowds, she frequently stood at her mother's side as she asked for voters' support. By taking off a semester from Stanford during the fall of 2000, Chelsea could also spend more time at the White House, filling in for her mother as hostess, and she accompanied her parents to Ireland and England in December on their final trip abroad as First Family.

After November 7, 2000, Hillary Rodham Clinton sought to balance the demands of her two roles—Senator-elect and First Lady. She attended briefing sessions with other newly elected legislators and hosted dozens of receptions and dinners. Her book, *Invitation to the White House,* detailed the Clinton years in the presidential mansion, picturing and describing the family gatherings and public functions. About a third of the pages were recipes for her favorite dishes—making the book look like something by any traditional presidential wife. Yet when she was interviewed in her role as Senator-elect, Hillary talked about the issues she had stressed throughout her campaign—health care, education, and problems facing families. She gave informed and careful responses to questions about a projected budget surplus and the proper role of the federal government. When the Clintons purchased a six-bedroom house in North-west Washington, D.C., in late December, the First Lady explained that she had sought a place large enough to accommodate researchers documenting her years as First Lady. It was a unique situation for a Senator-elect. An $8 million advance for her autobiography illustrated how very interesting her story had become.

Soon after Bill Clinton's election in 1992, Hillary's mother was asked what kind of First Lady her daughter would be, and she replied that she would combine the best of Eleanor Roosevelt and the best of Jacqueline Kennedy. That forecast set a high standard, but in many ways it proved correct by the time Hillary Rodham Clinton left the White House. The melding of glamorous, traditional hostess and thinking, issue-oriented spokesperson had never been so successfully accomplished, and that might explain why critics— who preferred a separation of these roles—remained so loud.

Into the Twenty-first Century

A s Americans moved into the twenty-first century, they could not help but notice how much the path to becoming First Lady had changed during the last one hundred years. The four women whose husbands headed their parties' tickets in the 2000 presidential election would have been viewed in amazement by their counterparts in 1900. In that earlier election, the sickly Ida McKinley was rarely seen and never heard; Edith Roosevelt, wife of the Republican vice presidential candidate Theodore Roosevelt, although competent and intelligent, considered any appearance in the national spotlight as definitely unladylike. Mary Bryan, the wife of William Jennings Bryan, the Democratic Party's nominee for president, had earned the same law degree as her husband and she often helped research his speeches. But the negative publicity she had received during the 1896 campaign, when she was criticized by national magazines as a woman "who aims to do too much," showed her the wisdom of keeping quiet. Letitia Stevenson, wife of Democratic vice presidential candidate Adlai Ewing Stevenson, (whose grandson would later win his party's presidential nomination twice), showed a strong intellectual bent, and she eventually wrote her own autobiography although she never attended college. None of the four would have dreamed of giving a political speech or submitting to an interview.

By the year 2000, candidates' wives took for granted that they would play important roles in the campaigns. Even before the nominating conventions made the choices official, George W. Bush and Al

Gore had been virtually assured of the top spots on their respective Republican and Democratic tickets, and their wives had begun working hard to help them win. Laura Bush, who joked that she had agreed to marry George W. on the condition that she would never have to give a political speech, had become his articulate, tireless advocate, chalking up dozens of interviews and thousands of miles. Tipper Gore, already familiar to many Americans after eight years in the vice presidential mansion, seemed at ease in front of cameras and even carried one herself to record the campaign from her side of the lens.

The wives figured prominently at the nominating conventions. A poised Laura Bush opened the Republican meeting with a speech aimed as much at millions of television viewers as at the delegates assembled in front of her. At the Democratic convention, Tipper Gore delegated the speaking to her daughter but then jubilantly celebrated Al's nomination with a dance across the stage, in full view of cameras. When her husband appeared, he delivered a long, passionate kiss that could have come out of Hollywood and was the subject of television talk shows for weeks. Never in their wildest dreams could Ida McKinley or Mary Bryan have imagined themselves the subject of so much attention.

The candidates' wives in the 2000 election illustrated how much American women's lives had changed. For the first time in history, all four (Laura Bush, Lynne Cheney, Tipper Gore, and Hadassah Lieberman) held graduate degrees, and Cheney boasted a Ph.D. All four had delayed marriage until they earned a college degree, and three went on to forge careers of their own. Cheney's record as Chair of the National Endowment for the Humanities and television talk show host had made her a national figure and, until her husband was tapped for vice president on the Republican ticket, she was sometimes mentioned as a possible cabinet appointee. Both she and Tipper Gore had published books, and all four women were polished speakers. Hadassah Lieberman had been divorced (as had Democrat Joe Lieberman), and now her family comprised children that were "his," "mine," and "ours." All together, the four women had given birth to a total of only ten children, far fewer than their counterparts in 1900.

Whether in volunteer work or in paid jobs, the four women had executive experience. They had assembled staffs, delegated responsibility, and assessed results. Perhaps, most importantly, they were all familiar with the nation's capital. Three had lived there, and the fourth (Laura Bush) had grown to know the city and White House well during her father-in-law's administration, 1989–1993. All four had had ample time to prepare for the national spotlight, and none showed signs of awe or discomfort at what might lie ahead for them if their husbands won.

LAURA WELCH BUSH

THROUGHOUT the closely contested 2000 campaign, November 7 was expected to be the cut-off date, when the results would finally become clear. But the recounts and debates over the legitimacy of the election continued for weeks, and not until December 18 did Laura Bush take the traditional tour that each outgoing First Lady conducts with her successor. The intervening weeks could not have been tranquil but her friends insisted it would take more than uncertainty to throw her off stride. She also profited from first-hand experience with the White House. "I have slept in the Lincoln bedroom and the Queen's bedroom," Laura noted, implying that she felt competent to manage the 132-room mansion.

Although political contests had shaped much of her adult life, it had started out differently. The only child of homebuilder Harold Welch and homemaker Jenna Hawkins Welch, Laura was born in Midland, Texas, on November 4, 1946. She often said that in spite of her parents' limited education, they set high standards and started a savings account to pay for her college almost as soon as she was born. Her mother fostered Laura's interest in books, and she became an avid reader. At public schools in Midland, Laura participated in Girl Scouts and studied ballet, but she had already decided to become a teacher. At an early age, she began lining up her dolls and acting the teacher to them.

At her graduation from Robert E. Lee High in 1964, only one event marred what would otherwise be a picture-perfect school record. A few months earlier, on November 6, 1963, she had been driving her Chevrolet outside Midland and ran a stop sign, hitting a car driven by another high school senior, Michael Douglas, and killing him. Friends who knew her well said the accident changed her life, impressing on her forever the necessity to take responsibility for one's actions. Years later she remained unable to discuss the tragedy, even with some of her closest friends. But at the time, she suffered no legal consequences and her driving privileges were not suspended.

Following graduation from Southern Methodist University in Dallas in 1968, Laura pursued her dream and taught second grade at Kennedy Elementary School in Houston where many of her students were African Americans. She later said that the experience had opened her eyes and made her "realize how unfair" life could be. In 1972, she earned a master's in library science at The University of Texas at Austin and then worked as a school librarian in both Houston and Austin.

Although her path presumably crossed with that of George W. Bush several times, both at the Midland School they attended and in a housing complex where they lived as young adults, the two did not meet until they were introduced by mutual friends in the summer of 1977. Four months later, on November 5, 1977, they married. Her

father-in-law was already contemplating a try for the White House
and her husband was poised to run for Congress in 1978, so she
could hardly avoid politics. She gave up working as school librarian
to devote full time to homemaking, volunteer work, and campaigning. But she emphasized that she never considered herself a political
adviser to her husband. To a reporter who queried her on this
subject in 2000, Laura replied, "I'm his wife, and don't you think
that's better?"

In the athletic Bush clan, Laura quickly established her independence as a reader and her own person. Her mother-in-law, Barbara
Bush, recalled that Laura had amazed the entire family with her
spunky response to Dorothy Bush, her husband's grandmother, on
their first meeting. When the matriarch of the competitive and
achieving Bush family inquired of young Laura what she did, Laura
answered, "I read, I smoke, and I admire." (Laura later insisted this
story was untrue, but Barbara Bush stood by it.) As a young wife,
Laura cultivated her own circle of women friends, with whom she
occasionally took bird-watching or rafting trips. People who knew
both Laura and her husband considered her the more intellectual
and steady of the two, and they noted that although she continued to
have a drink occasionally, she played a role in his decision to stop
drinking.

On November 25, 1981, Laura gave birth to twin daughters,
Barbara and Jenna, named for their two grandmothers. The girls
were fraternal twins, rather than identical, and differed in both
appearance and personality. Jenna, reportedly the more fun-loving
of the two, enrolled at The University of Texas at Austin in September, 2000, while Barbara, the more intellectual, chose Yale, her
father's alma mater. Neither enjoyed the spotlight focused on political families, and their parents respected their feelings and adamantly protected their privacy.

As the popular First Lady of Texas (1994–2000), Laura worked
hard to improve literacy. Her most notable achievement was starting
the Texas Book Festival, which featured local authors and, begin-

ning in 1996, raised hundreds of thousands of dollars to buy books for libraries. Laura later added breast cancer awareness to her agenda, along with attention to the problems of Alzheimer's sufferers and their families after her father died from that disease in April, 1995. She indicated that she would concentrate on similar causes as First Lady.

Two weeks before inauguration day Laura announced her White House staff, notable for its number of experienced veterans. From her Texas office she took both her chief of staff (who had worked with her since 1995) and her head of projects. For the sensitive, demanding jobs of social secretary and scheduler, she dipped into her mother-in-law's talent pool and chose people familiar with Washington. In an interview with Barbara Walters, broadcast the night before the inauguration, Laura rejected the tag of "traditional" to apply to herself as First Lady, and she stressed that she would shape the job to suit herself. It has been said that every incoming First Lady is given the equivalent of a "magic wand" but the rules for its use are left up to her. Now Laura Welch Bush had her chance to do just that.

Appendix

Presidents' Wives Who Served as First Lady

	Year Married*	Years as First Lady†
Martha Dandridge Custis Washington (1731–1802)	1759	1789–1797
Abigail Smith Adams (1744–1818)	1764	1797–1801
Dolley Payne Todd Madison (1768–1849)	1794	1809–1817
Elizabeth Kortright Monroe (ca. 1763–1830)[1]	1786	1817–1825
Louisa Catherine Johnson Adams (1775–1852)	1797	1825–1829
Anna Symmes Harrison (1775–1864)	1795	1841[2]
Letitia Christian Tyler (1790–1842)	1813	1841–1842[3]

* Date is that of marriage to man who became President. In some cases an earlier (or later) marriage also occurred.

† Terms of First Ladies coincide with the presidential term and run from one inauguration to another except as noted. Until 1937, Presidents assumed the office March 4.

1. Actual birthdate is disputed.

2. William Henry Harrison died one month after taking office, before Anna had arrived in Washington.

3. Letitia Tyler died September 10, 1842.

Presidents' Wives Who
Served as First Lady
(Continued)

	Year Married	Years as First Lady
Julia Gardiner Tyler (1820–1889)	1844	1844–1845[4]
Sarah Childress Polk (1803–1891)	1824	1845–1849
Margaret Mackall Smith Taylor (1788–1852)	1810	1849–1850[5]
Abigail Powers Fillmore (1798–1853)	1826	1850–1853
Jane Means Appleton Pierce (1806–1863)	1834	1853–1857
Mary Todd Lincoln (1818–1882)	1842	1861–1865[6]
Eliza McCardle Johnson (1810–1876)	1827	1865–1869
Julia Dent Grant (1826–1902)	1848	1869–1877
Lucy Webb Hayes (1831–1889)	1852	1877–1881
Lucretia Rudolph Garfield (1832–1918)	1858	1881[7]
Frances Folsom Cleveland (1864–1947)	1886[8]	1886–1889
		1893–1897
Caroline Scott Harrison (1832–1892)	1853	1889–1892[9]
Ida Saxton McKinley (1847–1907)	1871	1897–1901[10]
Edith Carow Roosevelt (1861–1948)	1886	1901–1909
Helen Herron Taft (1861–1943)	1886	1909–1913

4. Julia Gardiner married President John Tyler on June 26, 1844, only a few months before his presidential term ended.

5. Zachary Taylor died in office on July 9, 1850.

6. Abraham Lincoln was assassinated on April 15, 1865.

7. James Garfield died September 19, 1881, after having been shot on July 2.

8. Frances Folsom married President Grover Cleveland on June 2, 1886, after he had taken office in March 1885. He was defeated for a second consecutive term but was reelected in 1892 and served from 1893 to 1897.

9. Caroline Harrison died in the Executive Mansion, October 25, 1892.

10. William McKinley was assassinated on September 14, 1901, just months after beginning his second term.

Presidents' Wives Who
Served as First Lady
(Continued)

	Year Married	Years as First Lady
Ellen Axson Wilson (1860–1914)	1885	1913–1914[11]
Edith Bolling Galt Wilson (1872–1961)	1915	1915–1921[12]
Florence Kling Harding (1860–1924)	1891	1921–1923[13]
Grace Goodhue Coolidge (1879–1957)	1905	1923–1929
Lou Henry Hoover (1874–1944)	1899	1929–1933
Eleanor Roosevelt Roosevelt (1884–1962)	1905	1933–1945[14]
Bess Wallace Truman (1885–1982)	1919	1945–1953
Mamie Doud Eisenhower (1896–1979)	1916	1953–1961
Jacqueline Bouvier Kennedy (1929–1994)	1953	1961–1963[15]
Lady Bird Taylor Johnson (1912–)	1934	1963–1969
Patricia Ryan Nixon (1912–1993)	1940	1969–1974[16]
Betty Bloomer Warren Ford (1918–)	1948	1974–1977
Rosalynn Smith Carter (1927–)	1946	1977–1981
Nancy Davis Reagan (1921–)	1952	1981–1989
Barbara Pierce Bush (1925–)	1945	1989–1993
Hillary Rodham Clinton (1947–)	1975	1993–2001
Laura Welch Bush (1946–)	1977	2001–

11. Ellen Wilson died in the White House on August 6, 1914.
12. Edith Galt married President Woodrow Wilson on December 18, 1915.
13. Warren Harding died in office on August 2, 1923.
14. Franklin Delano Roosevelt died in office on April 12, 1945.
15. John F. Kennedy was assassinated on November 22, 1963.
16. Richard Nixon resigned from the presidency on August 9, 1974.

Index